International English in Its Sociolinguistic Contexts

D0071357

"... addresses a timely and attention-getting topic with expertise and perspective. There is both engagement with theoretical issues and an exploration of specific cases from all continents of the globe.... This book is a clear choice for courses in the TESOL master's program at my institution, which prepares both U.S. and international TESOL teachers. A particular virtue is the clarity of the writing style for non-native English speaking readers."

Nancy Hornberger, University of Pennsylvania

"... a substantive, well-organized, and authoritative volume ... Its appearance is timely indeed, as researchers, employers, school boards and ministries of education around the world are grappling with the implications of English as a global language."

David Nunan, University of Hong Kong

"The links to language planning, policy, and pedagogy make this a very valuable book that will be of great interest to many people involved in ELT around the world."

Christina Higgins, University of Hawaii at Manoa

Present-day globalization, migration, and the spread of English have resulted in a great diversity of social and educational contexts in which English learning is taking place. A basic assumption of this book is that because English is an international language, effective pedagogical decisions cannot be made without giving special attention to the many varied contexts in which English is taught and learned. Its unique value is the combination of three strands—globalization, sociolinguistics, and English as an international language—in one focused volume specifically designed for language teachers, providing explicit links between socio-linguistic concepts and language pedagogy.

International English in Its Sociolinguistic Contexts:

- Fully recognizes the relationship between social context and language teaching
- Describes the social and sociolinguistic factors that affect the teaching and learning of English
- Examines how the social context is influential in determining which languages are promoted in schools and society and how these languages are taught
- Is unique in directly relating basic constructs in sociolinguistics to English language teaching
- Features case studies that illustrate the diversity of English teaching contexts

Directed to a wide TESOL and applied linguistics professional readership, this text will be particularly useful and effective for pre-service and in-service professional development in TESOL for K-12 and higher education levels.

Sandra Lee McKay is Professor of English at San Francisco State University, United States.

Wendy D. Bokhorst-Heng is Assistant Professor at the National Institute of Education, Center for Research in Pedagogy and Practice, Singapore.

ESL & Applied Linguistics Professional Series
Eli Hinkel, Series Editor

Visit www.Routledge.com/Education for additional information on titles in the ESL and Applied Linguistics Professional Series

International English in Its Sociolinguistic Contexts

Towards a Socially Sensitive EIL Pedagogy

Sandra Lee McKay and Wendy D. Bokhorst-Heng

Routledge
Taylor & Francis Group

NEW YORK AND LONDON

First published 2008
by Routledge
270 Madison Avenue, New York, NY 10016

Simultaneously published in the UK
by Routledge
2 Park Square, Milton Park, Abingdon, Oxon OX14 4RN

*Routledge is an imprint of the Taylor & Francis Group,
an informa business*

Typeset in Sabon by
RefineCatch Limited, Bungay, Suffolk
Printed and bound in the United States of America on acid-free
paper by Edwards Brothers, Inc

Library of Congress Cataloging in Publication Data
McKay, Sandra.
   International English in its sociolinguistic contexts : towards a
   socially sensitive EIL pedagogy / Sandra Lee McKay, Wendy D.
   Bokhorst-Heng.
     p. cm.
   1. English language—Study and teaching—Foreign speakers.
2. English language—Social aspects.   3. Intercultural
communication.   4. Communication, International.
5. Sociolinguistics.   I. McKay, S. L. (Sandra Lee), 1945–
Bokhorst-Heng, W. D. (Wendy Diana), 1962–   II. Title.
   PE1128.A2M395 2008
   428.2′4—dc22   2007046123

ISBN10: 0–8058–6337–0 (hbk)
ISBN10: 0–8058–6338–9 (pbk)
ISBN10: 1–4106–1798–X (ebk)

ISBN13: 978–0–8058–6337–6 (hbk)
ISBN13: 978–0–8058–6338–3 (pbk)
ISBN13: 978–1–4106–1798–9 (ebk)

Contents

List of tables and figures

Tables

Figure

Preface

Present-day globalization, migration, and the spread of English have resulted in a great diversity of social and educational contexts in which English is being used and learned. The purpose of this book is to examine the sociolinguistic contexts of present-day English use and learning. It is addressed to teachers of English whose students will be using English for international purposes. In examining the sociolinguistic contexts of language learning, we focus on the manner in which English learning is affected by the larger social, political, and educational setting, so we also discuss how the linguistic features of English as an international language (EIL) interactions, both inside and outside of the classroom, are affected by the social context in which the interaction takes place.

One of the major debates in the field of sociolinguistics has been whether to take social or linguistic factors as primary in investigating the relationship between the social context and language variables. As evidence of this debate, Wardhaugh (1992) and others make a distinction between *the sociology of language* and *sociolinguistics*. Whereas the sociology of language investigates the manner in which social and political forces influence language use, sociolinguistics takes linguistic factors as primary in its investigations of language and society. Because we believe there is a constant interplay between the social context and language use and that ideologies typically mediate between these two variables, we have chosen not to employ this distinction as an overarching framework. Nevertheless chapters 3 and 4, "Multilingual societies" and "Language planning and policy," describe social and political forces that affect language use, whereas chapters 5 and 6, "Language variation and standards" and "Interactional sociolinguistics," discuss specific features of the structure and pragmatics of EIL.

The book begins with an overview of the development of EIL and the pedagogical contexts of EIL learning. The first chapter focuses on the role of English in an era of globalization. Employing a language ecology perspective, we examine how English has developed as a global language and how this development has impacted the status and use of English and other languages. The chapter also considers the dangers that can arise in the spread of English in terms of the loss of other languages, growing monolingualism in Anglophone countries, and an economic divide in access to English.

Chapter 2 also deals with the topic of EIL, describing various present-day English learning contexts. While recognizing the limitations of Kachru's (1986) model of Inner, Outer, and Expanding Circles to describe present-day English use, the chapter employs these contexts as a starting point to provide an overview of the various situations in which English is being used and learned today. Major pedagogical challenges faced by educators in each of these contexts are described and exemplified through the use of case studies of specific countries. One of the purposes of chapters 1 and 2 is to raise issues that will be addressed throughout the book.

Chapter 3 provides an analysis of multilingual societies by discussing countries in which there is both diglossia and widespread English bilingualism, such as India and South Africa, as well as countries in which there is English bilingualism without diglossia, such as in Great Britain and the United States. The chapter contrasts English learning contexts among countries with and without diglossia in terms of such factors as incentives and support for learning English, types of English input, status of the mother tongue, and support for mother tongue maintenance.

Chapter 4 focuses on language planning and policy decisions as they affect EIL learning. One of the primary issues addressed in language planning decisions is which language or languages should be designated as an official language. The designation of an official language has important consequences for language learning and teaching in terms of (a) the insight the designation provides into prevalent social attitudes toward particular languages, (b) the effect of government language policies on language-in-education directives, and (c) the setting of linguistic standards. Through the use of case studies, focusing on Singapore and the United States, each of these consequences is examined in depth. These case studies, together with China and Korea, are also used to examine educational responses to the nativization of English. The premise of our discussion is Pennycook's (1994) idea of the "worldliness" of language, and what that worldliness means for language planning and policy. The notion of language *politicking* is employed to capture the often non-linguistic imperatives driving language policy and language pedagogical practices.

The focus of chapter 5 is on how social factors influence specific syntactic, interactional and discourse features of English. Given this micro-level approach, the chapter focuses on linguistic features of present-day English use within their sociolinguistic contexts. Special attention is given to the development of World Englishes, their features and their relationship to identity issues. This discussion of linguistic variation is followed by a thorough analysis of the question of standards in EIL pedagogy. Various meanings of intelligibility are discussed, as well as criteria for determining when a linguistic innovation should be considered a norm.

Chapter 6 examines how interactional sociolinguistics can provide insight into the use of English in an era of globalization. The chapter begins with an overview of the central figures and tenets of interactional sociolinguistics and discusses the methods and premises of research in interactional sociolinguistics. Using this background, we examine existing research regarding EIL interactions. Specifically, we consider the ways in which interactional sociolinguistics research has been beneficial in providing insight into English as a lingua franca (ELF) interactions, the code-switching behavior of bilingual users of English, and bilingual users' attitudes toward code-switching. Throughout the chapter we emphasize the rich linguistic repertoire of bilingual speakers and argue for a greater role in the use of the L1 in L2 learning.

In the final chapter, the authors argue that in order to have a socially sensitive EIL pedagogy, language planners and educators should consider the following factors in making pedagogical decisions: the extent of multilingualism in the country, the language policies and practices of the nation, the linguistic features of the particular varieties of English spoken in the country, and the manner in which individuals in these contexts make linguistic choices to indicate their affiliation with particular speech communities and ideologies. The chapter concludes by outlining various assumptions that should inform a socially sensitive EIL pedagogy.

A basic assumption of the book is that being bilingual in the current era of globalization is a personal and social asset. While we support the acquisition of English for those who desire knowledge of the language, we believe every effort must be made to simultaneously encourage the development of the first language. For this reason, we encourage the development of educational programs that seek to develop proficiency in both English and the mother tongue and examine ways in which the L1 can be used productively to foster proficiency in English.

Woven throughout the text will be several themes. We take as our starting point the ideological basis of language, and the ways in which ideologies mediate between social structure and linguistic practices. We agree with Woolard and Schieffelin (1994) when they say, "Linguistic forms hinge on the ideologization of language use" (p. 56). That is, the kinds of decisions institutions, governments, communities, and individuals make about language and language use are directly linked to the ideologies underlying the socio-cultural context. Language ideologies can be defined as "sets of beliefs about language articulated by users as a rationalization or justification of perceived language structure and use" (Silverstein, 1979, p. 193), or, as defined by Kroskrity (2000), as representing "the perception of language and discourse that is constructed in the interest of a specific social or cultural group" (p. 8). Language ideologies are embedded in real, socio-historical contexts; and they are socio-political, operating in the contexts of relationships of power, forms of discrimination, social engineering, nation-building, and so forth. Thus, when we talk about international English, we assume there are complex ideological constructions of what international English means in different socio-historical and socio-cultural contexts. These ideological constructions have direct bearing on pedagogical practices in the classroom.

From this premise emerges three ideological constructions that are evident in the discourse of EIL The first is an idealization of globalization (e.g., Friedman, 2005). Those who wholeheartedly support globalization point to the manner in which globalization makes it possible for individuals to participate in a global space with equal access to material and intellectual resources. The key to this participation is English. Often lost in such discourse is the manner in which globalization can undermine local values and traditions. Throughout the book we document the ways in which in the current era of globalization there is a constant tension between the global and local. In reference to language planning, this is evident in the manner in which many countries today are formally encouraging the learning of English as a means of becoming part of the global order while at the same time emphasizing the uniqueness and importance of the national culture (Canagarajah, 2006; Tsui & Tollefson, 2007). On a pedagogical level, the tension between globalization and local values is evident in the choice of both pedagogical content and language methodology.

A second discourse we examine is the English-only discourse. Within the English-only discourse it is assumed that the teaching of English should be entirely through the medium of English, with only English allowed in the classroom. Various rationales are offered for this discourse, many of them unverified by language acquisition research. These include the contention that the more English is used in the classroom, the better, which ignores the fact that "the quantity of input is less important than its appropriacy and comprehensibility" (Phillipson, 1992, p. 210). Another common assumption informing English-only discourse is that reference to the L1 in language learning undermines the learning of the target language. Other rationales for using only English are broader in scope. Some schools, for example, advertising an English-medium school, argue that if this is what parents and learners are told is the policy of the school, this policy should be upheld throughout the school, even in social interactions. Such policies can go so far as to penalize students for using their mother tongue, marginalizing the use of the L1 and minimizing the resources of bilingual speakers.

The final discourse we emphasize throughout the book is the Self–Other discourse on both a socio-cultural and individual level. We will refer to this discourse as *Othering*, which "refers to the ways in which the discourse of a particular group defines other groups in opposition to itself; an Us and Them view that constructs an identity for the Other and, implicitly for the Self" (Palfreyman, 2005, pp. 213–214). Such discourse in EIL pedagogy has led to the idealization of the so-called native speaker, as well as to a lack of recognition of the benefits of local bilingual teachers. It has also resulted in an unwillingness to recognize the right of English speakers outside Inner Circle countries to nativize the language for the local cultural context. Finally, the Self–Other discourse has at times positioned certain groups as incapable of participating in "modern" methods of language learning that typically involve group participation and "critical thinking."

Definition of terms

Because the global spread of English into diverse multilingual contexts has brought with it the development of many varieties of English, it is important to examine some of the terminology presently used to describe these varieties. What follows is a clarification of how we will be using three key terms: World Englishes, ELF and EIL.

World Englishes

Our use of the term *World Englishes* is based on Kachru's (1986) early description of institutionalized varieties of English. Kachru distinguishes three major types of users of English: (a) native users of English for whom English is the first language in almost all functions, (b) nonnative users of English who use an institutionalized second-language variety of English, and (c) nonnative users of English who consider English as a foreign language and use it in highly restricted domains. Kachru refers to speakers in the first group as members of the Inner Circle, the second group as members of the Outer Circle and the last group as members of the Expanding Circle. Kachru argues that speakers in the Outer Circle have an institutionalized variety of English, which he describes in the following manner:

> The institutionalized second-language varieties have a long history of acculturation in new cultural and geographical contexts; they have a large range of functions in the local educational, administrative, and legal system. The result of such uses is that such varieties have developed nativized discourse and style types and functionally determined sublanguages (registers) and are used as a linguistic vehicle for creative writing.
>
> (p. 19)

We refer to what Kachru terms institutionalized second-language varieties of English as World Englishes. World Englishes have developed largely in former British colonies where English is used in many domains on a daily basis and has been influenced by local languages and cultures. While Kachru's model was instrumental in initially recognizing the validity of varieties of English, we believe the spread of English has brought with it far more complexity in use than can be captured by this model.

English as a lingua franca

Our use of ELF is based on two early definitions of the term by Firth (1996) and House (1999). They define ELF in the following manner.

> [ELF is] a "contact language" between persons who share neither a common native tongue nor a common (national) culture, and for whom English is the chosen *foreign* language of communication.
>
> (Firth, 1996, p. 240)

> ELF interactions are defined as interactions between members of two or more different linguacultures in English, for none of whom English is the mother tongue.
>
> (House, 1999, p. 74)

We will use the term ELF in the narrow sense described above to include only interactions between L2 speakers of English who do not share a common culture, hence excluding, for example, Indian speakers of English who choose to use English to communicate with other Indian speakers of English who have a different mother tongue, as well as the interactions between L1 and L2 English speakers.

English as an international English

We will use EIL as an umbrella term to characterize the use of English between any two L2 speakers of English, whether sharing the same culture or not, as well as L2 and L1 speakers of English. Our definition then includes speakers of World Englishes communicating within their own country, as well as ELF interactions. It also includes L2 speakers of English using English with L1 speakers. Our definition of EIL is thus much more comprehensive than some who equate EIL with ELF. We also view EIL as far more complex linguistically than is allowed for in either the World Englishes or ELF model. What we have today is a "heterogeneous global English speech community, with a heterogeneous English and different modes of competence" (Canagarajah, 2006, p. 211). One of the aims of this book is to suggest some of the causes and ramifications of this heterogeneity for effective communication, as well as for pedagogy and personal and social identity.

References

Canagarajah, S. A. (2006). Negotiating the local in English as a lingua franca. *Annual Review of Applied Linguistics, 26*, 197–218.

Firth, A. (1996). The discursive accomplishment of normality. On "lingua franca" English and conversation analysis. *Journal of Pragmatics, 26,* 237–259.

Friedman, T. (2005). *The world is flat.* New York: Farrar, Straus and Giroux.

House, J. (1999). Misunderstanding in intercultural communication: Interactions in English as a *lingua franca* and the myth of mutual intelligibility. In C. Gnutzmann (Ed.), *Teaching and learning English as a global language* (pp. 73–89). Tübingen: Stauffenburg.

Kachru, B. B. (1986). *The alchemy of English.* Oxford: Pergamon Press.

Kroskrity, P. V. (2000). *Regimes of language: Ideologies, polities, and identities.* Santa Fe, New Mexico: School of American Research Press.

Palfreyman, D. (2005). Othering in an English language program. *TESOL Quarterly, 39*(2), 211–233.

Pennycook, A. (1994). *The cultural politics of English as an international language.* London: Longman.

Phillipson, R. (1992). *Linguistic imperialism.* Oxford: Oxford University Press.

Silverstein, M. (1979). Language structure and linguistic ideology. In R. Clyne, W. Hanks, & C. Hofbauer (Eds.), *The elements: A parasession on linguistic units and levels* (pp. 193–247). Chicago: Chicago Linguistic Society.

Tsui, A. & Tollefson, J. W. (2007). *Language policy, culture, and identity in Asian contexts.* Mahwah, NJ: Lawrence Erlbaum Associates, Publishers.

Wardhaugh, R. (1992). *An introduction to sociolinguistics. Second edition.* Oxford, UK: Blackwell.

Woolard, K. A. and Schieffelin, B. B. (1994). Language Ideology. *Annual Review of Anthropology, 23*, pp. 55–82.

Acknowledgments

We wish to thank Christina Higgins, Nancy H. Hornberger, David Nunan, and G. Richard Tucker for their constructive feedback on earlier versions of the text, Naomi Silverman and Eli Hinkel for their support in completing this project and most of all our families for their patience and understanding. Special thanks go to Gerry McKay for the back cover image design.

Chapter 1

English in an era of globalization

The purpose of this chapter is to examine how English has developed as a global language and how this development has impacted the status and use of English and other languages. The authors argue that while there are many benefits to having a global language like English, it is essential that language educators work to ensure that the spread of English proceeds in a manner that supports the integrity and development of other languages. The chapter begins by examining the various meanings of globalization and relates this discussion to the teaching of English. Next the chapter explores the reasons for the spread of English, discussing historical, economic, educational and social reasons for its spread. This is followed by a consideration of the dangers that can arise from the spread of English in terms of the maintenance of other languages. The chapter ends with a discussion of two serious consequences of the spread of English, namely, growing English monolingualism and an economic divide in the learning of English.

Globalization and the use of English

Perhaps no other term has been as widely used and abused during the twenty-first century as the term *globalization*. For some, globalization has leveled the playing field, making it possible for everyone to have equal access to a global market and information exchange. This view of globalization forms the basis for Friedman's (2005) popular book, *The world is flat*, in which he argues that today the world is flat, allowing individuals to stay in their own locale while participating in a globally linked economic and information system. Others (e.g., Barber, 1996), however, see globalization as the cause of a loss of cultural and linguistic diversity which, rather than leveling the playing field, has contributed to greater disparity between the rich and the poor.

What is needed is a careful analysis of the varied meanings of the term. Scholte (2000) offers such an analysis by distinguishing several common connotations of the term, including the following.

- globalization as internationalization, or the growth of international exchange;
- globalization as liberalization, or the removal of government imposed restrictions;
- globalization as universalization, or the spreading of common objects and experiences to everyone;
- globalization as westernization, or modernization, suggesting the spread of capitalism, industrialism, and bureaucratism; and
- globalization as deterritorialization, or the change of social space so that space is no longer mapped in terms of territorial places, distances or borders.

Scholte argues that only the last meaning offers new insights into the current globalization; many of the other meanings have existed for several decades. Globalization as westernization, for example, was present in earlier eras of colonialism. He contends that what is new about present-day globalization is the reformulation of social space brought about by mass communication and transportation.

Giddens (1990) shares a similar view of globalization, which he defines as "the intensification of world wide social relations which link distant localities in such a way that local happenings are shaped by events occurring many miles away and vice versa" (p. 64). In our discussion of globalization, we will view globalization as a reformulation of social space in which the global and local are constantly interacting with one another; in addition, we will argue that neither one should be afforded a dominant position. Canagarajah (2005a) makes a similar point when he argues for the need to balance local and global concerns. As he puts it,

> The local shouldn't be of secondary relation or subsidiary status to the dominant discourses and institutions from powerful communities, whereby the global is simply applied, translated, or contextualized to the local. Making a space for the local doesn't mean merely "adding" another component or subfield to the paradigms that already dominate many fields. It means radically reexamining our disciplines to orientate to language, identity, knowledge and social relations from a totally different perspective. A local grounding should become the primary and critical force in the construction of contextually relevant knowledge if we are to develop more plural discourses.
>
> (p. xiv)

One of the goals of this chapter and indeed the book will be to examine the relationship between globalization and the spread of English. Currently, more and more books and articles are addressing the topic of globalization and English teaching (e.g., Block & Cameron, 2002; Canagarajah, 2005a; Crystal, 1997; Pennycook, 2007; Phillipson, 1992). In this chapter, we examine various perspectives of the global spread of English and its influence on English teaching. In sorting through these perspectives, it is helpful to consider Pennycook's (2003) categorization of current attitudes toward the spread of English. The first is what he calls the *homogeny position*, which views the spread of English as leading to a homogenization of world culture. For some, this homogenization is viewed favorably and almost triumphantly. Crystal (1997), for example, cites various statistics to document the pervasiveness of English today and tends to view this pervasiveness as a positive characteristic of globalization. Others, however, see homogenization as essentially a negative feature of globalization, reflecting imperialism and colonization (Phillipson, 1992), and leading to the loss of other languages (Nettle & Romaine, 2000). What is lacking in this perspective is an account of the agency of individuals to react to imperialism and language loss, a point raised by Brutt-Griffler (2002), as well as Canagarajah (2005b) and Pennycook (1998, 2007).

The second position delineated by Pennycook (2003) is the *heterogeny position* in which individuals like Braj Kachru describe the features of World Englishes as a sign of the pluricentricism that has been brought about by globalization. The goal of the World Englishes paradigm has been to describe the manner in which English has become localized, creating different varieties of English around the world. For Pennycook (2003), there is a major shortcoming in this perspective. As he puts it,

> While the homogeny argument tends to ignore all these local appropriations and adaptations, this heterogeny argument tends to ignore the broader political context of the spread of English. Indeed there is a constant insistence on the neutrality of English, a position that avoids all the crucial concerns around both the global and local politics of the language. Furthermore, by focusing on the standardization of local versions of English, the World Englishes paradigm shifts the locus of control but not its nature, and by so doing ignores power and struggle in language.
>
> (p. 8)

In the end, Pennycook (2003) argues that the ultimate effect of globalization on the use of English is neither homogenization nor heterogenization; rather it is "a fluid mixture of cultural heritage . . . and popular culture . . ., of change and tradition, of border crossing and ethnic affiliation, of global appropriation and local contextualization" (p. 10). This, he contends, is what the new global order is about. In the remainder of the chapter we will examine each of these perspectives in depth as we discuss the spread of English as a factor of colonialism, beliefs and incentives, and language loss.

Before we do so, let us explain why it is important to consider the various perspectives outlined above. Primarily, this is because we believe the effect of globalization on language teaching cannot be critically examined unless we consider the manner in which the discourses surrounding English teaching frame the topic of globalization. We agree with Fairclough (2006) that it is important to distinguish the actual process of globalization from the discourses of globalization. As Fairclough (2006) puts it,

> (a) there are real processes of (e.g. economic) globalization, independently of whether people recognize them or not, and of how they represent them; (b) but as soon as we begin to reflect upon and discuss these real processes, we *have* to represent them, and the ways in which we represent them inevitably draw upon certain discourses rather than others. So we might say that the problem turns into that of how we decide *which* discourses to draw upon in reflecting upon and discussing these real processes—how we determine whether and to what extent particular discourses provide us with representations which are adequate for these purposes. [emphasis in the original]
>
> (p. 5)

Our purpose then in describing various discourses that surround the topic of globalization and language teaching is to better assess which discourses are more adequate for representing and assessing the relationship between globalization and language teaching.

The spread of English

Colonialism

Any account of the spread of English would not be complete without a discussion of the role of colonialism. Colonialism is central to the spread of English for several reasons. First, as Pennycook (1998) notes, "English language teaching (ELT) was always a significant part of colonial policy. Where the empire spread so did English" (p. 20). Second, the growth of the British Empire led many to associate the use of English with power since those who knew English had greater access to jobs. This association of English with power resulted in strong incentives to learn English. Finally, colonialism fueled a discourse of the insider and outsider, or the Self and the Other, in which the native Other was often portrayed as "backward, dirty, primitive, depraved, childlike, feminine and so forth" while the colonizers, their language, culture, and political structures were seen as "advanced, superior, modern, civilized, masculine, and so forth" (p. 129). In reference to English language teaching, this viewpoint led to a preference for native-speaking teachers and an emulation of the culture and teaching methods of such speakers.

The role of British and American colonizers in the spread of English is an issue that has been widely debated. Phillipson (1992) and others have argued that the spread of English within British and American colonies is essentially one of linguistic imperialism, which Phillipson contends occurs when "the dominance of English is asserted and maintained by the establishment and continuous reconstitution of structural and cultural inequalities between English and other languages" (p. 47). Structural inequalities are material properties such as institutions and financial allocations that favor the use of one language over another. Cultural inequalities, on the other hand, refer to attitudes and pedagogic principles that favor one language over another.

For Phillipson, the spread of English is due primarily to the linguistic imperialism of British and American colonialism and more recently to a well-funded English teaching establishment. To support this assertion, Phillipson, in his widely circulated book, *Linguistic imperialism*, documents past and present colonial policies enacted by Britain and the United States. He also sets forth five tenets that he argues developed from colonial history and presently inform the English teaching profession.

> Tenet one: English is best taught monolingually.
> Tenet two: the ideal teacher of English is a native-speaker.
> Tenet three: the earlier English is taught, the better the results.
> Tenet four: the more English is taught, the better the results.
> Tenet five: if other languages are used much, standards of English will drop.

Whereas Phillipson presents what has become a popular view of colonial history and the spread of English, it has not gone unchallenged. One of the strongest opponents of this view is Brutt-Griffler (2002) who challenges the theory of linguistic imperialism on several grounds. To begin, she questions Phillipson's reading of colonial policies regarding the establishment of English. She concedes that in the case of American language policies in the Philippines, specific measures were taken to see that widespread English acquisition occurred. The Americans had a clear plan for making English the medium of instruction in all public schools and for pressuring private schools to do the same. However, Brutt-Griffler contends that there were significant differences between American and British colonial language policies. While the United States, as a large nation with a small colonial territory, could afford to implement large-scale

English teaching, Britain, as a small nation with a vast empire, could not afford to do the same.

In contrast to the American policy in the Philippines, the British linguistic policy in countries like India generally was to educate a small group of elite civil servants in English. Because these indigenous leaders often enjoyed social prestige among their people, they were the ideal candidates to implement British policies. At the same time, it was important that these leaders maintain proficiency in the local languages to communicate with the populous. In this way,

> both economic and sociopolitical factors in the colonies had a bearing upon the spread of English. Taken together, they dictated the need for training of an indigenous group of civil servants who would be able to maintain communication between the subjugated population and the imperial officials. This dual aim of "indirect rule," both economic and political, led to a modification of the drive for English education. Given these goals, English education was necessary for the relatively small group of civil servants, albeit not to the exclusion of the teaching of their native language.
>
> (Brutt-Griffler, 2002, p. 44)

Brutt-Griffler's (2002) strongest criticism of Phillipson's theory of linguistic imperialism rests on her conviction that this model, while recognizing the agency of colonizers to impose English, ignores the agency of learners to pursue the learning of English. As she puts it, "When agency in spread is taken one-sidely, it contributes to the writing of an imperial narrative of English spread . . . The conceptual lens of linguistic imperialism obscures the role of Africans, Asians, and other peoples of the world as active agents in the process of creation of world English" (p. 107). The view we will take in this book is that while there are indeed instances of colonizers insisting on the spread of English through educational policies, the agency of individuals to choose to study English cannot be overlooked in a comprehensive analysis of colonial history.

Canagarajah (1999), for example, describes an English classroom in a Tamil community in northern Sri Lanka in which teachers and students both pursue and reject the learning of English. For Canagarajah, the experiences of the learners in this Tamil classroom are representative of many colonized subjects. As he puts it,

> History is replete with examples of colonized subjects who have "betrayed" the claims of the vernacular for the advantages of English, and who now feel they are in some sense outsiders in both Western and local communities. Others, especially in the period since decolonization have rejected English lock, stock, and barrel, in order to be

faithful to indigenous traditions—a choice which has deprived many of them of enriching interactions with multicultural communities and traditions through the English language.

(p. 1)

Any complete account then of the historical and current spread of English must recognize the agency of individuals to both pursue and reject the learning of English. While much of the current and historical literature on language learners suggests that everyone shares a desire to acquire English, it is important to remember that there are many who resist the learning of English for ideological reasons. For those who do desire to learn English, one of the primary factors that has contributed to this desire is a belief in the power of the English language.

The alchemy of English

For many, English is seen as a key to knowledge and personal success. Kachru (1986) in a book entitled The *alchemy of English*, contends that "knowing English is like possessing the fabled Aladdin's lamp, which permits one to open, as it were, the linguistic gates to international business, technology, science and travel. In short, English provides linguistic power" (p. 1). The rhetoric surrounding the English language itself, starting during the colonial era, has often promoted this belief. As Pennycook (1998) notes, the nineteenth century was a time of "immense British confidence in their own greatness, and writing on English abounded with glorifications of English and its global spread" (p. 133). Perhaps one of the best known adulations of English was the comment by Meiklejohn (1891, p. 6 as cited in Pennycook, 1998): "The sun never sets on the British dominions; the roll of the British drum encircles the globe with a belt of sound; and the familiar utterance of English speech are heard on every continent and island, in every sea and ocean, in the world" (p. 133). Praise of the English language continues today with Crystal (1987) extolling the pervasiveness of English.

> English is used as an official or semi-official language in over 60 countries, and has a prominent place in a further 20. It is either dominant or well established in all six continents. It is the main language of books, newspapers, airports and air-traffic control, international business and academic conferences, science, technology, medicine, diplomacy, sports, international competitions, pop music, and advertising. Over two-thirds of the world's scientists write in English. Three quarters of the world's mail is written in English. Of all the information in the world's electronic retrieval systems,

80 percent is stored in English. English language radio programmes are received by over 150 million in 120 countries.

(p. 358)

More recently, Crystal (1997) contends that "there has never been a language so widely spread or spoken by so many people as English" (p. 139). He speculates that there may be no stopping the spread of English since it may have reached a critical number in which it is impossible to stop its growth. If this is the case, he wonders whether or not in the next 500 years, everyone will automatically be introduced to English.

Coulmas (2005) offers further praise of English as he lists reasons why someone today might choose to study English. These include the fact that English is

> the dominant language of the world's greatest military power;
> allocated (co-)official status in a third of the world's countries;
> spoken by the very rich and the very poor;
> used across a wide range of ethnicities and nationalities;
> employed for every conceivable literary genre;
> the basis of the world's biggest language industry;
> the most common second language;
> more widely taught as a foreign language than any other;
> the most valuable linguistic component of human capital;
> the foremost language of international scholarship;
> the language most connected with others by means of bilingual
>   dictionaries;
> involved in more language-contact situations than any other
>   language.

(p. 225)

A belief in the power of English is clearly present among the youth of many large urban centers today. Coulmas, for example, notes that a 2003 survey of city-dwellers in Beijing, Shanghai and Guangzhou found that the vast majority of respondents of all age groups believed that fluency in English was a key to success. This was particularly true of the under-35 age group in which 80 percent expressed this belief. Even though most of these young people speak only a little English, "the notion that English will help them to get on in the world has been implanted in their minds" (p. 224).

One way to view this prevalent belief in the power of English is to see it as a narrative that portrays imagined communities which learners of English strive to join. Fairclough (2006), for example, cites Cameron and Palan (2004) who argue that narratives of globalization can have a constructive effect on the processes and institutions of globalization. As

Fairclough (2006) puts it, "Narratives which are plausible for enough people and which they can come to believe in lead them to invest (their time, energy, money and other resources) in the imaginary futures which these narratives project, and through their commitment to an investment in them ('investment' in the widest sense), they can bring them into being" (p. 19). In reference to English learning there are powerful narratives of English acquisition that lead learners to believe that if they "invest" in English learning, they will reap the benefits of social and intellectual mobility.

Recent research on English learning has documented some of these narratives of imagined communities. Norton and Kamal (2003), for example, report on a study they conducted with middle-school children in Karachi, Pakistan in which young learners of English were asked to reflect on what they would like to do to help Afghan refugee children in Pakistan thrive. Many of the young Pakistani children believed that it was important for the Afghan refugees to develop literacy and to learn some English. Many of the reasons they gave for wanting the Afghan refugee children to learn English illustrate narrations that idealize the benefits of joining an imagined community of English speakers. The following statements, written by young Pakistani students, are representative of such narrations.

> English is the language spoken commonly. This language is understood throughout the world. If the Afghan children learn English, know English, speak English they will be able to discuss their problems with the people of the world.

> The English language is an international language spoken all over the world and it is the language of science. Therefore to promote their education and awareness with modern technologies, it is important to teach them English.

> (p. 309)

Niño-Murcia (2003) cites Peruvian narratives that recount the benefits of joining an imagined community of English speakers. Niño-Murcia examined the beliefs of English learners in Tupichocha, an agro-pastoral village of 1,543 inhabitants that is losing its population from emigration. While people over 40 generally do not express an interest in learning English, this is not true for the younger generation. Many of these young people want to learn English so that they can take distance-learning courses on the Internet; others want to learn English so that they can go to an English-speaking country and earn more money. For example, one respondent, Luz (age 25), when asked why she was studying English, responded that she wanted to learn English so she could go to the United

States and earn a good salary. In her mind English proficiency was the key to both immigration and making money. Yet as Niño-Murcia points out,

> For the participants, the United States is not only an imagined geo-graphical site, but also the land where their needs will be fulfilled. The irony is that the rhetoric of free trade, global market and capital flow comes together with tightening frontiers to prevent human flow. Luz's illusions aside, English is in reality a very minimal factor in whether people are able to surmount the barrier. While the popular media contain vast amounts of false information about both English and the countries where it prevails, they give little or no accurate information about how in fact the immigration/illegal migration sys-tem works. It is the financial requirements of the embassy, not the language factor at all, which actually sets limits on legal access to the USA. While capital and goods can "freely" move, the human element should stay where they "belong."
>
> (p. 132)

Incentives for learning English

A belief in the importance of learning English has gained further momentum by the existence of various incentives to learn English, some real and others part of the imagined benefits of language learning. In the following discussion we examine three areas of English learning incen-tives that are highly relevant to the teaching and learning of English, namely economic, educational, and mass media incentives.

Economic incentives

The groundwork for English to become the major language in the world market was laid with the development of industrial capitalism.

> With the development of industrial capitalism in the late eighteenth century, with England, and later also the United States, as its center, English more and more became the language of the world market. As commerce became a more intensive world phenomenon, and linked all parts of the world market ... the need for a central language of commerce exerted itself, and that language, was, by dint of England's commercial supremacy, naturally English. This circumstance is not attributable to any cultural aspirations of the English, but to the economic conditions that created their commercial supremacy.
>
> (Brutt-Griffler, 2002, p. 49)

Today English is central to many forms of capitalistic endeavors. There are, however, two growing facets of the global work force that provide powerful incentives for English learning. The first is the use of English in transnational corporations. Phillipson (2003) notes that the trend in transnational corporations throughout Europe is to shift to English as the in-house corporate language. A 2001 Danish survey, for example, reported that one third of Danish companies are planning on a shift to the use of English in the work context in the next ten years. In addition, Chrysler workers in Germany are required to learn English, though there is no comparable requirement for English-speakers to learn German (Phillipson, 2003). To the extent that this trend continues, English will be an important language to know in order to be employed in transnational corporations.

Outsourcing is another facet of the world market that is largely undertaken in English. Friedman (2005), for example, argues that even though India has few natural resources, its present economy is growing rapidly, largely because it is good at doing one thing—"mining the brains of its own people by educating a relatively large slice of its elites in the sciences, engineering and medicine" (p. 104). This mining of brains, however, is only economically rewarding in a global context if the educated workforce speaks English. Since India is one of the few places where one can find a surplus of English-speaking engineers, companies that need technical expertise can now get this help cheaply over the Internet. (See Vaish, forthcoming, for a complete discussion of the outsourcing industry in India.) Currently in many transnational corporations and outsourcing jobs, English is a condition for employment. This fact lends further support to the belief that English is like Aladdin's lamp.

The centrality of English in transnational corporations and outsourcing is an indication of changing work categories. Reich (1991, as cited in Warschauer 2000) categorizes the present work force into three categories.

1   *Routine-production service workers* include factory workers but also routine information workers, such as data processors and payroll clerks.
2   *In-person service workers* include workers such as janitors, hospital attendants, and taxi drivers.
3   *Symbolic analysts* spend much of their time analyzing symbol-based (numerical and textual) information. These workers include software engineers, management consultants, strategic planners, lawyers, real estate developers and research scientist.

(pp. 517–518)

It is the last category of employees that is increasing in the globalized economy. It is such workers who frequently use English in the work context and are experiencing a rise in income, status and career opportunities.

What do these changing trends in the work force suggest for the teaching of EIL? As Warschauer (2000) notes,

> First . . . they underscore the role of English as an international language for global communication. Secondly, they signal a change in the types of communication required in English. A large and increasing number of people, even if they never set foot in an English-speaking country, will be required to use English in highly sophisticated communication and collaboration with people around the world. They will need to be able to write persuasively, critically interpret and analyze information, and carry out complex negotiations and collaboration in English.
>
> (p. 518)

While routine-production workers and in-person service workers may need to use some English on the job, the type of English they will need is far more restricted than that required of the symbolic analysts. The fact that a high level of English proficiency is often required for symbolic analysts and that such individuals typically reap higher economic benefits than other workers indicate the manner in which English can contribute to an economic divide in which those who can afford to develop their English proficiency are those that may be able to reap the economic benefits that it brings.

Educational incentives

Current educational incentives for learning English tend to occur through two mechanisms. The first is policies within educational institutions and the second is government policies. In the case of the former, there is an increasing trend in European universities to offer courses and degrees in English. In addition, many English-speaking nations are actively recruiting learners from other countries on the grounds that students will benefit from an English-medium education. Finally, in many fields, but particularly in scientific fields, there is pressure for scholars to publish in English. Phillipson (2003) points out the negative effects of such a policy:

> the pressures to publish "internationally" rather than locally are intense, and are seen as applicable to all scholars. This can lead to a neglect of local or national topics. It can also lead to a false sense of priorities when posts are filled, if writing for an "international" journal is assumed to imply better quality than in a national one.
>
> (p. 81)

Another way in which educational incentives for learning English can occur is through government language policy decisions. Current Chinese language-in-education policies illustrate the manner in which the learning and teaching of English can be strongly influenced by government policies in regard to both the requirements for studying English and the methods promoted in the English language classroom. In 1976 Deng Xiaoping launched a national modernization program in which English education was seen as a key component: "English was recognized as an important tool for engaging in economic, commercial, technological and cultural exchange with the rest of the world and hence for facilitating the modernization process" (Hu, 2005, p. 8).

In 1978 the Ministry of Education issued the first unified primary and secondary curriculum for the era of modernization. This curriculum introduced foreign language learning at Primary 3. The directive also mandated that efforts in promoting English language proficiency were to be aimed at strengthening English language teaching in elite schools, which were expected to produce the English-proficient personnel needed to successfully undertake national modernization. In fact, in 1985 the Ministry of Education exempted poorly resourced schools from providing English instruction. In addition, the Ministry of Education gave several economically developed provinces and municipalities the autonomy to develop their own English curricula, syllabi and textbooks for primary and secondary education (Hu, 2005). These materials tended to be more innovative, learner-centered and communicative than earlier classroom texts and materials.

The directives summarized above illustrate the dangers that can arise from state mandated guidelines for language teaching. First, such mandates can determine when foreign language learning begins in the public school system. The Chinese Ministry of Education, like many other Asian countries, is formally promoting the early learning of English, even though the issue of early exposure to foreign language learning is still being debated. Second, state mandates can determine who has access to English language learning. In China, recent policies have tended to support English learning among Chinese elite, in this way exacerbating educational inequality. Finally, state mandates can determine how a language is taught. In China, as in many other Asian countries, current curriculum developments have tended to promote more learner centered, communicative methods, largely because these are the methods being promoted in the West and associated with modernization.

Government policies like those introduced in China can result in parental pressure for children to learn English. This is clearly the case in Korea today. In 1997 the Ministry of Education decided to have English become a regular subject in elementary schools so that presently third and fourth graders are required to take English classes for one hour a week while fifth and sixth graders take English classes for two hours a week.

Since English has become a compulsory subject in elementary schools, many Korean parents are sending their children to English-language kindergartens, even though such schools are typically three times more expensive than ordinary kindergartens (Park, 2006). In addition, the number of Korean students studying abroad in English-speaking countries has increased more than ten-fold in the past six years. In fact, the number of elementary students alone has increased from 212 in 1998 to 6,276 in 2004, marking a 30-fold increase (Chung, 2006). Such parental pressure for learning English has led to a heated discussion in the mass media as to the wisdom of pushing young people to learn English (e.g., Park, 2006).

Another Ministry of Education policy that provides incentives for English learning is standardized tests for entry to institutions of higher education. According to LoCastro (1996), in Japan English is a de facto requirement for higher education since almost all entrance examinations for high schools, colleges, and universities include some type of English language assessment. Because of this, many young Japanese state that their primary reason for learning English is to pass English exams. Furthermore, most of these exams focus on grammar, vocabulary, pronunciation and translation questions, making the acquisition of spoken English much less of an issue for language learners. Many contend that the exams have had a deleterious washback effect on language teaching since classroom teachers feel under tremendous pressure to teach for the exam no matter what they have learned in methods classes or what kind of methods are advocated by the Ministry of Education.

Mass media incentives

Four areas of the mass media that currently provide motivation for English learning, particularly among the younger generation, are advertising, music, movies, and electronic communication.

ADVERTISING

From Beijing to Paris to Cairo products today are typically promoted in English. In his analysis of the use of English in Mexican advertising, Baumgardner (2006) provides countless examples of the use of English as attention-getters in newspaper and magazine advertising. He also points to the use of English in Mexican shop names as, for example, *Le Pavillion Sports Bar*, *Status Men's Shop*, *Athlete's Foot* and *Payless Car Rental*. Mexican product names using English or English compounds are also common as, for example, *Boots*, *Chip's* and *Sandwichitas* (literally "little sandwiches"). Executives of advertising companies offer several reasons why these phenomena are occurring. First, by using English in product names, the product has a greater chance of becoming known in other countries due to the widespread use of English as a second language. In addition, many consumers seem to believe that if a product has an English name, it will be superior to a local product. Finally, the use of English seems to give products status and prestige. Ross (1997), for example, contends that Italians are using English in shop names because of its prestige.

> The simple reason for most of these shop signs [in Milan] is that English is today seen as an attractive and fashionable language. An English name lends an aura of chic prestige to a business, suggesting that it is part of the international scene, following the latest trends, up-to-date with the newest ideas. This aspect of English as an international language ... is perhaps too often underestimated. Yes, English is important for communication world-wide, but English is also important because of the prestige associated with English-speaking countries, America in particular.
>
> (as cited in Baumgardner, 2006, p. 263)

MUSIC

Because English is the dominant language in popular music today, music is another aspect of the mass media that can provide motivation for learning English. In many countries, exposure to popular songs in English has led to a good deal of code-mixing in locally produced pop music. As Kachru (2006) points out, such mixing can serve various purposes, such as providing social commentary or achieving satirical and humorous effects. For example, in her analysis of Hindi popular songs, she found that the purpose of a good deal of the code-mixing was to create humor by parodying Westernized youth.

In other contexts, code-mixing is used to challenge existing social and political norms and to portray a modern identity. Moody (2006), for example, asserts that the use of English in Japanese challenges a belief in the uniqueness of the Japanese language: "If English text is able to suggest a meaning in Japanese, and vice versa, then it is difficult to maintain the myth of Japanese uniqueness. Instead, the Japanese language begins to function within a domain that is also occupied by English" (p. 220). In addition, the mixing of Japanese and English in popular songs seems to express a "desire for a more cosmopolitan and globally influential language" (p. 220). English then is often used in both advertising and popular music as a symbol for modernity and globalization. Such connotations of English provide further incentives to learn the language, especially among urban youth.

One of the most persuasive accounts of the influence of English and globalization on music is Pennycook (2007). Based on his in-depth analysis of hip-hop culture in a variety of contexts from Malaysia to Senegal, Pennycook argues that hip-hop culture is a vivid illustration of *transcultural flows*. He maintains that in evaluating hip-hop culture

> we need to move beyond arguments about homogeneity or hetero-geneity, or imperialism and nation states, and instead focus on translocal and transcultural flows. English is a translocal language, a language of fluidity and fixity that moves across, while becoming embedded in, the materiality of localities and social relations. English is bound up with transcutlural flows, a language of imagined communities and refashioning identities.
>
> (p. 6)

Pennycook shares with Appadurai (2001) the idea that in an era of globalization, "we are functioning in a world fundamentally character-ized by objects in motion. These objects include ideas and ideologies, people and goods, images and messages, technologies and techniques. This is a world of flows" (p. 5). For Pennycook, pop music is a vivid illustration of these flows where global and local languages mix to create new language forms and images.

MOVIES

While advertising and songs provide little opportunity for extended input in English, this is not the case for movies. There is no doubt that American movies dominate the world film market, with some estimates that the United States controls about 75 percent of the world film market (Crystal, 1997). What is significant for language learning is that in many contexts, American films are being shown with the English sound track and visual subtitles in the local language(s). The same is true for a good deal of television viewing. Phillipson (2003) argues that this use of two languages provides a form of linguistic hybridization. As he puts it, this mixing of languages "is typical of cultural globalization, through which a diverse cultural landscape is being subjected to the commercial and consumerist pressures of large, privately owned media corporations. Television viewing with bilingual input . . . is a form of linguistic hybridization" (p. 87).

ELECTRONIC COMMUNICATION

Electronic communication provides another source of global exposure to English. Nowhere is this use so prevalent as in China. According to recent estimates there are 68 million users of the Internet in Mainland China with nearly 26 million computers connected to the Internet and over 474,000 web sites (Gao, 2006). In analyzing various Internet contexts in China, Gao (2006) found a prevalent use of Chinese–English code-mixing, leading to an Englishization of Mandarin Chinese. Gao maintains that this phenomenon has three significant sociolinguistic implications. First, what he terms Chinese Internet language (CIL) (i.e., the use of Mandarin Chinese with English influence) has a great deal of social prestige. Because of this prestige, such language will have an impact upon people's language use and be emulated by many young people. Second, because CIL is mainly used among young Chinese who tend to be the vanguards of language change, such vibrant use of language is likely to be contagious. Finally, the use of CIL is likely to have a cross-modality linguistic influence: "CIL, language mostly used in online communication, may also gradually spread to the domain of non-electronic communication, both spoken and written, and consequently lead to the changes in the Chinese language" (p. 306).

Lam's (2000) study documents another effect of computer-mediated communication (CMC), namely the ability of language learners to assume a new identity, one that can enhance literacy skills. Lam's study was a case study of a Chinese immigrant teenager to the United States, named Almon. When Lam first began studying Almon, he had little confidence in writing in English, which he contended was always his worst subject. However, after designing his own home page and joining an electronic community interested in Japanese pop culture, he gained confidence in his literacy through his online exchanges with pen pals. Lam contends that the community Almon joined on the web allowed him to develop a new identity, one that gave him self-confidence. She concludes that

> Whereas classroom English appeared to contribute to Almon's sense of exclusion or marginalization (his inability to speak like a native), which paradoxically contradicts the school's mandate to prepare students for the workplace and civic involvement, the English he controlled on the Internet enabled him to develop a sense of belongingness and connectedness to a global English-speaking community. Almon was learning not only more English but also more relevant and appropriate English for the World Wide Web community he sought to become a part of.
>
> (p. 476)

In light of the positive effect that pop culture and the World Wide Web can engender in learners' identity, confidence and literacy skills, we agree with Lam that "TESOL in today's global, multicultural world needs a broad and critical conception of language and literacy that is responsive to students' relations to multiple target languages and cultural communities"

(p. 478). Having documented the current spread of English and some of the incentives for learning English, we turn now to an examination of how the spread of English is affecting other local languages.

English and other languages

Demographics

It is estimated that today there are around 5,000–6,700 languages in the world and about half of these will become extinct in the next century. Furthermore, about 90 percent of the world's population speaks the 100 most used languages, leaving about 6,000 languages spoken by 10 percent of the population. Of the 100 most used languages, the top 15 languages in terms of numbers of native speakers are spoken by about half of the world's population (Nettle & Romaine, 2000). These top 15 languages are listed in Table 1.1

The geographical distribution of these languages differs significantly. While English, Spanish, Portuguese, French, and Mandarin have a large geographical reach, this is not true for the other languages on the list. In fact, about 83 percent of the world's languages are spoken in only one country and, in addition, there are 25 to 30 times as many languages in the world as there are countries (Nettle & Romaine, 2000). What this suggests is that bilingualism or multilingualism is the state of affairs in most countries today. For example, half the citizens of the European Union Member States report that they can speak at least one other

Table 1.1 Top 15 languages in terms of numbers of native speakers

Rank	Language	Population	% of world's population
1	Chinese, Mandarin	885,000,000	15
2	English	322,000,000	5.4
3	Spanish	266,000,000	4.5
4	Bengali	189,000,000	3.2
5	Hindi	182,000,000	3.0
6	Portuguese	170,000,000	2.8
7	Russian	170,000,000	2.8
8	Japanese	125,000,000	2.1
9	German	98,000,000	1.6
10	Chinese, Wu	77,175,000	1.3
11	Javanese	75,500,800	1.2
12	Korean	75,000,000	1.2
13	French	72,000,000	1.2
14	Vietnamese	66,897,000	1.1
15	Telegu	66,350,000	1.1

Source: Nettle & Romaine, 2000, p. 29.

language than their mother tongue at the level of being able to have a conversation (Eurobarometer, 2005).

Although English has far fewer native speakers than Mandarin and several languages have 100,000,000 speakers or more, clearly it is English that is considered the international language of the world today. What has greatly increased the geographical spread and significance of English today is the number of second language speakers of English. Indeed presently there are more second language speakers of English than there are native speakers. In addition, English is the dominant or official language in over 60 of the 185 nation-states recognized by the United Nations (Nettle & Romaine, 2000). Many of the reasons for the present-day dominance of English were discussed earlier in the chapter. We now turn to considering the relationship of English to other languages, considering to what extent English is replacing other languages in the world.

Language shift

Nettle and Romaine (2000) note that there are several ways in which a language can die. The first is language loss through population loss, that is, when speakers of the language disappear through disease or wars, as was the case with some colonized indigenous populations. The second way is through language shift, either a forced or voluntary shift. In forced language shift, populations are often required through colonization to acquire the language of the conqueror, a clear case of what Phillipson (1992) terms linguistic imperialism. There are many cases of forced language shift. Nettle and Romaine (2000), for example, document the loss of the Hawaiian languages and the decline of the Celtic languages. In voluntary shift, individuals perceive that it is to their benefit to acquire another language. Both types of shift have contributed to the widespread growth of English; however, in many contexts aspects of both forced and voluntary shift are present, as was the case in the Philippines.

When the United States acquired the Philippines, it undertook an extensive documentation of the demographics of the country, noting some 87 indigenous languages. Aware that the Spanish had had little impact in unifying the country linguistically, the Americans drafted a detailed plan to spread English within the country. At the base of the plan was a decision to use English as the sole means of instruction in the public schools. Whereas the official reports of the Bureau of Education contended that the plan would be successful so that within 15 years English would be the common unifying language of the country, "in practice, the great majority of the population continued using local languages, despite the reported 97 percent of the Filipino children who passed through the colonial educational system by the late 1920s" (Brutt-Griffler, 2002, p. 36). Although the policy would seem to have been a failure from the

Americans' perspective, the fact is that today English is widely used in Filipino society. The question is why.

Part of the answer lies in Nettle and Romaine's (2000) account of the influence of economic takeoff on languages. They distinguish the pull and push factor of economic development in the following manner:

> On the one hand, the developed economies have a strong pull factor, offering as they do the apparent possibility of wonderful new technologies, more profitable occupations, and a rising standard of living. On the other hand, economic takeoff gives the elite classes extraordinary power, by furnishing them with ever-better weapons, larger armies, and many other technologies for controlling and brainwashing people. Such elites have a strong interest in compelling people to join their sphere of economic interest—a larger sphere of interest means more profits—and they often do. This "push" factor is just as significant as the intrinsic "pull" of economic development in understanding subsequent history.
>
> (p. 132)

In the case of the Philippines, what the American plan for the imposition of English did was to establish a "push" factor, namely a tradition of English medium education and use. However, it may well be that it has been the pull factor of economic development that has led to the widespread use of English in the Philippines today. In this way, language shift is often a result of complex processes, some of them related to push factors (i.e., linguistic imperialism) and others clearly related to pull factors. In the Philippines, as in many other countries around the world today, individuals have chosen to learn English but they "did not themselves generate the conditions under which they had to choose" (Nettle & Romaine, 2000, 142).

Cases like the Philippines demonstrate that language shift or endangerment is often a far more complex process than some of the literature on linguistic imperialism would suggest. Drawing on examples of African colonization, Mufwene (2002), for example, contends that "the vitality of a language often depends on factors other than merely power. They show that if power has any role to play, basic cost-and-benefit considerations having to do with what a speaker needs a particular language for, or to what extent a particular language facilitates survival in a changing socio-economic ecology, determine what particular languages are given up and doomed to attrition and eventual extinction" (p. 164). Although there are those who see the global spread of English as the culprit for today's language loss, we would argue, first, that the local linguistic ecology often has a far greater impact on language shift and maintenance than does the global spread of English, and second, that current discourse on the spread of English is often assessed in reference to the elite of a country rather than the population in general.

One of the central questions that will be addressed throughout this book is to what extent it is a good thing that today more and more people speak an international language. Clearly there are benefits in being able to use English to access information and perhaps to achieve greater economic development. What is at issue is how this can be done in a manner that gives individuals real freedom of choice in deciding which languages to use when and where. As we shall see in the following chapters, there is a good deal of ambivalence today regarding the spread of English. Whereas the speakers of many of the minority languages in the world today want to take part in the benefits of knowing English, they do not want to do this at the expense of the other languages they speak or their culture. One goal of this book is to explore how the teaching and learning of English can be undertaken in such a way as to maintain linguistic diversity while providing equal access to the acquisition of English. We share with Joseph & Ramani's (2006) a belief in "the right of people to have access to English—the language of modernity and globalism" (p. 186). Yet as they point out, the spread of English has brought with it two alarming phenomena:

> The first is the danger of educated, middle-class people worldwide becoming monolingual in English. The second is the social exclusion and isolation from mainstream life for many people in the "developing world" who have inadequate levels of competence in English. This latter phenomenon is linked to the rapid displacement of local languages by English, and lack of support for maintenance and promotion of these languages.
>
> (p. 187)

We turn now to an examination of these two potential dangers of the spread of English, namely growing monolingualism and an economic divide in the learning of English.

Monolingualism

As Ellis (2006) points out, things that are taken for granted usually do not have articles describing and examining them; hence, there is a dearth of books that examine *monolingualism* as a construct. In light of this situation, Ellis' article on monolingualism is a welcome addition to the literature on language use. Ellis begins by exploring various definitions of monolingualism, some of which demonstrate the complexity of defining the term. Richards & Schmidt (2002), for example, in the *Longman dictionary of language teaching and applied linguistics*, define it as

1   A person who knows and uses only one language.
2   A person who has an active knowledge of only one language, though perhaps a passive knowledge of others.

(as cited in Ellis, 2006, p. 175)

This definition suggests that an individual who has some familiarity with another language could still be considered monolingual. The question then becomes how much knowledge must one have of a second language to be considered monolingual. The answer clearly is a matter of degree and just as bilingualism is best regarded as a continuum, "it follows that the point on the continuum which separates a bilingual from a monolingual will vary according to the interests and focus of those proposing it" (p. 175). For Ellis, "an individual is *monolingual* who does *not* have access to more than one linguistic code as a means of social communication" [emphasis in the original] (p. 176).

Ellis (2006) then goes on to characterize three prevalent representations of monolingualism. The first perspective views monolingualism as the unmarked case against which bilingualism and multilingualism are measured. Unfortunately, this is the perspective reflected in some second language acquisition research that assumes a monolingual starting point rather than recognizing that for many users of English the goal of learning English is to achieve bilingualism.

The second perspective of monolingualism delineated by Ellis is one that emphasizes the cognitive, communicative, social and vocational limitations of monolingualism. This is the stance promoted in much of the literature that encourages the acquisition of a second language, particularly for what is sometimes termed *elite bilingualism*, that is, the learning of a foreign language primarily for travel or cultural purposes. Ellis (2006) points out that when the Australian government in the early 1980s argued that languages need not form part of a core curriculum for Australian schools, the Australian Linguistic Society and Applied Linguistic Society of Australia presented a variety of educational, sociopolitical and personal reasons for supporting the study of foreign languages in Australia, arguing that studying a second language is educationally, culturally and intellectually enriching.

The third perspective of monolingualism outlined by Ellis (2006) is one that is the most critical of monolingualism, employing metaphors of disease, sickness and disability to describe monolingualism. Ellis cites Skutnabb-Kangas (2000) for example, who writes, "Like cholera or leprosy, monolingualism is an illness which should be eradicated as soon as possible" (as cited in Ellis, 2006, p. 186). In reference to ESL teachers, Skutnabb-Kangas (2000) writes,

To me monolingual ESL teachers are [by] definition incompetent to teach ESL: they simply lack several of the capacities or proficiencies that a learner needs and can reasonably expect from the teacher (. . .) a starting point for all ESL teachers is to eradicate monolingualism among themselves.

(as cited in Ellis, 2006, p. 188)

It is difficult to accept such an extreme view until far more is known about the effects of monolingualism both on cognitive development and on the teaching of a second language. Because of this, we agree with Ellis (2006) that "monolingualism is deserving of study as a phenomenon in its own right, and not just as the invisible and unexamined corollary of bilingualism" (p. 189).

However, assuming monolingualism as a starting point in reference to the spread of English has several dangers. First, it can result in a type of complacency among monolingual English-speaking individuals so that, as Crystal (1997) points out, the spread of English as a global language "will cultivate an elite monolingual linguistic class, more complacent and dismissive in their attitudes toward other languages" (p. 12). Evidence for such complacency is demonstrated by the decline in foreign language education in many Anglophone countries. For example, in institutions of higher education in the United States, the number of students studying modern foreign languages as a percent of college students has steadily declined since the 1960s (Welles, 2004). As we shall see in chapters 2 and 3, similar trends are occurring in Great Britain and Australia.

The second danger of assuming monolingualism as a starting point, as we noted earlier, is that second language acquisition research often fails to recognize that the goal of second language acquisition for most learners of English is to become bilinguals rather than monolinguals (Sridhar & Sridhar, 1994). Finally, taking monolingualism as a starting point is also dangerous for ELT pedagogy in that it can support the view that an English-only classroom is the desired approach to second language learning without examining the benefits of using the students' other languages to productively facilitate the learning of English. We turn now to an examination of a second danger in the spread of English, namely, inequality in access to English language learning.

An economic divide in English language learning

As we pointed out earlier, current language policies enacted by the Chinese Ministry of Education have tended to promote English language learning for the elite in China. The same situation is presently occurring in Hong Kong, where in 1997 the Department of Education announced a sweeping change in the medium of instruction in Hong Kong schools so that most schools were asked to adopt Chinese as the medium of instruction. At the same time, the government made an exemption for a minority of schools that had been operating successfully in English to continue using English as the medium of instruction (Choi, 2003). According to Choi (2003), the policy, "which provided for the selection of the best primary school graduates for monolingual education, was designed to be a cost-effective way of training in English skills for those who had the economic and cultural capital to benefit from it. Meanwhile, the majority of students were barred from sufficient exposure to English, the language of power and wealth" (p. 673). Choi contends that the policy was basically engineered by business interests right before the change over in 1997 and that its ultimate effect was to "perpetuate a form of linguistic imperialism" (p. 673).

In order to justify the policy, the government extolled the benefits of mother tongue education; however, many parents believed that what would be best for their children was for them to go to English-medium schools and potentially gain the economic capital they believed, rightly or wrongly, would come from proficiency in English. Many parents strove to get their children into the small number of English-medium schools or enroll them in expensive international schools and even send their children overseas to Anglophone countries to study, options that were available only to a small proportion of economically elite families. The Hong Kong language policy then had several negative effects brought on by globalization and the spread of English: first, it encouraged an economic divide in the learning of English; second, it minimized the value of using the mother tongue in education with its implicit suggestion that this option was in some ways less desirable; and finally, it promoted the idea of the desirability of an English-only classroom in the acquisition of English.

An economic divide in the teaching of English is also evident in South Korea where Park and Abelman (2004) argue that "English has long been a class marker in South Korea: namely knowledge of and comfort with English has been a sign of educational opportunity, and for some of the experience of travel or study abroad and contact with foreigners in South Korea" (p. 646). Park and Abelman contend that today in South Korea "there is a veritable English language mania" (p. 646). The size of the English language market in South Korea is estimated to be about $3,333 million dollars a year with another $833 million spent on study abroad programs. The private after-school education market is also booming, particularly after it was announced in 1995 that English would become an elementary school subject. However, participation in this English-education market is not within the reach of those with fewer economic assets.

As a vivid illustration of this economic divide, Park and Abelman (2004), drawing on their extensive interviews with three South Korean mothers, document the manner in which class affected these mothers' management of their children's English after-school education. For the mother with fewer economic assets, her inability to provide her children with the kind of English education she desired reminded her of her own educational deprivation and her economic limitations. For the middle-class mother, who spoke English and whose study abroad experience led her to realize that life abroad is also stratified, she worried how far her children's English would really take them. Finally, the upper-class mother tended to celebrate the acquisition of English as a source of personal satisfaction and a necessary condition for cosmopolitan membership. Indeed, for Park and Ableman (2004), English among South Korea's growing middle class is intimately related to South Korea's cosmo-politan striving, i.e., a desire to be part of the global order. The story of these three mothers highlights an important dimension of globalization, the spread of English and an economic divide in the learning of English, namely, that these themes play a very influential role in family life in which parents' desire for their children's acquisition of English can engender a sense of personal inadequacy and dissatisfaction. Because we believe the issue of an economic divide in English learning is a critical issue in the teaching of English, we will return to this theme at various points in the book.

Summary

In addressing the issue of the use of English in an era of globalization, we began by arguing that globalization, in the sense of an intensification of social relations across distant localities, necessitates a shared language, which at the present time is English. In order to understand how English has achieved international status, we examined reasons for the historical and present-day spread of English. We devoted special attention to recent economic, educational and mass media incentives for learning English. We also emphasized the fact that in evaluating the role of linguistic imperialism in the spread of English, it is important to recognize the power colonizers have exerted to impose English, but equally important to rec-ognize the agency of learners to both pursue and resist the acquisition of English.

The chapter then explored the effect of the spread of English on the other languages of the world. Although there is little question that the use of some languages has been severely curtailed through linguistic imperial-ism, at the same time many individuals have acquired English because of the many pull factors that entice learners to learn English. The final section of the chapter examined two potential dangers of the spread of English, namely, growing monolingualism among English speakers and an economic divide in English learning. We turn in the next chapter to an analysis of the various social contexts in which English is currently being learned.

References

Appadurai, A. (2001). Grassroots globalization and the research imagination. In A. Appadurai (Ed.), *Globalization* (pp. 1–21). Durham, NC: Duke University Press.

Barber, B. (1996). *Jihad vs. McWorld: How globalism and tribalism are reshaping the world*. New York: Ballantine Books.

Baumgardner, R. (2006). The appeal of English in Mexican commerce. *World Englishes, 25*(2), 251–266.

Block, D. & Cameron, D. (Eds.) (2002). *Globalization and language teaching*. Mahwah, NJ: Lawrence Erlbaum Associates.

Brutt-Griffler, J. (2002). *World English: A study of its development*. Clevedon: Multilingual Matters.

Cameron, A. & Palan, R. (2004). *The imagined economies of globalization*. London: Sage.

Canagarajah, A. S. (1999). *Resisting imperialism in English teaching*. Oxford: Oxford University Press.

Canagarajah, A. S. (2005a). Introduction. In A. S. Canagarajah (Ed.), *Reclaiming the local in language policy and practice* (pp. xiii–xxx). Mahwah, NJ: Lawrence Erlbaum Associates.

Canagarajah, A. S. (Ed.) (2005b). *Reclaiming the local in language policy and practice*. Mahwah, NJ: Lawrence Erlbaum Associates.

Choi, P. K. (2003). "The best students will learn English": Ultra-utilitarianism and linguistic imperialism in post-1997 Hong Kong. *Journal of Education Policy, 28*(6), 673–694.

Chung, A. (2006). Children driven to learn English. *The Korea Times*. Retrieved November 20, 2006 from http://search.hankooki.com/times/times.

Coulmas, F. (2005). *Sociolinguistics: The study of speakers' choices*. Cambridge: Cambridge University Press.

Crystal, D. (1987). *The Cambridge encyclopedia of language*. New York: Cambridge University Press.

Crystal, D. (1997). *English as a global language*. Cambridge: Cambridge University Press.

Ellis, E. (2006). Monolingualism: The unmarked case. *Estudios de Sociolingüistica. 7*(2), 173–196.

Eurobarometer. (2005). Europeans and Languages. Retrieved October 18, 2006 from http://ec.europa.eu/public_opinion/archives/eb_special_en.htm.

Fairclough, N. (2006). *Language and globalization*. London: Routledge.

Friedman, T. (2005). *The world is flat*. New York: Farrar, Straus and Giroux.

Gao, L. (2006). Language contact and convergence in computer-mediated communication. *World Englishes, 25*(2), 299–308.

Giddens, A. (1990). *The consequences of modernity*. Cambridge: Polity Press.

Hu, G. (2005). English language education in China: Policies, progress, and problems. *Language Policy, 4*, 5–24.

Joseph, M. & Ramani, E. (2006). English in the world does not mean English everywhere: The case for multilingualism in the ELT/ESL profession. In R. Rubdy & M. Saraceni (Eds.), *English in the world: Global rules, global roles* (pp. 186–199). London: Continuum.

Kachru, B. B. (1986). *The alchemy of English*. Oxford: Pergamon Press.

Kachru, Y. (2006). Mixers lyricing in Hinglish: Blending and fusing in Indian popular culture. *World Englishes, 25*(2), 223–233.

Lam, W. S. (2000). L2 literacy and the design of the self: A case study of a teenager writing on the Internet. *TESOL Quarterly, 34*(3), 457–482.

LoCastro, V. (1996). English language education in Japan. In H. Coleman (Ed.) *Society and the language classroom* (pp. 40–58). Cambridge: Cambridge University Press.

Moody, A. (2006). English in Japanese culture and J-Pop music. *World Englishes, 25*(2), 209–222.

Mufwene, S. (2002). Colonization, globalization, the future of language in the twenty-first century. *International Journal on Multicultural Societies, 4*(2), 162–193.

Nettle, D. & Romaine, S. (2000). *Vanishing voices: The extinction of the world's languages*. Oxford: Oxford University Press.

Niño-Murcia, M. (2003). English is like the dollar: Hard currency ideology and the status of English in Peru. *World Englishes, 22*(2), 121–142.

Norton, B. & Kamal, F. (2003). The imagined communities of English: Language learners in Pakistani school. *Journal of Language, Identity and Education, 2*(4), 301–317.

Park, C. (2006). Parents push early English learning. *The Korea Times*. Retrieved November 20, 2006, from http://search.hankooki.com/times/times.

Park, S. J. & Ableman, N. (2004). Class and cosmopolitan striving: Mothers' management of English education in South Korea. *Anthropological Quarterly*, 645–672.

Pennycook, A. (1998). *English and the discourses of colonialism*. London: Routledge.

Pennycook. A. (2003). Beyond homogeny and heterogeny: English as a global and worldly language. In C. Mair (Ed.), *The politics of English as a world language* (pp. 3–17). Amsterdam: Rodopi.

Pennycook, A. (2007). *Gobal Englishes and transcultural flows*. London: Routledge.

Phillipson, R. (1992). *Linguistic imperialism*. Oxford: Oxford University Press.

Phillipson, R. (2003). *English-only Europe?* London: Routledge.

Richards, J. C. & Schmidt, R. (2002) *Longman dictionary of language teaching and applied linguistics. Third edition*. Harlow, Essex: Longman.

Scholte, J. A. (2000). *Globalization: A critical introduction*. London: Palgrave.

Skutnabb-Kangas, T. (2000). *Linguistic genocide in education—or worldwide diversity and human rights?* Mahwah, NJ: Lawrence Erlbaum Associates, Inc.

Sridhar, S. N. & Sridhar, K. K. (1994). Indigenized Englishes as second languages: Toward a functional theory of second language acquisition in multilingual contexts. In R. K. Agnihotri & A. L. Khanna (Eds.), *Second language acquisition: Socio-cultural and linguistic aspects of English in India* (pp. 41–63). London: Sage Publications.

Vaish, V. (forthcoming). *Biliteracy and globalization in India.* Clevedon: Multilingual Matters.

Warschauer, M. (2000). The changing global economy and the future of English teaching. *TESOL Quarterly, 34,* 511–535.

Welles, E. B. (2004). Foreign language enrollments in the United States institutions of higher education, fall 2002. *ADFL Bulletin, 35*(2–3), 7–26.

Chapter 2

Social contexts for
EIL learning

In classrooms around the world today, many individuals are involved in
English teaching and learning. Just as the British could say at one point in
history that the sun never set on the British empire, today it would be fair
to say that the sun never sets on English learning classrooms. The belief
that English provides access to global communication and knowledge has
led many individuals to enroll in formal English language classes. But not
all English learners today do so voluntarily. Many young people are in
English classes today because they are required to do so by educational
officials or by immigration regulations.

The purpose of this chapter is to describe the various contexts in which
English is currently being learned. In order to highlight the diversity of
present-day English learning contexts and the uneven socioeconomic
spread of English, we begin by introducing Kachru's (1985) model of
concentric circles of English speakers. We then analyze each of the three
major English use contexts delineated by Kachru in terms of the social
attitudes and educational and institutional policies that can influence
English pedagogy.

EIL learning contexts

In 1985, Kachru presented a seminal model of English use contexts. He
maintained that the spread of English could "be viewed in terms of three
concentric circles representing the types of spread, the patterns of acquisition and the functional domains in which English is used across cultures
and languages" (p. 12). These circles were (a) the *Inner Circle*, where
English is the primary language of the country, such as in Australia,
Canada and the United Kingdom; (b) the *Outer Circle*, where English
serves as a second language in a multilingual country, such as in Singapore,
India, and the Philippines; and (c) the *Expanding Circle*, where English is
widely studied as a foreign language, such as in China, Germany and
Korea.

Due to changes in the use of English around the globe, the lines separating these circles have become more permeable. To begin, the tremendous influx of immigrants to some Inner Circle countries has led to growing multilingualism, resulting in some individuals in these countries using English for very limited purposes. Second, the widespread use of English in some Outer and Expanding Circle countries has resulted in individuals in these countries using English for a variety of purposes and developing native-like intuition. This situation led Kachru (1999) to argue that some speakers in Outer Circle countries have what he terms *functional nativeness*, similar to what Pakir (1999) refers to as *English-knowing bilinguals*. Although Kachru coined this term to refer only to speakers in Outer Circle countries, there is no doubt that in many Expanding Circle countries today, particularly in Europe, many individuals are using English in a great variety of domains and gaining functional nativeness.

The growing number of English bilinguals who now have functional nativeness has led some to argue for a modification of Kachru's model. Bruthiaux (2003), for example, criticizes the model because he believes it overlooks the variation of English used within specific geographical areas, particularly in areas where there is a large discrepancy between those who know English and those who do not. It also does not address variation in use within specific contexts as, for example, the use of African–American English vernacular within the United States.

An alternative model that answers these criticisms is one presented by Yano (2001) who posits a series of cylinders to represent English speakers today. Each cylinder represents a country. Within each country there are fluent speakers of English, represented at the top of the cylinders, whose English standards are almost identical to highly fluent speakers of other countries. These fluent speakers of English are able to use English for communicative purposes across national boundaries. In this way the boundaries at the top of the cylinders, representing fluent speakers of English, are permeable. On the other hand, the bottom of the cylinders represents those individuals in the country who speak a local variety of English, largely for use within the country. Since these varieties are more distinct than the varieties spoken by fluent bilinguals, Yano represents these varieties, at the bottom of the cylinders, with solid lines showing that these varieties are not permeable.

Although we agree with Bruthiaux, Yano and others that Kachru's concentric circles present an oversimplified model of English speakers today, nonetheless we use this model as a heuristic to discuss current English learning contexts. We do so because we see the circles as representing three major types of English learning contexts at the social level. In the first type of context, what Kachru terms Inner Circle countries, English learners often have not been exposed to English as a child; rather they come to learn English through an immigration process.

Furthermore, there is tremendous pressure for immigrants to learn English since most social and employment situations require the use of English. In the second type of learning contexts, what Kachru terms Outer Circle countries, learners are often exposed to English at an early age but often in more formal contexts outside of the home environment. Finally in the third type of learning context, the Expanding Circle, learners are acquiring a language that has little relevancy to day-to-day communication within the country's borders. Clearly within each country all of these situations could occur on an individual basis. For example, within a Japanese context, an Expanding Circle country, a child of an American–Japanese couple could be exposed to English at an early age and acquire native English fluency. However, since in this chapter we will be describing prevalent learning contexts within a society rather than focusing on individual learners, we have chosen to use Kachru's model. Within each context, we will focus on social attitudes, as well as educational and institutional policies, that influence the parameters of the English learning context. We will also highlight the diversity of language proficiency and use that exists within each of these contexts.

Inner Circle learning contexts

Within Inner Circle countries, the most prevalent type of English learning context involves recent immigrants to the country. In our discussion we will focus on public institutions since these are the ones that educational policies regulate and typically they provide students with their initial exposure to English. Within many Inner Circle countries, individuals who do not speak English are referred to as *language minority students*. These students include immigrants (i.e., foreign-born children who emigrate with their parents), refugees (i.e., foreign-born citizens who enter a country under special conditions), and long-term residents who come from non-English-speaking homes. For our purposes language minority students who lack proficiency in English will be referred to as *English learners (ELs)*, a term that we believe is less discriminatory than the commonly used phrase, *language minority/limited English proficient* (LM/LEP) students.

Language development and social integration

In considering educational policies as they apply to ELs in Inner Circle countries, we will focus specifically on the United States and Great Britain because of their large and growing immigrant population. Many parallels exist between the educational policies enacted for ELs in the United States and Great Britain. During the 1960s, both countries experienced a tremendous influx of immigrants with varied countries of origin. In both countries, new immigrants tended to settle in large industrialized urban area for employment purposes. Because of this fact, the EL population in urban centers increased tremendously. School districts, however, were largely unprepared for this shift in demographics and had no language program in place for the new students. Since 1960 both countries, like other Inner Circle countries, have experimented with various types of educational programs to meet the needs of ELs. Historically British policies tended to support mainstreaming for ELs while U.S. polices tended to promote English as a second language (ESL) pull-out programs or bilingual programs to the extent they were mandated by legislation or Supreme Court decisions. What is ironic is that in both countries the same rationale was offered for these very different approaches, namely, the rationale of protecting equality of opportunity for language minority students. (For a more complete comparison of British and U.S. policies, see McKay & Freedman, 1990.)

British EL language policies

In spite of tendencies in Great Britain toward a nationally centralized system of education, with a tradition of national examinations and a national curriculum, British school districts, called Local Educational Authorities (LEA), have considerable autonomy. During the 1960s, one of the first programs local school districts established for ELs were separate language centers, termed *induction centres*. In 1985, a major educational policy statement regarding ELs was issued with the publication of the Department of Education and Science's report, *Education for all*, commonly known as the Swann Report. The Swann Report strongly endorsed the mainstreaming of ELs. It argued that withdrawal classes "establish and confirm social and racial barriers between groups" and "whilst not originally discriminatory in intent" were "discriminatory in effect" because they deny children "access to the full range of educational opportunities available . . . by requiring them to miss a substantial part of the normal school curriculum" (p. 389). The report argued strongly that the informal interaction that occurs in schools is as important for language development as the formal context of language development, and thus it is important for ELs to be placed in a context where they could interact with native speakers.

The Swann Report did not support bilingual education "principally on the grounds that to implement it, minority children would have to be segregated. They feared that this might highlight differences and have a detrimental effect on race relations" (Edwards et al., 1988, p. 81). While the report argued that LEAs should make school buildings available for native language instruction, the Swann Committee viewed the maintenance and development of ELs' native language as a responsibility of the ethnic community itself rather than the school. The committee argued that by putting ELs in mainstream classes, schools could provide a framework for promoting a pluralistic society:

> We also see education as having a major role to play in countering the racism which still persists in Britain today and which we believe constitutes one of the chief obstacles to the realization of a truly pluralistic society. We recognize that some people may feel that it is expecting a great deal of education to take a lead in seeking to remedy what can be seen as a social problem. Nevertheless we believe that the education system and teachers in particular are uniquely placed to influence the attitudes of all young people in a positive manner.
>
> (Department of Education and Science, 1985, p. 319)

Critics of the report (see, for example, the National Council for Mother Tongue Teaching, 1985) challenged the report's definition of pluralism, arguing that the report, by not advocating native language instruction in the schools, was promoting a type of linguistic assimilation in which the ability to speak English was equated with being British. The critics further argued that the Swann Report failed to recognize the important link between first and second language development and the important role that first language maintenance can have on both cognitive development and the acquisition of a second language. Finally, critics challenged the Swann Report for its failure to see the intimate connection between language and culture

Both the Swann Report committee members and the advocates of mother tongue maintenance shared the idea of promoting an ethnically pluralistic society, but for the Swann Committee this pluralism meant promoting *cultural* pluralism while for proponents of mother tongue maintenance, this pluralism meant *linguistic* pluralism even if it resulted in cultural segregation. What is significant, however, is that in all instances a discussion of the relationship between ethnicity and language programs was considered necessary to the educational decision-making process.

United States EL language policies

In the United States, educational and government leaders who favor programs that take ELs out of regular classes argue that the programs are necessary to support students' language development. Unlike their British counterparts, they rarely address the potential social effects of these programs on cultural isolation, segregation, and racism. In order to understand the different emphases that underlie United States and British education policies for ELs, we turn now to the United States language minority policies since the 1960s.

Like Britain, the United States experienced a large increase in immigrants during the 1960s, largely due to the change in immigration laws of 1965, which abandoned the national origins quota system and gave preference instead to family reunification and occupational skills. As in Britain, these recent immigrants tended to come from varied countries of origin and to settle in large industrialized urban centers so that urban schools in the United States were faced with a large influx of nonnative speakers of English with very diverse language backgrounds. As in Britain, local school districts in the United States have a great deal of autonomy.

The United States education policies develop largely from constitutional, statutory, and judicial sources. Most EL programs have arisen from legal issues regarding the entitlement of ELs to language education services. The major judicial foundation for EL language education programs is the 1974 *Lau v. Nichols* Supreme Court decision. In this case, the parents of 12 Chinese American ELs filed a class action suit against the San Francisco Unified School District, arguing that they had been denied an education because of a lack of language classes with bilingual teachers.

The case raised the issue of discriminatory intent versus discriminatory impact. The Court argued that placing ELs in regular classrooms was discriminatory in effect while not discriminatory in intent because ELs did not have the basic skills needed to function in the regular classroom. The Court argued that some program must be devised for ELs other than to leave them in regular classrooms, but it left the implementation of the remedy to the local school boards. United States educational policy has tended to interpret this directive to mean that some type of language development must occur *before* an EL is placed in the regular classroom. In fact, according to the decision, the placing of ELs in regular classrooms without support services would be a violation of fundamental rights. In Britain, however, the educational policy of mainstreaming assumes that the development of language skills of ELs can best occur while they are in regular classes, if some type of language support service is provided.

The contrasting language policies of the United States and Britain rest on very different pedagogical and social assumptions and language ideological frameworks. In the United States, the policy of removing ELs from regular classes rests on a definition of equality of opportunity as linguistic opportunity in which the development of English language skills is taken to be primary, even if the language programs result in racial segregation. In Britain, on the other hand, advocates of the Swann Report equate educational opportunity with the idea of social equality and racial integration. Language programs for ELs are to be undertaken in the mainstream classroom where there are a large number of native speakers.

The different definitions of equality of opportunity evident in the U.S. and British EL programs provide a framework for examining the social and linguistic assumptions that inform language programs for ELs. The first social question raised is one of social segregation in educational programs. In designing educational programs for ELs, educators in many Inner Circle countries must confront the decision of whether to give primary emphasis to social integration, and in the process perhaps compromise language support services, or to make language support services primary, even if this results in social segregation. The second social concern raised is one of promoting language shift or language maintenance in the school system. Educational programs that focus exclusively on English language development are intended to promote language shift rather than bilingualism. Such programs reflect a social orientation of language diversity as a problem rather than as a resource.

EL programs in Inner Circle countries also raise questions about theories of language learning. One of the major questions raised in this regard is to what extent development in a learner's first language can have beneficial effects on second language development. Can becoming proficient readers and writers in one's first language carry over to second language literacy? Another question involves the extent to which interaction with native speakers of a language is important for second language development. Are the benefits of separate language programs for ELs greater than what might occur if planned interaction with native speakers were to occur in mainstream classrooms?

What do educational policies and programs in Britain and the United States demonstrate about the role of English in Inner Circle countries in an era of globalization? First, the promotion of English is typically viewed as a vehicle for cultural and social assimilation rather than as a means for accessing knowledge and developing communicative skills. Second, English teaching often takes place in an English-only environment, suggesting that bilingualism is a problem rather than a resource. The long-term consequences of such policies are that Inner Circle countries may become English monolingual countries at a time in which the majority of the world is becoming bilingual, with many individuals learning English as one of their additional languages.

In many ways, Australia's language policies present a contrast to those of the United States and Great Britain in that they were designed to promote bilingualism for all Australians. In the mid-1980s Australia passed a report entitled *A national language policy*, which specified that language policies at the national level should be formulated on the basis of four guiding principles:

1   competence in English;
2   maintenance and development of languages other than English;

3   provision of services in languages other than English;
4   opportunities for learning second languages.

(Lo Bianco, 1990, p. 59)

These principles resulted in three educational objectives for Australian language policies. The first was "English for All," which was designed to promote English instruction for both native-speakers and learners of English. While funds were allocated to provide free English education for immigrants and refugees, the program did not adequately provide services for all of those in need of English learning. In fact by some estimates, almost half of Australian students who needed extra help in English at school did not receive help (Lo Bianco, 1990). The second educational objective, "Support for Aboriginal and Torres Strait Islander Languages," involved elements of bilingual and bicultural education for native speakers of English. Finally, the third objective, "A Language Other than English for All" (LOTE) entailed teaching community languages, as well as foreign languages, to first and second language speakers of English. In general, the LOTE initiative has had little success. As Smolicz and Secombe (2003) point out, "languages other than English still remain an unpopular option at senior secondary school level. This is particularly striking for students from the majority English speaking background, many of whom see no obvious benefits of investing the effort required to learn a new language, in view of the availability of what they perceive as 'easier options', as well as the global dominance of English" (p. 16). This trend reflects the growing complacency of monolingual English speakers to learn another language, a problem highlighted in chapter 1. Before leaving our discussion of English learning in Inner Circle countries, we consider the consequences of government language policies on English learners' identity.

Identity and English learning

Examining the identity of second language learners is a relatively recent interest in second language acquisition research. In the past, major attention was devoted to interlanguage analysis, with little recognition given to learning processes, individual variables, or the social context in which a second language is learned. However, recent work, informed by post-structuralist approaches and critical theory (e.g., McKay & Wong, 1996; Norton, 1997; Peirce, 1995; Rampton, 1995), has begun to examine how educational institutions can position students in particular ways. Work that is especially relevant to our discussion examines how school discourses can position second language learners within the educational context.

Harklau's (2000) ethnographic study of three ELs transitioning from a U.S. high school to a community college is particularly insightful on the relationship between educational institutions and learner identity. Within the high school context investigated by Harklau, the three target students tended to be "affiliated with and the responsibility of the English to speakers of other languages (ESOL) program and teacher" (p. 45). Harklau found that in the high school, the students and teachers "collaboratively regenerated and perpetuated" (p. 46) a representation of ELs as highly motivated students who provide an inspiration for everyone by their heroic struggles during their immigration to the United States and their acquisition of a second language.

At the same time, the teachers in the school often expressed doubts about the students' academic and cognitive ability. Given prevalent negative social attitudes in the United States toward bilingualism and an educational context in which English is the exclusive medium of instruction, Harklau didn't find it surprising that "teachers cast these students' ability to communicate in two languages not as a special talent or strength but rather as a disability, emphasizing what immigrant students could not do relative to monolingual, standard English speakers. One teacher, for example, commented, 'It must be like somebody who's very bright and has a stroke. And can't express themselves' " (p. 50). In our study of Chinese junior high school students (McKay & Wong, 1996), we too found that in general teachers, by refusing to recognize any knowledge that students might have brought with them (including native-language literacy and school experiences), tended to see the ELs as linguistically and cognitively deficient. In this way, the social and educational context often positions English learners in particular ways, frequently as deficient learners.

Encouragingly a good deal more work on learner identities in relationship to the educational context is currently underway. Lam's (2000) study, mentioned in chapter 1, for example, documents how the use of computer-mediated communication (CMC) can provide students with new identities that can enhance literacy skills. In a similar vein, Zuengler (2004) examines how in a sheltered U.S. high school class, the teacher and teacher aide use popular cultural icons like McDonalds, Michael Jordan and Jackie Chan to clarify the principles and content of the American constitution. While the teacher and the teacher aide use these cultural icons to position students as consumers who are easily attracted to consumption, the comments of the students suggest that they are far more product-savvy and critical than the teachers assume. In addition, the use of popular icons seemed to allow the less-proficient students to participate in class discussions because of their familiarity with the topics. Ultimately, Zuengler (2004) concludes that the use of popular icons can be beneficial for language learning, but that clearly more research is needed in this area. As she puts it,

> Considering that in North America and no doubt elsewhere, classrooms are becoming increasingly heterogeneous in language and

culture, it is important to know the dynamics, the potential, and the implication of popular culture in such classrooms, not only for the students' language and subject matter learning, but for their identities as individuals in societies which are new to many of them.

(p. 300)

The use of popular culture also raises the issue of the tension between the global and local. Although the use of popular culture provides students access to aspects of globalization, it is equally important, as we emphasized in chapter 1, to afford local concerns equal status in the language classroom.

Whereas the choice of topic in classrooms is highly relevant to issues of personal identity, Duff's (2002) study is helpful in examining the manner in which peer dynamics are also influential in matters of identity. Duff's study focuses on language use and socialization in a Canadian social studies class composed of local students of various ethnic backgrounds and non-local second language speakers, many of whom were Mandarin and Cantonese speakers. Class discussions were quite common, as were topics dealing with Chinese culture. In examining several class discussion excerpts, Duff found that the contributions of ELs tended to be "short, muted, tentative, and inaccessible to others. As a result, they forfeited—or resisted—opportunities to convey aspects of themselves, their knowledge, interests, and opinions to others, or to make the personal connections for others" (p. 305). When asked in an interview context about their participation, non-local students said that they were afraid of being laughed at or criticized by their peers for their comments. This presented them with a significant dilemma.

> Silence protected them from humiliation. However, interactional withdrawal attracted disdain from local students (who confirmed this), for whom silence represented a lack of initiative, agency, or desire to improve one's English or to offer interesting material for the sake of the class. The NNES [nonnative English speakers] students were therefore caught between what appeared to be two unfavorable options: silence or mockery and hostility.
>
> (p. 312)

Gee (2004) argues that teaching and learning language and literacy is not just about teaching and learning English but also about teaching and learning specific social languages. He maintains that what students need to get right is not just the language but what he calls Discourse, that is, "multiple ways of acting-interacting-speaking-writing-listening-reading-thinking-believing-valuing-feeling with others at the 'right' times and in the 'right' places so as to be recognized as enacting an 'appropriate socially-situated identity' " (p. 25). Although there is little doubt that the non-local students referred to in Duff's (2002) study needed to enact the "right" way of acting in order to be accepted members of the social studies class, the question is whether or not the non-local students had the desire or language ability to do this. As Duff (2002) points out, what is clearly needed is more investigation of

> the extent to which students actually *want* to display their identities and personal knowledge in class or to conform to the dominant, normative local sociolinguistic behaviors—that is, whether they consider those behaviors and disclosures as signs of competence or incompetence, of strength or weakness—a community standard and ideology toward which they *choose* to become socialized, or rather something they just endure, resist, or circumvent by demonstrating their capabilities in other ways.
>
> [emphasis in the original] (p. 313)

Outer Circle learning contexts

In Outer Circle countries, English is one of the officially recognized languages of the country. Frequently English is used primarily outside of the home in formal social contexts. In the realm of education, English typically serves as the medium of instruction in tertiary education and in some instances in secondary education. Although there are tremendous differences between Outer Circle countries, many of them grapple with two important issues regarding the learning of English. These are (a) how to address the social inequities that permit some individuals to acquire the English fluency needed to succeed in higher education while others do not, and (b) how to allocate the use of English and other local languages in the school system in order to promote multilingualism. In order to illustrate the complexities of these issues, we examine a particular Outer Circle country in relation to each issue.

Equality in educational access

Promoting equality of educational opportunity for all citizens is one of the major problems facing post-apartheid South Africa. One of the critical decisions that South Africa faced in the establishment of a post-apartheid government was the creation of an official language policy. As a way of redressing the discrimination of the past and building a non-racial nation in South Africa, the new constitution recognized English, Afrikaans, and nine indigenous languages as official languages at the national level. In 1996, after a good deal of negotiation, a language-planning task group submitted its final report, *Towards a national language plan for South*

Africa, in which it mapped the overall goals of a language-in-education policy for the new South Africa. In it, the report states that

> Language policy in the education sector should:
>
> (a) facilitate access to meaningful education for all South African students;
> (b) promote multilingualism;
> (c) promote the use of the students' primary languages as languages of learning and teaching in the context of an additive multi-lingual paradigm and with due regard to the wishes and attitudes of parents, teachers and students;
> (d) encourage the acquisition by all South African students of at least two but preferably three South African languages, even if at different levels of proficiency, by means of a variety of additive bi-, or multilingual strategies; it is strongly recommended that where the student's L1 is either Afrikaans or English, an African language should be the additional language.

Although the report allowed for choice from a range of language-in-education policy models, it identified additive bilingualism/multilingualism as the normative orientation of the language-in-education policy. Underlying the report was the assumption that learners learn other languages (including the dominant language) most effectively when there is continued educational use of the learners' first languages. This assumption, however, contradicts widely held assumptions in South Africa today about the best way to acquire English. These include the assumptions that learning English should commence as early as possible, that maintenance of the first language is unnecessary and perhaps undesirable, and that the best way for speakers of other languages to acquire English is submersion, that is, a *subtractive approach*. Currently this essentially English-only program is the only option offered by most schools that in the racially-segregated schools of the apartheid era served exclusively Indian, "Coloured" or English-speaking white learners.

To contextualize the school structure in South Africa under the apartheid system, there were basically four separate school systems—one for the white community, one for the Indian community, one for the so-called coloured (or mixed-race) community, and one for the African community. The available resources for the white schools far surpassed those of the black community in the townships and rural areas. The Indian and coloured schools, while better funded than those of the black townships, still did not match those of the white community. Because of this historical advantage, schools in the former white community have far better facilities than former Indian schools, Indian schools better than the coloured schools and the latter better than the African schools in the township and rural areas. As a consequence, following the establishment of a single educational authority, there has been a major flux of African students into the Indian (and coloured) schools located near African townships, and of many Indian students and some African students into former white schools. However, it is important to note that only those families with higher economic resources are able to attend the more privileged schools since they require higher school fees, as well as a means of transportation to schools outside of the children's neighborhood.

Given the focus of the National Language Plan on promoting multi-lingualism, one would imagine that schools would be concerned with promoting literacy in the child's first language, as well as English. Yet this is generally not what is happening in the more privileged primary and secondary schools in South Africa. In our work in the Durban area of South Africa, (McKay & Chick, 2001), we found that in the former white and Indian primary and secondary schools we examined, there was an exclusive use of English, with little or no attention to Zulu, the first language of many of the African students attending the school.

In our discussions with school principals on the place of Zulu and English in the social and educational context, we found that the use of English is related to issues of power. For most of the principals, English represents a unifying force, a vehicle for economic advancement, and an appropriate choice in prestigious domains such as the classroom. By contrast Zulu represents a potentially divisive force and is appropriate only for non-prestigious domains; that is, it is more of a handicap than a resource. Learners who choose to use Zulu in class are represented as either rebellious or as deficient in English. (See Vavrus, 2002, for a comparison of the use of Swahili in Tanzania.)

Most of the teachers in these schools expressed views that were closely aligned to those of the principals. For example, one of the teachers at the former Indian high school told her students not to use Zulu in class and would not let them explain things to one another in Zulu. She believes that if learners are to improve their English and be able to produce criti-cal analyses in English, they must use English in class. Another teacher argued that if Zulu speakers have chosen an English-medium school staffed by native English speakers they must accept that Zulu will not be used in class.

In general we found that the teachers and administrators at the schools we visited were promoting extensive and, at times, exclusive use of English under the banner that this was an English-medium school. Gen-erally code-switching was permitted only in non-prestigious domains such as the playground or when learners were viewed as lacking English proficiency. Thus in the schools we visited there is little indication that the additive policy of multilingualism promoted in the language-in-education policies of South Africa was being actively pursued. The question is why is English being so rigorously promoted? Clearly the answer to this is complex, but one clear advantage of achieving proficiency in English in South Africa is the access English provides to higher education.

Leibowitz's (2005) case study of black students at the Western Cape in South Africa, an institution that caters to predominately black students, illustrates how English is a key to academic success. In the 1990s the language of instruction at the university shifted mainly from Afrikaans to English. Many of the black students attending Western Cape went to township schools under apartheid where little English was heard and where the content emphasis was on domestic and agricultural work rather than intellectual or professional work.

In her case study, Leibowitz (2005) documents the disadvantages that students face coming to the university with less developed English skills. Students reported that their lack of proficiency in English affected their ability to follow lectures, their interpersonal communication with teachers and classmates, and their essay writing. Reading in English was also a far more time-consuming task than reading in the students' first language. But perhaps most importantly Leibowitz found that many of the black students had not been exposed to the kind of academic discourse that was necessary to succeed in a university setting. Several students reported that in their previous education, they had not been asked to employ the kind of critical evaluation that was asked for at the university. All of these factors made it far more difficult for these students to succeed in a university setting than for students from a middle-class background with high levels of English proficiency.

Leibowitz (2005) concludes that access to English in South Africa is a necessary but not sufficient condition for academic success. Students need exposure to both English and to the discourse of schools in order to succeed, both of which are far more likely to occur in the more privileged schools in South Africa. The situation in South Africa is far from unique. Ramanathan (1999), for example, reports on the difficulties that the lower caste groups in India have in succeeding in India's institutions of higher education. The same is clearly true for African–Americans in the United States (see Delpit, 1998; Heath, 1983; Smitherman, 2000).

The current state of English education in South Africa raises several critical issues. The first is how to convince parents and students of the value of having a bilingual/biliterate population. At the present time in many Outer Circle countries, parents, school administrators and teachers support an English-only agenda in the schools in the belief that this is best for their children. As in many Inner Circle countries, a child's first language is viewed as a problem rather than a resource. The second issue is how to provide less advantaged children in the society with equal access to English so they can succeed in institutions of higher education. However, even when Outer Circle countries support the development of bilingualism and the use of local languages in higher education, many problems can arise. The Philippines educational program provides a good example of some of these problems.

Bilingual programs

As was pointed out in chapter 1, the Philippines contact with English dates from its colonization by the United States. The role of English in the schools was initiated with President William McKinley's Letter of Instruction to the Philippine Commission in April 1900 stating that English was to be the medium of instruction at all levels of education. The rationale for the English-only policy was that American teachers could more effectively teach in English; English would unite the people; and English was the language "that would provide the Filipinos access to civilization . . . the life of reason and prudence" (Martin, 1999, as cited in Bernardo, 2004, p. 18). Hence, from the very beginning, educational language policies were driven by social, ideological, and political agendas.

When the constitution was drafted in 1935, English was designated the official language, but there was great interest in developing one of the local languages into a national language. Since then a number of constitutions have been debated and adopted involving different notions of a national language and creating a number of national agencies to deal with the matter. In 1936 the National Institute of Language was formed and Tagalog, a language of the Manila area, was chosen to provide the basis for the development of a national language. The institute was charged with the task of cultivating the language so that it could be used in the schools. However, in response to protests from other major language groups in the Philippines, Tagalog was modified, incorporating elements of other local languages, to form the basis for Pilipino. By 1946 Pilipino was designated as the national language of the Philippines.

One of the first challenges to the English-only policies of the schools came in 1939 when Jorge Bocobo became Secretary of Education and ordered that English be continued as a medium of instruction but that local languages could be used for support in the primary grades (Bernardo, 2004). By 1940, instruction in the national language, Pilipino, was required for senior high school students. Then during the 1940s and 1950s various experiments using the local languages as the medium of instruction were undertaken in the schools. These experiments culminated in the passage of the Revised Philippine Education program, which provided for the use of vernacular languages as the medium of instruction in the first two grades with a shift to English as the medium of instruction from third grade through college. It also provided for using the local language as an auxiliary language in grades 3 and 4 and Pilipino as the auxiliary language in grades 5 and 6 (Bernardo, 2004).

In 1969, during a period of student activism, students began to demonstrate against the continued use of English as the medium of instruction in the schools, which some viewed as a continuation of the cultural and linguistic imperialism of the United States. In response to this concern, in 1974 the Department of Education ordered that beginning in grade 1 "English was to be used as the medium of instruction for science and mathematics with Pilipino for all other subjects, with the major vernaculars as 'auxiliary' languages" (Gonzalez, 1990, p. 323). In contrast, then, to South Africa, the Philippines put in place an educational policy that was clearly designed to promote multilingualism in the country. The question is, how successful was the program in developing nationalism and promoting academic achievement?

An answer to this question can be found in the nationwide evaluation of the bilingual education program undertaken by the Linguistic Society of the Philippines. Using a multidimensional model of investigation (see Gonzalez, 1990), the study yielded some instructive findings. To begin, the main predictor of student achievement in all subjects was found to be socio-economic status. In addition, living in the Metro Manila area had a positive effect on student achievement. In the fields of math, science and social studies, the second best predictor of student achievement was the teacher's competency in the subject. Some other findings of the study are as follows (Gonzalez, 1990).

- The best predictor for academic success in the Philippines was being a Tagalog speaker living in Metro Manila and studying in a private school; the formula for failure was the opposite—being a non-Tagalog speaker, living in a rural setting, and studying in a public or government school.
- Students who achieved well in English also achieved well in Pilipino, but the reverse was not true. In other words, the transfer of language skills seemed to be one-directional from English to Pilipino. One of the reasons for this finding appears to be that Pilipino has not yet been adequately developed to be used for cognitive activities.
- Outstanding schools in terms of student achievement were good at teaching both English and Pilipino, suggesting that bilingual education can be successfully implemented in a country, provided local institutions have competent teachers.
- Most people in the Philippines accept Pilipino as a linguistic symbol for national identity, but they also accept the need for the maintenance of English for economic reasons.

Perhaps the main finding of the bilingual evaluation project was that "it is not programming and allocation of time or subjects which will spell success or failure in learning but such factors as socio-economic status, overall quality of schools, competence of faculty" (Gonzalez, 1990, p. 328). This study then, like the Leibowitz study in South Africa, seems to suggest that English proficiency is a necessary but by no means a sufficient condition for academic success. Rather, socio-economic status and urbanization are also important factors, along with a competent teaching faculty.

Expanding Circle learning contexts

As was pointed out at the beginning of the chapter, the lines between Kachru's Inner, Outer and Expanding Circle have become much more permeable due to growing migration and increased use of English. For example, Phillipson (2003) notes that today in continental Europe, an Expanding Circle context, English is becoming less "foreign" in that it is not learned for use abroad but often for internal purposes within the country, such as in higher education and employment. Phillipson contends that in such countries there are good grounds for considering English as a second rather than a foreign language, as is increasingly done in the Netherlands and Scandinavia. Seidlhofer et al. (2006) make a similar point, arguing that

> The current role of English in Europe is thus characterized by the fact that the language has become a lingua franca, a language of wider communication, and has entered the continent in two directions as it were, top-down by fulfilling functions in various professional domains and, simultaneously, bottom-up by being encountered and used by speakers from all levels of society in practically all walks of life. So English functions as a lingua franca, enabling people to connect based on common interests and concerns across languages and communities.
>
> (p. 5)

Since English seems to have assumed the role of a lingua franca in Europe rather than a foreign language, we will not be dealing with European countries here, although we will deal with the use of English as a lingua franca in chapter 6. Rather we will focus on countries where English is not generally used on a daily basis and is learned as a foreign language, often as a requirement specified by the Ministry of Education. Because of the number and diversity of such countries, we have chosen not to describe a limited number of case studies in this section but rather to identify key issues that exist in many Expanding Circle countries.

Many of the countries that fit Kachru's characterization of an

Expanding Circle country are grappling with the issue of how to balance globalization and nationalism, a dilemma faced earlier by many Outer Circle countries during post-colonialism. On the one hand, these countries recognize the benefits that English can bring in terms of global trade, tourism, and employment. On the other hand, these countries take pride in their own language, culture, and traditions, and hence have a strong sense of nationalism. In dealing with these tensions, Expanding Circle countries have adopted various policies and discourses. While Brazil has introduced a controversial bill to curb the use of English, the public at large has a very ambivalent attitude toward English, both loving it and loathing it (Rajagopalan, 2003). In South Korea official rhetoric has highlighted the importance of English competence in order to develop its foreign trade. At the same time, English textbooks extol the beauty of the Korean languages and highlight how Korean customs and cultural values are more desirable than American traditions (Yim, 2007). In Japan, English is promoted as a way of becoming part of the global community. Yet the uniqueness of Japanese culture is highlighted in most of the discourse on learning English. Hashimoto (2007) contends that Japaneseness is promoted by "deconstructing" English (p. 49), treating it as only a tool for international relations and emphasizing the unique cultural values of the Japanese.

While the issues of globalization and nationalism are a central concern for language planners in many Expanding Circle countries, language planners face few of the issues faced by planners in Inner Circle countries. Typically, there is no concern about a loss of the first language as speakers shift to English, nor with balancing social integration and language development. Also language planners in Expanding Circle countries generally do not see language diversity as a problem, as is done in many Inner Circle countries, but rather as a resource. Furthermore, Expanding Circle countries do not face the problem faced by Outer Circle countries of designing bilingual education programs since the focus in Expanding Circles is on English as a subject. In contrast, educators in Expanding Circle countries have other issues to address. Chief among these are (a) motivating learners, (b) educating competent and confident English teachers, and (c) designing locally appropriate methods.

Student motivation

In many Expanding Circle countries, students have little motivation to learn English. In fact, several ELT acronyms have been developed to describe this situation including TENAR (Teaching English for No Apparent Reason), TENOP (Teaching English for No Obvious Purpose) and TENOR (Teaching English for No Obvious Reason). All of the acronyms describe learning situations where the purpose for learning the language is quite vague. These acronyms apply to many Expanding Circle countries where large English classes are typical and where students are in English classes because they are required to be there. On the other hand, there are many learners in Expanding Circle countries who are working diligently to acquire proficiency in English and they are doing so even when there is not an immediate use for English for interacting with others on a daily basis. The question is, what is motivating these students?

The answer to this question, of course, is extremely complex. However, to start it is necessary to consider how motivation might be conceptualized in an Expanding Circle context. Most discussions of motivation recognize a distinction between *integrative motivation* (i.e., motivation that is based on a desire to participate in social groups in which the target language is used) and *instrumental motivation* (i.e., motivation that derives from achieving some gain such as a job or entrance to a university). Because a good deal of research on motivation has been undertaken in Inner Circle countries where the social context provides occasions for integrative motivation, educators have often stressed the value of integrative motivation, at times suggesting it is more beneficial than instrumental motivation. However, Expanding Circle countries do not provide a social context to engender integrative motivation. Current research, however, seems to suggest that there are other factors that come into play.

Because of the diversity of current English learning contexts, motivation must be examined in light of the values and attitudes of a specific social context. For some, it may be the desire to do well on an English exam in order to gain social prestige; for others, it may be the ability to access information in English on a particular subject; and for others it may be the ability to speak with other English speakers. Most of these factors are beyond the reach of the classroom. However, what educators can do is strive to determine what social factors are motivating their learners and then to build on these incentives in their own classrooms.

In a survey of Taiwanese learners of English, Chen et al. (2005) asked learners how important a variety of factors were in studying English, including the following: passing job and entrance exams, changing jobs, understanding movies, books, and magazines, traveling overseas, getting higher job security, obtaining raises, passing required classes, gaining social prestige, making social connections, and getting higher paying jobs. What they found was that integrative motivation was not a significant factor in motivating students; rather requirements appear to have an important role to play in motivating learners. Chen et al. (2005) point out that typically in China a person is lauded for scoring high on an exam. The drive to excel in language learning derives both from passing an exam and from the social recognition of excelling. The authors label this kind of motivation the *Chinese Imperative*, that is, motivation based on gaining the social recognition that comes from excelling on some type of socially required exam.

Still there will be learners for whom gaining proficiency in English is not necessary for their goals and social context. Hu (2005), for example, in his investigation of educational practices in China, found that a large number of students living in underdeveloped areas of China are enrolled in English classes because they

> are forced to do so because it is part of a compulsory curriculum. These students have no use for English and are not motivated at all to study the language. As a matter of fact, an overwhelming majority of these students will never move beyond a 9-year compulsory educa- tion. For these students the question is not how to teach them English but whether to teach them at all.
>
> (p. 656)

Nunan (2003) raises a similar question in reference to his study of English teaching in a variety of Asia–Pacific countries (specifically China, Hong Kong, Japan, Korea, Malaysia, Taiwan, and Vietnam). He main- tains that in the countries he examined, English language policies and prac- tices have been implemented "without a clearly articulated rationale and without a detailed consideration of the costs and benefits of such policies and practices on the countries in question. Furthermore, there is a widely articulated belief that, in public schools at least, these polices and practices are failing" (p. 609). Educators in Expanding Circle countries then need to consider whether or not English instruction is necessary for all of its young people. In addition, there is a need to examine what factors, along with a lack of motivation, are contributing to a lack of success in English teach- ing. In many Expanding Circle countries two factors seem to be operative, namely, teachers' competence and the choice of teaching methods.

Teacher competence

In investigations of English teaching in Asia–Pacific countries, (e.g., Bolton & Tong, 2002; Cortazzi & Jin, 1996; Kwon, 2000; LoCastro, 1996; Nunan, 2003; Tsui & Tollefson, 2007), often teacher education and teachers' lack of English skills are identified as problems. Clearly in countries where a decision has been made to require English instruction, adequate resources need to be directed to both pre-service and in-service teacher education so that bilingual teachers have opportunities to develop their fluency in English as well as their pedagogical knowledge. However, another factor that is contributing to poor teaching results, one that is rarely acknowledged, is the lack of confidence that many English teachers have in their own abilities.

Many studies have verified the lack of confidence that bilingual English teachers have, especially in relation to native speakers of English. Tang (1997), for example, reports on a survey she conducted in a teacher-retraining course in Hong Kong in which she asked local teachers about their perceptions of the proficiency of native- and nonnative-speaking teachers of English. A very high percentage of the teachers believed that native English-speaking teachers were superior to nonnative English-speaking teachers in speaking (100 percent), pronunciation (92 percent), listening (87 percent), vocabulary (79 percent) and reading (72 percent). Seidlhofer (1999), in her survey of English teachers in Austria, found that a majority (57 percent) of respondents stated that being a nonnative speaker of English made them feel insecure. Several factors contribute to bilingual teachers' feelings of insecurity.

To begin, bilingual teachers are often compared to first language speakers of English. Frequently in hiring practice, native speakers, even untrained native speakers, are hired over competent bilingual teachers. This is all part of the native speaker fallacy that assumes that native speakers of the language should provide the model for English training (see Braine, 1999; Davies, 1991; Medgyes, 1994). This is most frequently done in relation to achieving native-like pronunciation. As Canagarajah (1999) notes,

> Many Periphery professionals feel compelled to spend undue time repairing their pronunciation or performing other cosmetic changes to sound native. Their predominant concern is in effect "How can I lose my accent?" rather than "How can I be a successful teacher?" The anxiety and inhibitions about their pronunciation can make them lose their grip on the instructional process or lack rapport with their students.
>
> (pp. 84–85)

Teachers' self-confidence is further undermined by demands placed on them by Ministries of Education. In many Expanding Circle countries, just as in the Outer Circle countries we looked at, there is tremendous pressure for teachers to conduct an English-only classroom. For example, the Korean Ministry of Education has repeatedly asked teachers to use more English in their classes and to conduct English-only classes (Liu et al. 2004). This goal places a tremendous burden on teachers, particularly those with large classes and beginning level students. What is ironic is that studies on the use of the L1 in language classrooms have documented the ways in which the first language can be used very effectively in language classrooms. Liu et al. (2004), for example, in their investigation of the code-switching used by South Korean secondary English teachers, found that teachers did not use Korean indiscriminately in their classroom. Rather they used Korean for explaining difficult vocabulary and grammar, giving background information, saving time, and highlighting important information. Although the students in this study found the use of Korean in the classroom very helpful, teachers felt uncomfortable using Korean because they had been encouraged by the Ministry not to do so. This feeling contributed to a belief that they were not competent teachers.

The lack of self-confidence expressed by many bilingual teachers in Expanding Circle countries needs to be seen against an overall discourse in the TESOL profession referred to earlier as the colonial Self–Other discourse. In this discourse the native speaker is viewed as the giver of knowledge, a member of the "inner" circle who teaches English to speakers of "other" languages. Within this discourse, bilingual teachers, no matter how fluent they are, can never achieve insider status. What is most unfortunate about such discourse is that it minimizes the unique value of bilingual teachers as teachers of English in an era of globalization. As was mentioned in chapter 1, globalization has brought with it a constant interplay between global and local space. The strength of local bilingual teachers is that they can bring to the classroom an understanding of local conditions and how they interact with global concerns. Clearly, the local needs for English can vary widely. As Lin et al. (2005) note,

> English as appropriated by local agents serves diverse sets of intentions and purposes in their respective local contexts, whether it be the acquisition of a socially upward identity, or the creation of a bilingual space for critical explorations of self and the society. Learning English in the new information age is increasingly oriented toward global, cross-cultural communication in multilingual contexts, and yet there also exist side-by-side local forces and structures which shape a learner's investment and understanding of what it means to learn English in the specific context in which he or she is situated.
>
> (p. 217)

Local bilingual teachers are ideally placed to understand the localized English needs of their learners and to design a pedagogy appropriate for the particular local context. Unfortunately, their own lack of self-confidence and top-down ministry directives do little to encourage them to undertake this task. The impetus for their being involved in situated practices is further undermined by top-down designated teaching methods, particularly in reference to Communicative Language Teaching (CLT).

Appropriate methods

In many Expanding Circle countries, Ministries of Education are concerned with identifying a teaching methodology that is appropriate for use throughout the educational system and will increase the success of English teaching in their country. At the present time, this method is often CLT. Nunan (2003), for example, in his survey of Asian Pacific Rim countries found that most of the countries he studied subscribe to the implementation of CLT, though in fact in many classrooms, due to a variety of constraints, the method is not actually being implemented. While there are many definitions of CLT, typically CLT can be characterized by the following features:

1   An emphasis on learning to communicate through interaction in the target language.
2   The introduction of authentic texts into the learning situation.
3   The provision of opportunities for learners to focus not only on language, but also on the learning process itself.
4   An enhancement of the learner's own personal experiences as important contributing elements to classroom learning.
5   An attempt to link classroom language learning with language activation outside of the classroom. (Nunan, 1991, p. 279)

Due to large classes and expectations about the role of teachers and learners, the implementation of such a method in many Expanding Circle countries is extremely difficult.

What has led to the widespread promotion of CLT in many Expanding Circle countries? Tollefson (1991) suggests one reason. He argues that the spread of English is linked to what he terms the *modernization theory*. In modernization theory "Western 'experts' … are viewed as repositories of knowledge and skills who pass them on to elites who will run 'modernized' institutions" (p. 97). As applied to ELT teaching, so-called experts from Inner Circle countries have been involved in teacher training programs in Expanding Circle countries designed to pass on their "expertise" regarding language teaching methodology to help "modernize" English language teaching. Such programs reflect the Self–Other discourse referred to earlier in that teacher educators from Inner Circle countries are taken as the "insiders" who pass on their knowledge to the Other.

Another factor that is contributing to the promotion of CLT is top-down directives by Ministries of Education. Japan is a case in point. In 1989 and 1990, the Japanese Ministry of Education released new guidelines for the study of foreign languages in junior and senior high schools. One of the primary aims of the new curriculum was to require teachers to promote speaking and listening skills as a way of developing the communicative language ability of the students. Furthermore, teachers were to strive to adopt CLT methods in their classrooms (LoCastro, 1996). Many Japanese educational leaders supported this change. Koike and Tanaka (1995), for example, maintained that whereas the grammar translation method was effective in absorbing aspects of foreign culture, now was the time "for a change from the traditional to the communication-centered approach to foreign language teaching" (p. 23).

Korea is another country that is encouraging the use of CLT. Convinced that the grammatical syllabus does not develop students' communicative competence, in 1992, the Ministry of Education published a new curriculum, which clearly states that CLT should replace the audiolingual and translation methods currently used in the schools. According to Li (1998),

> In the new curricula, the goal of English teaching is "to develop the learner's communicative competence in English through meaningful drills and communicative activities, such as games, with the aid of audio-visual equipment" (Development Committee, 1992, p. 180). Students are to learn by means of authentic materials, such as newspapers, magazines, English news on the radio and English TV programs. The curricula reflect the belief that "CLT is characterized by learner-centredness" (p. 181), and teachers are encouraged to organize materials based on students' needs.
>
> (p. 682)

Thus, in a variety of Expanding Circle countries educational leaders have chosen to implement the use of CLT in the belief that this is the most modern and productive way to teach English.

Li's (1998) interviews with Korean secondary school teachers on the difficulties involved in implementing CLT in Korea illustrate some of the problems that have arisen in the implementation of CLT. Li's study revealed three sources of difficulty in using CLT. The first comes from the educational system itself in which large classes, grammar-based examinations, insufficient funding, and a lack of support for teacher education undermines the implementation of CLT. Second, the students' low English proficiency, lack of motivation for developing communicative competence, and resistance to class participation make it difficult to use CLT. Finally, the teachers believe that their own inadequacies contribute to the problem. Clearly teachers' feelings of inadequacy are compounded by the fact that the current Ministry of Education guidelines promote the use of CLT. Li, however, argues that it is essential for Korean educators to look within their own context for approaches to teaching English rather than depending on Western expertise. As he says,

Rather than relying on expertise, methodology, and materials controlled and dispensed by Western ESL countries, EFL countries should
strive to establish their own research contingents and encourage
methods specialists and classroom teachers to develop language
teaching methods that take into account the political, economic,
social, and cultural factors and, most important of all, the EFL
situations in the countries.

(p. 698)

Li's belief in the importance of local input in the designing of methods
and materials is in keeping with Kramsch and Sullivan's (1996) contention that the most appropriate pedagogy for teaching a global language is
one that is based on global thinking but local teaching. Such a pedagogy
suggests that local educators need to be involved in appropriating a
method for a particular teaching context. Kramsch and Sullivan (1996),
for example, describe how one Vietnamese teacher successfully appropri-
ated a textbook designed for communicative group work to suit a particular university classroom in Vietnam. Because the students in this
classroom knew each other quite well, having studied together for several
years, and because they expected a teacher-centered classroom in which
the teacher had responsibility for engendering moral values, the local
teacher implemented a pedagogy informed by these factors. Activities
that according to the text were to be done in pairs were enacted in a
teacher-centered classroom in which there was a good deal of display of
students' knowledge of one another. The teacher also used the content
to make moral comments on the topic being discussed. In short, this
Vietnamese teacher designed a pedagogy appropriate for this particular
localized context.

Luk (2005) describes a similar situation in a Hong Kong secondary
school. In this classroom the fact that students shared an L1, had little
motivation to study English, and were often unruly, resulted in the unsuccessful implementation of the kind of information-gap pair work used
in CLT. One strategy, however, that proved successful for one teacher was
a teacher-fronted activity that forced students to take a stand on a controversial local issue and to voice their opinions in English. In this particular activity, the teacher asked students to symbolize their position on
various topics by moving to a particular part of the room where they
could then express why they took the stance they took. The statements
ranged from whether or not the teacher was the "best" teacher to
whether or not Hong Kong was a good place to live to whether or not
violent Japanese comic books should be sold to children. Because the
issues were related to students' immediate concerns, they became involved
in the activity, using English to a far greater degree than students were
doing in some CLT classes that were using contrived information-gap

activities. Both examples illustrate how the most effective method must be one locally produced by educators who, aware of the global reach of English, are also fully informed of the learning parameters of the local context. (For further examples of localized appropriate methodologies, see Edge, 2006; Lin & Luke, 2006; Lin & Martin, 2005.)

Summary

In this chapter we identified English teaching and learning issues that exist in Inner Circle, Outer Circle and Expanding Circle countries. In Inner Circle countries, language diversity is often viewed as a problem. Because of this, programs are designed to encourage the acquisition of English, with little emphasis on developing students' first language. In the process of designing such programs, educators grapple with how to provide necessary language support while avoiding social segregation. In addition, in some Inner Circle countries, language minority students are positioned as outsiders, with some educators questioning their cognitive academic abilities.

In many Outer Circle countries, English proficiency is necessary for tertiary education. One of the issues facing Outer Circle countries is how to provide equal access to English education so that less advantaged students can successfully complete a higher education. Although some Outer Circle countries support a policy of multilingualism, the designing of educational programs that develop academic literacy in both English and the national language present many practical problems.

Finally, in Expanding Circle countries, educators are faced with the problem of motivating learners, particularly those who see no apparent reason for studying English. In addition, many English teachers do not have sufficient proficiency in English. Compounding the problem of teachers' proficiency is teachers' lack of confidence in their English ability. This lack of confidence is at times exacerbated by ministry of education methodology policies that are not appropriate for the local context. Having examined the globalization of English and the present-day contexts of English learning, in the next chapter we turn to an examination of the social and sociolinguistic context of English use today. We do so in the belief that such an examination will provide insight into how the pedagogical issues raised in this chapter might be approached.

References

Bernardo, A. (2004). Mckinley's questionable bequest: Over 100 years of English in Philippine education. *World Englishes*, 23(1), 17–32.

Bolton, K. & Tong, Q. S. (Eds.) (2002). English in China [Special issue]. *World Englishes*, 21(2).

Braine, G. (Ed.) (1999). *Non-native educators in English language teaching.* Mahwah, NJ: Lawrence Erlbaum Associates, Inc.

Bruthiaux, P. (2003). Squaring the circles: Issues in modeling English worldwide. *International Journal of Applied Linguistics*, *13*(2), 159–178.

Canagarajah, A. S. (1999). Interrogating the "native speaker fallacy": non-linguistic roots, non-pedagogical results. In G. Braine (Ed.), *Non-native educators in English language teaching* (pp. 77–92). Mahwah, NJ: Lawrence Erlbaum Associates.

Chen, J., Warden, C., & Chang, H. (2005). Motivators that do not motivate: The case of Chinese EFL learners and the influence of culture on motivation. *TESOL Quarterly*, *39*(4), 609–633.

Cortazzi, J. & Jin, L. (1996). English teaching and learning in China. *Language Teaching*, *29*, 61–80.

Davies, A. (1991). *The native speaker in applied linguistics.* Edinburgh: Edinburgh University Press.

Delpit, L.D. (1998). What should teachers do? Ebonics and culturally responsive instruction. In T. Perry & L. Delpit (Eds.), *The real Ebonics debate: Power, language and the education of African–American children* (pp. 17–26). Boston, MA: Beacon.

Department of Education and Science. (1985). *Education for all: Report of the Committee of Inquiry into the Education of Children from Ethnic Minority Groups (The Swann Report).* London: Her Majesty's Stationery Office.

Duff, P. (2002). The discursive co-construction of knowledge, identity and difference: An ethnography of communication in high school mainstream. *Applied Linguistics*, *23*(3), 289–322.

Edge, Julian (Ed.) (2006). *Relocating TESOL.* London: Palgrave.

Edwards, C., Moorhouse, J., & Widlake, S. (1988). Language or English? In M. Jones & A. Wests (Eds.), *Learning me your language: Perspectives on the teaching of English* (pp. 77–95). London: Mary Glasgow.

Gee, J. P. (2004). Learning language as a matter of learning social languages within discourses. In M. Hawkins (Ed.), *Language learning and teacher education: A sociocultural approach* (pp. 13–31). Clevedon: Multilingual Matters.

Gonzalez, A. (1990). Evaluating bilingual education in the Philippines: Towards a multidimensional model of evaluation in language planning. In R. Baldauf & A. Luke (Eds.), *Language planning and education in Australasia and the South Pacific* (pp. 319–335). Clevedon: Multilingual Matters.

Harklau, L. (2000). From the "good kids" to the "worst:" Representations of English language learners across educational settings. *TESOL Quarterly*, *34*(1), 35–67.

Hashimoto, K. (2007). Japan's language policy and the "lost decade." In A. Tsui & J. W. Tollefson (Eds.), *Language policy, culture and identity in Asian contexts* (pp. 25–36). Mahwah, NJ: Lawrence Erlbaum Associates.

Heath, S. B. (1983). *Way with words: Language, life, and work in communities and classrooms.* Cambridge, UK: Cambridge University Press.

Hu, G. (2005). Contextual influences on instruction practices: A Chinese case for an ecological approach to ELT. *TESOL Quarterly*, *39*(4), 635–660.

Kachru, B. B. (1985). Standards, codification and sociolinguistic realm: The

English language in the outer circle. In R. Quirk & H. G. Widdowson (Eds.), *English in the world* (pp. 11–30). Cambridge: Cambridge University Press.

Kachru, B. B. (1999). *Asian Englishes: Contexts, constructs and creativity*. Paper presented at the 12th World Congress of the International Association of Applied Linguistics, Tokyo.

Koike, I. & Tanaka, H. (1995). English in foreign language education policy in Japan: Toward the twenty-first century. *World Englishes, 14*(1), 13–25.

Kramsch, C. & Sullivan, P. (1996). Appropriate pedagogy. *ELT Journal, 50*, 199–212.

Kwon, O. (2000). Korea's English education policy changes in the 1990s: Innovations to gear the nation for the 21st century. *English Teaching, 55*, 47–91.

Lam, W. S. (2000). L2 literacy and the design of the self: A case study of a teenager writing on the Internet. *TESOL Quarterly, 34*(3), 457–482.

Leibowitz, B. (2005). Learning in an additional language in a multilingual society: A South African case study on university-level writing. *TESOL Quarterly, 39*(4), 661–681.

Li, D. (1998). "It's always more difficult than you plan and imagine:" Teachers' perceived difficulties in introducing the communicative approach in South Korea. *TESOL Quarterly, 32*(4), 677–704.

Lin, A. & Luke, A. (2006). Postcolonial approaches to TESOL. Special volume of *Critical Inquiry in Language Studies, 3*, 65–200.

Lin, A. & Martin, P. (Eds) (2005). *Decolonisation, globalisation: Language-in-education policy and practice*. Clevedon: Multilingual Matters.

Lin, A., Wang, W., Akamatsu, N., & Riazi, M. (2005). International TESOL professionals and teaching English for glocalized communication (TEGCOM). In A. S. Canagarajah (Ed.), *Reclaiming the local in language policy and practice* (pp. 197–224). Mahwah, NJ: Lawrence Erlbaum Associates.

Liu, D., Ahn, G., Baek, K., & Han, N. (2004). South Korean high school English teachers' code switching: Questions and challenges in the drive for maximal use of English in teaching. *TESOL Quarterly, 38*(4), 605–638.

Lo Bianco (1990). Making language policy: Australia's experience. In R. B. Baldauf, Jr. & A. Luke (Eds.), *Language planning and education in Australasia and the South Pacific* (pp. 47–79). Clevedon: Multilingual Matters.

LoCastro, V. (1996). English language education in Japan. In H. Coleman (Ed.), *Society and the language classroom* (pp. 40–58). Cambridge: Cambridge University Press.

Luk, J. (2005). Voicing the "self" through an "other" language: Exploring communicative language teaching for global communication. In A. S. Canagarajah (Ed.), *Reclaiming the local in language policy and practice* (pp. 247–268). Mahwah, NJ: Lawrence Erlbaum Associates.

McKay, S. L. & Chick, K. (2001). Positioning learners in post-apartheid South African schools: A case study of selected multicultural Durban Schools. *Linguistics and Education, 12*(4), 393–408.

McKay, S. L. & Freedman, S. W. (1990). Language minority education in Great Britain: A challenge to current U.S. policy. *TESOL Quarterly, 24*(3), 385–405.

McKay, S. L., & Wong, S. C. (1996). Multiple discourses, multiple identities: Investment and agency in second-language learning among Chinese adolescent immigrant students. *Harvard Educational Review, 66*, 577–608.

Medgyes, P. (1994). *The non-native teacher*. London: Macmillan.

National Council for Mother Tongue Teaching (1985). The Swann Report: Education for all. *Journal of Multilingual and Multicultural Development*, 6(6), 497–508.

Norton, B. (1997). Language, identity and the ownership of English. *TESOL Quarterly*, 31, 409–429.

Nunan, D. (1991). Communicative tasks and the language curriculum. *TESOL Quarterly*, 25(2), 279–295.

Nunan, D. (2003). The impact of English as a global language on educational policies and practices in the Asia-Pacific region. *TESOL Quarterly*, 37(4), 589–613.

Pakir, A. (1999) Connecting with English in the context of internationalism. *TESOL Quarterly*, 33(1), 103–113.

Peirce, B. (1995). Social identity, investment, and language learning. *TESOL Quarterly*, 29, 9–31.

Phillipson, R. (2003). *English-only Europe?* London: Routledge.

Rajagopalan, K. (2003). The ambivalent role of English in Brazilian politics. *World Englishes*, 22(2), 91–102.

Ramanathan, V. (1999). "English is here to stay:" A critical look at institutional and educational practices in India. *TESOL Quarterly*, 33(2), 211–233.

Rampton, B. (1995). *Crossing: Language and ethnicity among adolescents*. New York: Longman.

Seidlhofer, B. (1999). Double standards: teacher education in the expanding circle. *World Englishes*, 18(2), 233–245.

Seidlhofer, B., Breiteneder, A. & Pitzl, M. (2006). English as a lingua franca in Europe: Challenges for applied linguists. *Annual Review of Applied Linguistics*, 26, 3–34.

Smitherman, G. (2000). *Talkin that talk: Language, culture and education in African America*. New York: Routledge.

Smolicz, J. & Secombe, M. (2003). Assimilation or pluralism: Changing policies for minority languages in Australia. *Language Policy*, 2, 3–25.

Tang, C. (1997). On the power and status of nonnative ESL teachers. *TESOL Quarterly*, 31(3), 577–583.

Tollefson, J. (1991). *Planning language: Planning inequality*. London: Longman.

Towards a national language plan for South Africa: Final report of the Language Plan Task Group (LANTAG) (1996). Presented to the Minister of Arts, Culture, Science and Technology, Dr. B. S. Ngubane, 8 August.

Tsui, B. M. & Tollefson, J. W. (Eds.) (2007). *Language policy, culture, and identity in Asian contexts*. Mahwah, NJ: Lawrence Erlbaum Associates.

Vavrus, F. (2002). Postcoloniality and English: Exploring language policy and the politics of development in Tanzania. *TESOL Quarterly*, 36(3), 373–397.

Yano, Y. (2001). World Englishes in 2000 and beyond. *World Englishes*, 20(2), 119–131.

Yim, S. (2007). Globalization and language policy in South Korea. In A. Tsui & J. W. Tollefson (Eds.), *Language policy, culture and identity in Asian contexts* (pp. 37–54). Mahwah, NJ: Lawrence Erlbaum Associates.

Zuengler, J. (2004). Jackie Chan drinks mountain dew: Constructing cultural models of citizenship. *Linguistics and Education*, 14, 277–303.

Chapter 3

Multilingual societies

Within many multilingual societies today, one language (the high, or H-language) is typically used in formal domains, while other languages (the low, or L-languages) are used in informal domains. English is often the language of choice in the formal domains of the society, while national or indigenous languages are used in the home. Building on our discussion in chapter 2, this chapter will analyze two countries in which there is both *diglossia* and widespread English bilingualism, India and South Africa. The language situation in these countries will illustrate how the use of English within the larger social context has important implications for English teaching and learning. Multilingualism in India involves about 200 languages (that have 10,000 or more speakers, with another 1,248 mother tongues with fewer than 1,000 speakers) for a population of about 940 million people. Forty-seven languages are used in education as a medium of instruction, 87 in the press, 71 in radio, 13 in the cinema, and 13 in state-level administration (Annamalai, 2001). English is the most widely spoken *second* language, followed by Hindi, involving approximately 3 to 4 percent of the population; there are virtually no monolingual speakers of English using English in all domains. English proficiency is mostly restricted to the upper echelons of society. Similar linguistic diversity characterizes South Africa, where there are 11 official languages, in addition to the approximately 70 other languages used in the country. According to the 2001 census, English is spoken as a home language by approximately 8 percent of the population, mostly within the urban and middle and upper classes; the Bantu[1] languages, or the languages of the people, are more commonly the languages of the rural and working class.

The chapter will also examine countries in which there is English bilingualism *without* diglossia, meaning situations where many people

---

1 Bantu contains hundreds of languages spoken by more than 200 million people in various parts of Africa. The most common Bantu languages in South African include Zulu and Xhosa.

are bilingual but do not restrict one language to a specific set of purposes or functions. Examples would include some speech communities in
Britain and the United States. According to data from the U.S. Bureau of
the Census (2005), there were 10.5 million children (age 5–17) living in
the United States in 2005 who spoke a language other than English at
home, representing 20 percent of the school-age population. These students are twice as likely to live in poor families compared to children
who speak English well. The linguistic minority population as a whole
increased by 130 percent since 1980, while the English-only population
declined by 1.3 percent. This means that over the last 25 years virtually all
of the 5 million additional school age children in the United States were
linguistic minorities (UC–LMRI, 2006). Regarding bilingual speakers,
the 2000 U.S. Census (Censusscope, n.d.) reported that the number who
speak a language other than English at home increased by 47 percent
during the 1990s. The number of minority language speakers who also
speak English "very well" also increased, by 44 percent in the 1990s. And
in Britain, the Department for Education and Employment (Harris et al.,
2002, p. 44) statistics indicate that in 1999 children from ethnic minority
backgrounds—representing over 200 languages—form one tenth of the
student population.

We will contrast these two English learning contexts (diglossic versus
non-diglossic) with respect to four key areas: (a) incentives and support
for learning English; (b) type of English input; (c) status of the mother
tongue; and (d) and support for mother tongue maintenance. We will
argue for the benefits of designing English learning environments that
support the development of bilingualism.

Diglossic multilingualism

We noted earlier that the increasing status of English as an international
language is not because of a growth in the number of native speakers, but
more due to a dramatic increase in the number of individuals around
the world who are acquiring English as a second language. This does not
necessarily mean that such (or indeed, any) multilingual speakers have
native-like command of English (or of the other languages in their verbal
repertoire). It is more typical that multilinguals will have varying degrees
of proficiency, ranging from conversational fluency to a grasp of specialized language to full competence. Furthermore, many L2 speakers in
English-knowing bilingual/multilingual contexts will not necessarily use
English as their dominant language in all domains. Rather, they have
specific purposes in learning English, usually confined to particular interactional contexts. Many multilingual speakers therefore develop *selective
functionality*. That is, they develop a level of competence only to the
extent needed to fulfill a particular function and within a particular

context. These aspects of multilingualism are important to keep in mind as we turn to our discussion of diglossic multilingual societies, particularly with respect to the pedagogical implications of multilingualism. But before we go to that discussion, we first turn to an overview of diglossia as a sociolinguistic concept to better understand the implications that such patterns of language use have on language learning in multilingual contexts.

Diglossia

When speakers have two or more languages in their repertoires, they don't necessarily use them all in the same situation. Using Fishman's (1972) terms, what language(s) to use with whom and for what purposes is an important communicational consideration for multilingual speakers. These choices are not random, and are largely connected to the linguistic norms, values, and practices of the sociolinguistic context of the particular speech community. In his seminal article published in 1959, Ferguson introduced the term *diglossia* to describe a community where two or more varieties of the same language have different roles to play in society. For example, Singapore English can be described as an example of such *classic diglossia*: SSE (Singapore Standard English), the H-variety similar to the standard variety taught in schools; and SCE (Singapore Colloquial English, or, Singlish), the L-variety widely used in informal situations and acquired informally (Gupta, 1992).

Fishman (1967) extended Ferguson's classic diglossia to other multilingual situations where two mutually unintelligible languages occupy the H and L niches. In such *extended diglossia*, the notion of domains is important. According to Fishman (1972), domains are used to explain "who speaks what language to whom and when in those speech communities that are characterized by widespread and relatively stable multilingualism" (p. 437). Domains include, for example, the family, religion, education, government, friendship, and so forth. What makes a bilingual situation diglossic then is that the linguistic differences must be *functionally distinguished* within the particular society. They are also typically in hierarchical relation to each other, with one representing power, prestige, purity, and so forth. The H-language is used in the formal domains. For example, Sanskrit in India is used for religious, educational, literacy and other such formal domains. In contrast, the L-language (e.g. Kannada in India) is rarely used for such purposes, being only used for more informal situations, such as local markets and conversations between friends.

Other researchers (e.g. Hornberger, 1989; Martin-Jones, 1989) have argued against the strict distinction between two languages, and suggest diglossia needs to be seen more as a continuum, or as overlapping patterns of language use. They argue that in many multilingual situations, it is very difficult to draw distinct lines around particular situations and domains and say that a particular language variety is only used there. It is also the case that many multilingual speakers employ three or more languages in various combinations, suggesting a much more complex situation than diglossia implies. In some regions of East Africa one language is clearly identified with one ethnic group (the L variety), English is a lingua franca and bears greater status (the H variety), and Swahili is a general lingua franca somewhere in between H and L. To complicate the picture even more, code-switching between the H and L varieties can occur in any domain. In the classroom, for example, a teacher may be using the H variety while teaching content, but then switch to the L variety to reinforce a point or for classroom management. Or a politician may switch to the L variety in his or her campaign speeches for comic effect or to signal solidarity with the electorate.

Finally, if we consider the ideological basis of language (see chapter 4), it becomes clear that the particular belief systems underpinning a language —what Schiffman (1997) identifies as the "origin myths, beliefs about 'good' and 'bad' language, taboos, shibboleths, and so on" (p. 211)—are essential to understanding diglossic situations. Schiffman refers to these belief systems as "linguistic culture," a kind of shorthand referencing the set of behaviors, beliefs, attitudes, and historical circumstances that are typically associated with a particular language in that society. The linguistic culture thus has an impact on how people value their particular languages and varieties and how they allocate them. An example Schiffman provides is that of Tamil, where beliefs about the antiquity, beauty, and purity of Tamil maintain its H-variety.

In the next section, we will look at two diglossic multilingual societies, India and South Africa. These two countries fall within Kachru's Outer Circle in that English is one of the officially recognized languages of the country, following a history of colonial rule. As in many Outer Circle countries, they are grappling with how to address the social inequalities related to access to English—inequalities that are further reinforced by the diglossic boundaries of use. English is used primarily outside the home in formal and higher-status contexts, and is mostly learned in the context of formal education. And English is the language of political and economic power, of scientific knowledge, modernization and development. Furthermore, diglossic multilingualism means that English is acquired in addition to the existing languages in the individual and social linguistic repertoires. Indeed, given that English is mostly acquired in school, a key issue facing educational policy and pedagogy is how to allocate the use of English and the other local languages in order to promote multilingualism. As we will discuss later in this chapter, this latter point in particular is a key distinguishing factor between the educational practices in diglossic and non-diglossic countries.

EIL and diglossia

As we consider English learning in India and South Africa, it is important to remember that educational attainment is quite low for both countries. In India one third of all school-aged children (6 to 14 years old) were out of school in 1991, and two thirds of all adults did not complete middle school (eight years of schooling) (Annamalai, 2004). Eighty-nine percent of all primary schools are in rural areas. In South Africa in 2001 about 18 percent of persons aged 20 and over have no schooling; 22.4 percent have, at most, primary education. Only 20 percent have completed secondary education. Of the 5 million persons older than 4 years of age who had no formal education in 1994, 70 percent were Black; of the professionally unqualified teachers in 1992, 99.9 percent were Black (Statistics South Africa, 2001). School enrollment rates have since drastically improved; some 2000 estimates indicate a 133 percent increase in enrolment in primary school and 95 percent in secondary; however, at the same time, it is estimated that about three-quarters of children fail school and thus many of these are repeat students. Thus, when we talk about diglossia and English, it does not refer to all members of society; however, it does refer to the relationship English has with the other languages operant in these multilingual societies.

As described by Schiffman (1996), "diglossia is so deeply rooted in Indian culture that it is not only probable that we will find it no matter which language we look at, it is almost an *inevitable* feature of the Indian linguistic scene" (emphasis in original) (p. 156). The following are some important characteristics of such diglossia in India:

1   English is one of the official languages in India, and there is strong environmental support for English in the mass media and indigenous literature.
2   English is the most widely spoken *second* language, followed by Hindi; there are virtually no monolingual speakers of English using English in all domains.
3   The approximate 5 percent (about 50 million) of India's population that do speak English are mostly professionals and elite, who typically speak a variety of indigenous languages and therefore use English as a link language.
4   What all this means is that, while English may be a 'neutral' link language for those within the top tier of society, it has also had a stratifying effect, disadvantaging those who are unable to access English-medium education and therefore unable to participate in the domains wherein English is the dominant medium of communication, like education or global/international business, and benefit from what such access provides.

5 Finally, English is a diglossically H-language; the use of English increases in the more formal domains of education, government, and employment while very few use English in their private domains.

Diglossia also characterizes South Africa's multilingual society. As in India, English is not a major language in statistical terms; the Bantu languages are statistically more dominant. However, socio-politically and socio-economically, English is far more hegemonic than any other language, particularly in metropolitan and urban areas. English is the medium of instruction at most schools, except at some historically Afrikaans-medium schools and universities. Even these are under pressure to change. For example, in response to the demands of students, the formerly Afrikaans-medium University of Pretoria is now a dual-medium (Afrikaans and English) institution. English is widely used in the print media, on radio and television; it is the language of science and technology, job opportunities, parliament, and international popular culture, and is the language most used in business. It is the language of interethnic communication, and thus is also seen as a unifying language.

With this brief introduction to diglossia in South Africa and India, we now turn to a discussion of several common themes in each, with an eye to implications for EIL pedagogy and learning.

Incentives and support for learning English

In broad strokes, the overriding incentive for the learning of English in diglossic multilingual societies is the very status of English as the H-language, and its use in H-domains. The general belief in such societies is that learning of English will thus also provide access to the domains in which English is dominant, particularly higher education, government, and the national and global economies. There are a number of factors contributing to this H-positioning of English, including the *colonial legacy*, the *post-colonial/democratic government's response to that legacy*, and *globalization*.

Colonial legacy

We discussed in chapter 1 how the British linguistic policy generally was to educate a small group of elite civil servants in English. The British colonial legacy thus positioned English as a language of status, power and socio-economic mobility, making English a desirable acquisition for many. This legacy is clearly evident in India and South Africa.

In India, the Macaulay *Minute on Indian Education* of 1835—the ordinance that made English the medium of instruction in all schools and universities—was unambiguous in its elitist intent: to create "a class who may be interpreters between us and the millions we govern, a class of persons, Indian in blood and colour, but English in taste, in opinion, in morals and in intellect" (quoted in Bhatt, 2005, p. 26). There were three forms of education under colonial rule: English-medium, in urban areas and reserved for the elite members of society; two-tier medium which entailed vernacular education for primary and English for advanced education, mostly in smaller towns; and vernacular medium for primary education in the rural areas, where there was education at all. Vernacular education was viewed as inferior and English medium as better. Bhatt (2005) describes the colonial legacy in India as "social-linguistic apartheid" (p. 27): on one hand there are the upper and middle classes, with relatively easy access to English and who now represent an inner circle of power and privilege; and on the other, groups of people who do not have such access. At the same time, the use of English has become dominant in public domains, replacing the use of former elite languages such as Sanskrit, which was formerly under the control of elite groups like the Brahmins. Furthermore, English has come to be viewed as the language of rational and scientific (as opposed to religious) thought and material (as opposed to spiritual) progress. The dominance of English is thus seen differently than the previous dominance of native languages, and contributes to an open access view of English, distinct from other native dominant languages.

English in South Africa came via the British occupation of the Cape of Good Hope, now Cape Town, in 1795 when they took over from the Dutch. Under the British policy of Anglicization, all official posts and positions of political, economic, legal, educational, and social prestige were reserved for those proficient in English. For a time, these efforts were supplanted by policies of Afrikanerization under the Afrikaner government. The 1953 Bantu Education Act made Afrikaans, rather than English, the medium of instruction in all Black African schools. There was strong resistance to this policy, leading to the bloody Soweto uprisings of June 16, 1976. What emerged from these uprisings was a perception among Black South Africans of Afrikaans as the language of oppression, and English as the language of liberation against apartheid.

Post-colonial/democratic government policy

Faced with inequalities that were steeped in language ideology and practice, an immediate concern facing post-colonial and democratic governments was to implement ways to redress these inequalities. For both India and South Africa, multilingualism was central to the governments' response. But at the same time and in each case, English diglossia, and its associated inequality, was further entrenched. Largely because of historical (colonial) outcomes discussed above, both countries today continue to have socioeconomic divisions that make it impossible for the majority of the citizens to access English equally. Finally, harking back to our discussion in chapter 1, it is also significant to note how governments and citizens in both countries have been active agents in the continued spread of English, beyond any imperialist tendency of colonial rule.

In India, the post-colonial Indian government formulated the 1957 (revised in 1968) "Three Languages Formula" as an attempt to provide some kind of linguistic balance. All children are to be exposed to at least three languages during their time at school: the regional language or the mother tongue, Hindi (in Hindi-speaking areas, it would be another Indian language), and English. While the policy was originally meant for secondary education, parents are increasingly demanding English be taught at earlier levels, including primary 1. The assumption is that increasing the hours of instruction will lead to better learning. However, as Annamalai (2004) notes, starting English early does not work in many schools for a variety of reasons. For example, many primary school teachers in India do not have a college education and generally do not come from families with exposure to English at home. Hence, the goals of early English instruction would in effect be undermined.

While India's Three Languages Formula was an attempt to equalize the status among the various languages, its implementation shows continued hierarchical ordering. Greatest status continues to be given to the two official federal government languages, Hindi and English, followed by the other official languages. These are followed by languages that have no official government function at the federal or state level, but are spoken by more than one million people. And finally, at the bottom are the languages spoken by small groups and tribal languages. This hierarchy is particularly evident as we consider the medium of instruction. As evident in Table 3.1, only a very small percentage of students receive English-medium instruction, with the majority learning English as a second language. This in effect is a "bifocal" (Annamalai, 2001, p. 35) language policy: one with English-medium bilingual education for the select few,

Table 3.1 Percentages of schools that teach English in India

	Primary (classes 1 to 4/5) (%)	Middle (classes 4/5 to 8) (%)	Secondary (classes 9–10) (%)
English as a first language	2.9	4.3	6.6
English as a second language	21.7	55.0	54.1
English as a third language	6.6	38.0	35.8
Total for English	30.4	97.3	96.5

Source: Annamalai, 2004, p. 178.

and another with Indian language-medium instruction for the masses. For those in English-medium schools, the English used and taught tends to be the Standard, global form. At the mass level where English is taught as a subject, English is usually taught by teachers who themselves have low levels of English proficiency and in non-standard forms.

As in India, the South African democratic government's response to colonial and apartheid policy was a policy of multilingualism. Its language policies were guided by the government's national ideals, which included (Webb, 2004, p. 218):

- establishing democracy;
- promoting equality and human rights;
- developing national unity and promoting mutual tolerance and respect among the different cultural, linguistic, religious, racial and sociopolitical groups;
- implementing affirmative action;
- retaining the country's cultural diversity.

The official multilingual policy was outlined in a language-planning task group's report, *Towards a national language plan for South Africa* (see page 39), making 11 languages official in the nation (for a critique of the policies, see Webb, 2004): nine indigenous languages and the two former colonial official languages of English and Afrikaans.

The 11-languages policy specifically challenged the hegemony of English and Afrikaans, and attempted to eliminate negative stereotypes linked to indigenous languages and their speakers. Furthermore, it aimed to promote national unity, respect and tolerance for linguistic and cultural diversity. In keeping with this national multilingual policy, a "Language in Education Policy" was put in place in 1997 to ensure that all South Africans become multilingual: "being multilingual should be a defining characteristic of being South African" and the "learning of two or more languages should be general practice" (cited in Sutton, 2006, p. 41). Each school decides on its own language policy regarding medium of instruction and languages to be taught as subjects. One of the required two official languages is English, meaning all students in school are exposed to English instruction.

Globalization

The dominant status of English has been further heightened around the world as a result of its status as a global language (see chapter 1).

In India, the rapid rise of urbanization, industrialization, technologization, and general modernization has brought with it a dramatic increase in the status and dominance of English (and challenges to the Three

Languages Formula). An example we discussed in chapter 1 is how the Internet in particular has opened up jobs for English proficient Indians as a result of outsourcing or off-shoring by U.S. and other international companies: India gets about 70 percent of all outsourcing opportunities from the United States alone (Bhatt, 2005).

South Africa's re-integration with the global economy after the fall of apartheid in 1993 has also raised the status of English in that country. Its new language policy was intended to give greater prominence to several African languages; however, instead, English has gained new ground. McLean and McCormick observe (1996) "this policy thrust towards multilingualism is often intended and perceived as a symbolic statement, and that for instrumental purposes English remains the dominant language in South Africa" (p. 329).

The results of these historic and contemporary conditions in India and South Africa have thus contributed in significant ways to the continued and entrenched H-status of English. And from these conditions have emerged very specific discourses about English that increase the incentive to learn English. Among the more prevalent discourses is the equation of English with being educated, cultivated, and intellectual, and a widespread view of English as capital. As noted by Sheorey and Nayar (2002), "in the general educational discourse of India, to be 'educated' is commonly considered to be English-literate. That alone speaks volumes for the prominence of English as a language of general mental and intellectual cultivatedness in India" (p. 14).

The view of English as the "Aladdin's lamp" that we discussed in chapter 1 is particularly motivating for learners of English. English is widely regarded in India as the means towards better jobs and therefore towards upward socioeconomic mobility. What Gupta wrote in 1995 holds even more true today with the rise of EIL and the economic impact this has had on India: "Indians secretly believe, if not openly say, that competence in English makes a considerable difference in their career prospects . . . Politicians and bureaucrats denounce the elitism of [English-medium] schools but surreptitiously send their children to them" (p. 76)—a phenomenon similarly seen in Hong Kong in 1998 when law-makers continued to send their children to English-medium schools while at the same time passing legislation that required most schools to switch from English to Cantonese.

Such views are similarly held in South Africa, where English is widely seen as "the language of power, prestige and status, and as an 'open sesame' by which one can acquire unlimited vertical social mobility" (Kamwangamalu, 2002, p. 3). Webb (2004) cites a survey conducted in predominantly Black residential communities in the Pretoria area which reported that English was regarded as the most valuable language for getting a job (94 percent of respondents), with Afrikaans in second place (74 percent) and the Bantu languages scoring between 38 percent and 49 percent (p. 229). Furthermore, English was regarded as the language that will help one earn respect from others (87 percent), followed by Pedi (76 percent), Tswana (62 percent), Zulu (59 percent) and Afrikaans (49 percent). As observed by Webb (2004), "the strong position of English is striking, clearly indicating the continued asymmetric power relations among the languages of the area" (p. 229). Thus, as in India, increasingly parents in South Africa are opting for English-medium schools, and in increasingly earlier grades. For example, Appalraju's study (cited in de Kadt, 2002) in a Zulu-speaking rural community showed that the majority of parents were electing, often at considerable expense, to send their children to English-medium high schools in neighboring towns instead of the closer and less expensive Zulu-medium high schools in their own towns.

Support for learning English in both India and South Africa thus comes directly through its status as an official language and through the language-in-education policies, making English a medium of instruction and a language to be learned in all schools. It also comes through strong environmental support in the mass media and indigenous literature. And it comes through the prevalent discourses associated with it being a language of high status and prestige. However, at the same time, the large rural populations challenge effective implementation of the policies. There are real financial constraints that limit the availability of sufficiently trained English educators, and the provision of textbooks, particularly in rural schools. Furthermore, within the education systems of both India and South Africa, what has emerged is the bi-polar implementation of English education.

Type of English input

Ramanathan and Atkinson's (Ramanathan, 1999) ethnographic study at an English-medium college in India provides some detail of various practices that influence the type of English input students receive. The objective of their study was to examine how Dalits (lower-caste) and OBC (Other Backward Classes) students coming from vernacular K-12 schools adjust to the use of English at the tertiary level. They focused on three educational practices that influence these students' access to Indian English: (a) tracking students into college-level streams that bar some from English-medium instruction; (b) grammar-translation methods, which, they argue, inhibit the communicative competence of some students; and (c) teaching English literature rather than English language throughout India. Based on how many years of English education they had received, some students were placed in streams that continued to teach English as a subject, rather than using it as medium of instruction. Pedagogical practices followed much the same as those they had received in their K-12 years.

First, teachers made extensive use of Gujarati and Hindi in the classroom. Faculty members felt the use of students' primary language(s) was necessary because it was the only way to "get through to the students" (Ramanathan, 1999, p. 221). Almost all of the language—the directives, vocabulary items, entire paragraphs from short stories—were translated. Teachers frequently required students to read a passage aloud from their textbooks, or instructions in a grammar workbook, and to then translate them into either Gujarati or Hindi as a way to check comprehension. There was little or no attention given to developing speaking skills, as "developing fluency in speaking English was not part of the university-mandated curriculum" (Ramanathan, 1999, p. 221). The focus of the curriculum was exclusively devoted to the teaching of grammar, usually in decontextualised exercises, rather than on speaking.

On the one hand, one could argue that such pedagogical practices are commensurate with pedagogy in other content areas, and as such, is an example of how English pedagogy needs to be embedded in the local context. As Ramanathan (2005) points out in her discussion of pedagogical practices at a women's college, the teachers there recall their own vernacular-medium schooling practices, where the use of the vernacular was both heavily used and regarded as valuable and integral to language teaching (p.74). However, on the other hand, when students in the above segment were asked about such pedagogical practices, the students responded that they did not feel prepared to actually use the language in their pursuit for a career: "*Amne tho ahinya grammaraj sikhwade chhe*; English *ma vaat karvani* practice *nathi malthu . . . tho* job interviews *maa mushkil hoye amne*" [We only get taught grammar here; we don't get to practice speaking English ... so we find job interviews difficult] (Ramanathan, 1999, p. 222). Ramanathan went on to note that, although the students felt they were not learning what they needed, they nonetheless continued to maintain belief that these classes would somehow improve their social status and life chances.

The second pedagogical practice noted by Ramanathan (1999) was how the curriculum is mostly dominated by the study of literature rather than language use (the faculty themselves were literature teachers, not language teachers). Recall that literacy in English is synonymous with "being educated". Most of the literature texts were British and rooted in colonial tradition. However, the students expressed a sense of cultural dissonance between themselves and what was portrayed in the literature, particularly around issues of romantic love (as opposed to arranged marriages) and issues of power and race (as opposed to caste). The result is a feeling of cultural dissonance between themselves and what is portrayed in their textbooks, and feelings of alienation. Such emotions are further exacerbated by the heavy reliance on translation and the use of the vernacular in teaching English literature. Ramanathan (2005) documents how one teacher laboriously translated each sentence of an English play, and attempted to explain the sarcasms and subtleties in the text—all of which were lost in translation.

Thus, although there is strong motivation to learn English in India, practices such as these actually keep the poorest and most disadvantaged students from learning in ways that would allow them to access the benefits that English proficiency accords. This is a clear example of a key characteristic of today's learners of EIL: they do not necessarily want to learn or internalize the cultural norms of native speakers of English from the Inner Circle. Rather, they want to learn English for very particular purposes, to gain access to the benefits that knowledge of English brings. Learning British colonial literature and being denied the opportunity to speak English in class subvert such goals and ultimately leaves such learners without the skills they desire and need.

Turning to South Africa, the South African Department of Education's language-in-education policy encourages the principle of *additive* multilingualism, but allows the governing body within each public school to determine the school's medium of instruction. While it does not stipulate any specific model, it does suggest two: the use of a first language as the medium of instruction (with the requirement that an additional language also be taught); and, particularly in cases where the students' home languages are not the medium of instruction, a "structured bilingual approach", understood as initial instruction through L1, with a gradual transition to English. However, if we compare the medium of instruction with students' home language (see Table 3.2), it is clear that there is a strong preference for English, regardless of the home language. While only 5.7 percent of the school population uses English as a home language, 51 percent of schools reported using English as the medium of instruction (although what this means in practice may be quite different).

Probyn (2006) observes that even though English is increasingly the medium of instruction from the beginning of Grade 4, and in some cases

Table 3.2 Medium of instruction in school and home language

	Medium of instruction	*Home language*
Afrikaans	11% of schools	11.3% of school population
English	51% of schools	5.7% of school population
A Bantu language	37% of schools	83% of school population

(*Source:* 1996 Department of Education statistics, cited in Webb, 2004, p. 233).

even Grade 1, the majority of African learners in township and rural schools (over 80 percent of learners) have little exposure to English outside of the formal classroom apart from television and popular music. Furthermore, these learners have limited access to English reading materials both in and out of school. There is thus a "gap between learners' English proficiency and the linguistic demands of learning through the medium of English" (Probyn, 2006, p. 393).

However, while parents may be requesting English education earlier, English medium instruction is not necessarily what parents want. Webb (2004, p. 234) cites data from a survey which indicated that only 12 percent of those surveyed said they preferred English as a medium of instruction, whereas 37 percent preferred instruction through their primary (Bantu) language. Another 39 percent preferred English and their primary language to be used jointly. Along the same vein, Heugh (2002) cites a national sociolinguistic survey conducted in 1999 by the PANSALB that showed at least 88 percent of parents desired the maintenance and development of the home language alongside English. Thus, while there is a strong desire to learn English, as in India, this desire is not to be interpreted as a desire for English-only.

The use of code-switching between English and the mother tongue is also prevalent in African schools, as it was in India. Even in schools where the governing bodies appointed English as the medium of instruction, a significant degree of code-switching in content subjects occurs. One study reported 53 percent of teachers reporting the use of Zulu alongside English (Webb, 2004, p. 234). However, there are three caveats here that suggest the use of code-switching is not so much to support and reaffirm the mother tongue languages, but rather for support in learning English and reinforcing the H-status of English. First, all formal assessment is conducted in English, and does not take into account mother tongue learning. Second, as Probyn (2006, p. 394) observes based on her research in Eastern Cape schools, many teachers tend to regard code-switching "as a sign of failure rather than a legitimate classroom strategy". And third, as was discussed in chapter 2 regarding McKay and Chick's work in South Africa's Durban area (see also discussion below), English-only programs tend to be offered in most privileged primary and secondary schools, where there is the exclusive use of English with little or no attention to Zulu. These elite schools tend to be held as the pedagogical and ideological model for others to emulate, thus again reinforcing the H-status and privilege of English.

As in India, the curriculum used in South African English classrooms mostly originates from Inner Circle countries. The British overtones are clear in the following segment of a phonics textbook, taken from a chapter titled "Oh boy" (reproduced by Sutton, 2006):

The royal boy took his toys to enjoy on the voyage. He annoyed his loyal servant when he destroyed all his toys. He will have to take care not to annoy all the other people in his employ.

(p. 78)

The cultural and class divide between the "royal boy" and the average South African student is wide, with the result of similar disconnect and alienation to that mentioned earlier in the Indian context.

In India and South Africa we thus see common themes emerge from the types of English input and the circumstances within which they occur. There is a heavy emphasis on the use of literature, and of a literature and pedagogy divorced from the cultural realities of the everyday lives of the students; in pedagogy and curriculum, there is an emphasis on monolingual English use, and content divorced from its multilingual contexts. And ultimately, the dominant status of English is reinforced in all of these practices.

Mother tongue status

In both India and South Africa, current language and language-in-education policies and practices of diglossia perpetuate the historical language status hierarchies. English continues to be the language of highest status, and dominates the H domains; the mother tongues, with varying degrees, continue to be relegated to the lower status domains. This is particularly perpetuated through practices and ideologies of English-only, which is seen in many schools in both countries—particularly in urban schools which are then held as models for others to follow.

For example, in spite of South Africa's official commitment to promote multilingualism and the mother tongue in the classrooms, the curriculum continues to assume an English-only, or monolingual, model (see chapter 2). Not only does this mean students are not learning literacy in their first language, but this emphasis on English also undermines the productive use of the mother tongue in the learning of English. McKay and Chick's (2001; Chick, 2002) study documents how the principals of the schools examined were not in favor of using Zulu or any language other than English in the classrooms. Diverse languages are generally seen as obstacles to the learning of the target language. Rather than multilingualism, or at least bilingualism, operant in the classroom, they found the ideological assumptions of English-only discourses in the six schools they visited. In one school, Zulu was taught as a subject in all grades by teachers who are all English first-language speakers, and whose own formal preparation for teaching Zulu comprised of twelve one-hour Zulu lessons. In two of the other schools, Zulu was taught as a subject in the higher grades. And in the others, there was no Zulu instruction. All but one of the principals were not in favor of using Zulu in the classroom. Among the reasons given were: (a) this is an English-medium school and therefore students are told to only use English; (b) English is necessary for economic advancement and therefore they should not "revert" to Zulu; and (c) the use of English at school was in line with the government's objectives to reduce racial lines and build a unifying force. Sutton's (2006) research in two classrooms in a school in the Eastern Cape found similar practices, where all learners were strongly encouraged to speak only English in the classroom and discouraged from using their home language.

The net effect of such practices, Chick argues (2002), is that they help maintain the hegemony of English in school and in society in general; the Bantu languages and their speakers are constructed within a deficit model; Bantu languages continue to be stigmatized with low social and economic value. "By such strategic means," he argues, "English-only discourse helps maintain the existing power relationships, providing native speakers of English with a distinct advantage in the educational realm" (p. 270).

Support for mother tongue maintenance

In diglossic multilingual societies, there is, in theory anyway, no threat to one's mother tongue language(s) when learning the H-language. The H-language is learned and acquired through additive bilingualism, in addition to one's mother tongue language. This support for the mother tongue is further enhanced in the allocation of numerous mother tongue languages as official languages and within multilingual education policies. This is evident in both India and South Africa where both countries have a multilingual policy, have numerous languages holding official status, and encourage multilingual education. The governments of both countries have sought to directly redress the social inequalities related to language. South Africa's post-apartheid language and education policy advocates that all students learn their home language and at least one additional official language. The school curriculum also recommends that the learner's home language should be used for learning and teaching wherever possible.

However, the intent of such policies to redress social inequalities has not materialized in significant ways. Classroom pedagogical practices often continue to uphold the dominance of English, and marginalize the value of the mother tongue languages. In South Africa, while there were promises to "develop" the indigenous languages in terms of corpus, status, and prestige in the areas of education, commerce, science and technology, little has been done and the use of indigenous languages continues to be contained to the low domains. Probyn (2006) provides the following summative observation:

Given the problems in teaching and learning through the medium of English as an additional language, it might seem surprising that schools have not taken up the recommendations of the Language-in-education-policy for strengthening the position of African languages in the curriculum, particularly as languages of learning and teaching. However, a number of factors that have little to do with the realities of the classroom teaching and learning strongly direct schools towards retaining English as the language of teaching and learning. These include the social, economic, and political power of English in the country, the under-development of African languages as languages of science and technology, the link of African languages as media of instruction with the apartheid education system and a lack of learning materials in African languages.

(p. 394)

In diglossic multilingual societies, we thus see a variety of policy initiatives initiated to redress many of the inequalities resulting from colonial language policies and to level the playing field between English and indigenous languages through giving greater access to English education and through supporting indigenous languages. At the same time, we see how the very diglossic structure of language use, the colonial legacy of English-language superiority, the continued ideological update of the dominant status of English, and pedagogical and curricular practices of an English-only paradigm work against some of the objectives such policies seek to realize. It is not a story of English imperialism and the unstoppable killer effect of a global English. Rather, it is a story of the mediations between languages and their ecologies, and of the negotiation of power relationships between languages. As we noted in chapter 1, the economic divide in the learning of English is one potential danger of the spread of English, and one that is particularly evident in diglossic multilingual countries such as India and South Africa. In the next section, we will see multilingual situations faced with another real danger evident in the spread of English, namely: growing monolingualism.

EIL without diglossia

There are, of course, many societies with bilingual or multilingual populations that are not diglossic. According to Fishman, bilingualism without diglossia is a situation where there are large numbers of bilingual individuals, but they do not restrict the use of their languages to any one set of circumstances. In such situations, either language may be used for almost any purpose, and there is considerable overlapping or code-switching and code-mixing (see chapter 6). Also, in such multilingual situations (distinguishing them from diglossic ones), the linguistic codes may not be so sharply hierarchical in terms of H- and L-varieties. But perhaps the most outstanding characteristic of many multilingual situations without diglossia, such as in the United States and Great Britain, is the general goal of monolingualism in bilingual education and the lack of support for language maintenance—in spite of increasing numbers of immigrants for whom English is not the L1. Canada is one of the few countries in this category that has attempted to actively reject the monolingual model, adopting instead a policy of "multilingualism within a bilingual framework." Through its Heritage Language Policy, heritage languages are encouraged and maintained in the formal education setting, with the ultimate aim of preparing bilingual people to participate within a multicultural society. Faculties of education in universities throughout Canada have developed courses in pre-service and in-service teacher education that address issues of diversity and equity, including language diversity. However, even here there are limits: of the two official languages, English has increasing dominance. The 2001 Census reveals, for example, that 1,863,000 new Canadians experienced a language shift towards English, while only 96,000 transferred to French (Cardinal, 2005). Furthermore, shifting foci within the state's priorities have resulted in declining financial support for Heritage Language education since the late 1990s. Nonetheless, the 2001 Census of Canada reports that 21 percent of Canadians aged 20 to 49 are bilingual.

In contrast to the Canadian experience, the United States has been described by Myers-Scotton (2006) as a "graveyard of languages" (p. 402). And Britain has the lowest rate of bilingualism (30 percent), except for Hungary, among all of the EU nations (European Commission, 2006). Britain devotes less time to language learning at school than its European counterparts—they start learning languages later, they stop earlier, and there is less amount of curriculum time devoted to languages than elsewhere in the European Union. In contrast to the limited commitment to bilingualism/multilingualism, there is a strong economic interest in Britain to promote the hegemony of English. According to the British Council, the export of English language services and products is second in importance to the British economy only to North Sea Oil (Graddol, 2006).

Once again, we will explore the dynamics of multilingualism and English language learning in such multilingual contexts on the basis of themes explored earlier: the incentives and support for learning English; the type of English input; the status of the mother tongue; and support for mother tongue maintenance. But first we provide a brief introduction to multilingualism in the United States and Britain since that will be our focus in this discussion. We have chosen to focus on these countries because of the marked contrast between their large bilingual population and the policies that seek to minimize or fail to support such diversity.

Whereas in chapter 2 we examined these countries in reference to educational policies and social integration, here we examine them in reference to the themes listed above.

Looking first at the United States, much of the country's controversy surrounding language diversity and educational language policies stem from a number of common myths underlying the hegemonic, monolingual English language ideology. Ovando and Wiley (2003, p. 141) summarize some of the key ones as follows:

- Language diversity in the United States is an "abnormal" condition that is attributable to immigration.
- Past immigrants quickly and willingly learnt English, but recent immigrants resist learning English.
- Language diversity has a disuniting impact on national harmony.
- Language diversity threatens the dominance of English.
- Social and regional varieties of English weaken the purity of "standard" English.
- State and federally supported bilingual education is a failed program that keeps language minorities from learning English and doing well in school.
- "Foreign" languages—if studied at all—should be taught in the higher grades.

These ideologies are central to understanding the particular themes we will be discussing concerning the teaching and learning of English, and the kinds of support there is for mother tongue maintenance. Bilingualism in the United States is largely transitional and results in shifts toward the majority language within a few generations—and often sooner.

Turning to Great Britain, we find that, in spite of the increasing diversity of its populace through immigration, there are few discussions of any commitment to bilingualism. Language instruction itself received little attention in British educational policy until the mid-1960s, when there was a marked increase in immigration from non-English speaking countries. These immigrants were generally viewed according to a deficit model, as "having no English." And, rather than examining a bilingual model, the immediate priority was one of assimilation into the dominant English culture, through language. As described by Thompson (2004, p. 85), "This focus was frequently at the expense of a wider range of curriculum subjects (e.g. maths, science, geography, and so on) and always at the expense of the pupils' home language(s) and their potential to become bilingual, if not multilingual." Leaping forward to 1985, we come to the Swann Report. Significantly, the report favored a move away from separate ESL teaching and recommended that the needs of bilingual learners be met within mainstream schools. It also firmly opposed any separate provision for language maintenance classes or bilingual forms of education. More will be said about the Swann Report below.

These views about language are only underscored by the wider attitudes prevalent in Britain towards language learning. As verified by a survey conducted by the European Commission (2006), Britain has been notorious in its failure to produce competent bilinguals. And in fact, there has been a steady decrease in support for the learning of languages other than English. In 2004, the British government dropped the requirement that all British 14- to 16-year-olds should study at least one foreign language. Naturally, there has been a steady decline in the numbers of students studying foreign languages ever since. As noted in chapter 1, there appears to be a certain amount of comfortable complacency given the global dominance of English—with everyone else learning English, there is no need to learn a foreign language.

Incentives and support for learning English

In both the United States and Britain, incentives for learning English are predominantly (a) *citizenship* and *social integration*, and (b) *socioeconomic factors*.

Citizenship and social integration

English is seen as the language required to fully participate in all aspects of U.S. society. The words of President Theodore Roosevelt hold valid for many today (cited in Nieto, 2000, p. 192): "We have room for but one language here, and that is the English language; for we intend to see that the crucible turns our people out as Americans, of American nationality, and not as dwellers in a polyglot boardinghouse." About three-quarters of a century later, President Ronald Reagan uttered similar views (cited in Nieto, 2000, p. 192): "It is absolutely wrong and against American concept to have a bilingual education program that is now openly, admittedly dedicated to preserving their native language and never getting them adequate in English so they can go out into the job market." President Bush's requirement that longstanding illegal immigrants learn English is premised on this same view, that learning English is a sign that they accept and are willing to integrate into U.S. culture. In this context, the only bilingual education programs that would be most palatable to U.S. citizens would be ones that promote rapid transition to English. Such is the dominant discourse in the English-only movement as well, whereby English is seen as a language of cohesion, unity, and common identity.

Similar assumptions around English and citizenship are evident in Britain, where foreigners applying for British citizenship or permanent residence are required to take an English language test, in addition to a quiz on life in Britain. The Swann Report (and reaffirmed by the sub-sequent Cox Report on which the 1988 National Curriculum was based) stated that, "The key to equality of opportunity, to participation on equal terms as a full member of society, is a good command of English" (Department of Education and Science, 1985, p. 426).

Socio-economic factors

Better English generally means better jobs and higher income, and con-versely, not speaking English largely means being trapped in low-paying jobs with little opportunity for advancement. Bleakley and Chin's (2004) analysis of the outcomes of English-speaking and non-English-speaking immigrants in the United States confirmed that poor English skills meant less schooling and substantially lower wages for immigrants, and often for their children as well. Non-English speakers are much more likely to drop out of school and therefore have significantly lower-paying jobs when working.

In chapter 2 we discussed some of the primary ways support for learn-ing English occurs in the United States and in Britain. By way of review, such support in the United States comes from constitutional, statutory and judicial sources (see chapter 2). Most programs for English learners have come from legal issues regarding the entitlement of such students to language education services. Through various legal rulings, it was deter-mined unconstitutional to place ELs directly in regular, all-English class-rooms without support services. In this context, most bilingual education programs have focused almost exclusively on transition to English-only instruction, with the goal of promoting language shift rather than bilin-gualism. Recent policy has resulted in a dramatic and increasing decline in the availability of bilingual education programs.

Britain does not have the broad constitutional, statutory and judicial support as is evident in the United States, and like the United States, it does not have an official policy for language education. In chapter 2 we out-lined a number of key initiatives regarding English education, including:

- 1966, the need for intensive ESL teaching was first officially recog-nized and funded through the Local Government Act. This separate funding scheme led to pull-out classes where ELs were taught English in isolation from their peers. Language centers, or *induction* centers, were also established for 11 to 16-year-old ELs newly arrived in England.
- 1975, the Bullock Report published the findings of a committee look-ing into the teaching of reading in primary schools that supported the idea of bilingualism. It recommended that schools make provision for ESL instruction.

- The 1980s saw greater support for bilingual and ESL education under the rubric of multicultural education, although the medium of instruction and all national and school assessments continued to be in English.

However, particularly since the 1985 Swann Report and similar to the United States, while the assumption is that all citizens should be proficient in English and that such proficiency is essential for integration into mainstream society, governments in many English-dominant countries are actually cutting back on support for learning English. For example, the British government announced late December 2006 that free English language lessons for adult asylum seekers would be cut. There is thus a contradiction—on the one hand, the government requires immigrants to pass an English test; on the other, it denies them the means by which to be able to do so.

Finally, in both the United States and Britain, support for learning English comes through the lack of support for mother tongue maintenance. While there have been important efforts in some school districts and communities to support heritage languages, the dominant discourse in most departments of education in both countries is that language diversity is a liability, rather than a resource. Thus, not only is there incentive to learn English, but to *only* learn English at the expense of one's mother tongue.

Type of English input

Perhaps the most prevalent view guiding language learning policy and pedagogy in many Inner Circle countries such as the United States and Britain is the notion that ELs learn English better and faster if they are in regular classes with native speakers of English—the submersion/mainstream, or "sink-or-swim" paradigm that we saw in chapter 2. New ELs are often placed in mainstream classes as soon as they arrive, sometimes concurrent with ESL classes with the goal to transition them to English-only as quickly as possible—even though, as Harklau (1994, p. 242) notes, language learners may take up to seven years to develop the level of proficiency needed to compete on an equal footing with native speakers.

Harklau's (1994) ethnographic study, which compares the instructional contexts and pedagogy of ESL versus mainstream classes in the United States, helps us understand the different kinds of English input in these two different contexts. The school in her study offered a number of ESL classes, and a number of sheltered content classes for ESL learners. Most of the courses were taught by a non-certified, but highly experienced, ESL teacher who also coordinated the ESL program; the rest were taught by mainstream teachers untrained in ESL, indicative of the the fact that the U.S. Department of Education does very little to promote knowledge of bilingualism, multilingualism or even second language acquisition among its pre- and in-service public school teachers. Harklau's comparative analysis of the two L2 learning environments suggested that, indeed, a primary benefit of mainstream classes was the "plentiful, authentic input" of English "that served a genuine communicative purpose—to transmit the content of school subject matter" (p. 266). However, the predominant pedagogical practice of teacher-led "discussion" provided little opportunity for extended interaction. She notes how mainstream classroom teachers rarely adjusted input in order to make it comprehensible to ELs: for example, they did not reduce the speed and complexity of speech, did not increase repetition or pausing, nor provided comprehension checks. Teacher talk containing puns or irony was particularly difficult for ELs, as was the frequent switch between instructional talk versus asides. Teachers in mainstream classes also rarely gave explicit feedback or instruction on the target language, leaving students on their own to just pick it up. Explicit language teaching only occurred in English classes. In these classes, the focus was mostly on formalizing what native speakers intuitively knew about English usage, and did not provide instruction on the specific rules or principles that nonnative speakers without such intuitions would need. Teachers in mainstream classes also rarely elicited output from ESL students, with the result that ELs were often withdrawn and non-interactive in mainstream classes.

In contrast to the mainstream classes, the ESL classes at the school observed by Harklau (1994) did provide students with explicit language instruction, and provided many opportunities for the productive use of both spoken and written language, for which there was ongoing feedback. There was greater participation of students in class discussion. However, students often found the lessons too easy, and the teacher found it difficult to manage the different language abilities of the students.

Harklau (1994) concludes with the following observation: "The fact is that there was no truly appropriate educational environment for L2 learners at Gateview. Rather, students' educational experience was a makeshift response to a system fundamentally geared towards the instruction of native speakers of the language" (p. 267). Her comment is particularly noteworthy in the context of the high-stakes English-medium assessments operant in both the United States and Britain. Los Angeles Unified, California's largest school district, seen as a leader in bilingual education, currently assigns most ELs to classrooms that use *Open Court*, a phonics-intensive reading program designed for native speakers of English. Not insignificantly, the publisher of Open Court, CTB McGraw-Hill, also is the publisher of the state's two high-stakes assessments, the

California Achievement Test (CAT/6) and the California English Development Test (CELDT). In the same vein, the 1988 Education Reform Act in Britain assumes English to be the first language and medium of instruction for all pupils in England (cited in Thompson, 2004, p. 94). And it requires annual testing and assessment procedures that place ELs alongside monolingual English speaking students, leading to a curriculum undifferentiated from that of monolingual speakers.

Finally, in thinking about the types of input learners have available to them, it is important to remember that language learning does not take place only in the classroom. In Inner Circle countries the input of English is predominantly monolingual, is widespread, is robust, and there are "native speaker" models. In Outer Circle countries, the input of English in official contexts is also often monolingual; however, in television, radio and popular culture, there is often the concurrent use of multiple languages through code-switching and code-mixing. In its diglossic manifestations, English is often more limited to the upper echelons of society, and thus not as widespread. The models are most often "nonnative speaker" models, speakers for whom English is also a second language.

Mother tongue status

Sonia Nieto, a well-known author on diversity and multicultural education in the United States, tells of her daughter Marisa who could speak Spanish fluently by the time she was three, but no English. On hearing her speak Spanish on her first day of day care, one of the teachers said, "Oh, I see she doesn't have language." Such comments, Nieto (2000) argues, are indicative of a prevalent ideology in the United States, that "children who do not yet speak English lack language altogether" (p. 189). Such is the status of mother tongue languages in the United States. In most U.S. classrooms, linguistic diversity is commonly seen as a temporary barrier to "real" learning. Once students learn English, learning can proceed. Sacrificing one's mother tongue then is seen as necessary for education— and ultimately, for the benefits of citizenship. Language and patriotic loyalty are widely seen as synonymous, with patriotism measured by how quickly one has abandoned a native language and replaced it with English.

The mother tongue languages (usually referred to as home languages or first languages) in Britain have similar non-status. Thompson (2004) interprets this as the government's denial of Britain's multicultural and multilingual population, and Britain continues to operate on the assumption of English monolingualism as being the ideal state of affairs for the nation. In this context, the "first priority in language learning" (Department of Education and Science, 1985, p. 426) is given to the learning of English, and not to bilingualism.

Support for mother tongue maintenance

Support for mother tongue maintenance in the United States and Britain is embedded in bilingual education.

In the United States, bilingual education is premised on the principles of civil rights. The Equal Educational Opportunity Act of 1974 states that:

> No state shall deny equal educational opportunities to an individual on account of his or her race, color, sex, or national origin, by the failure by an educational agency to take appropriate action to overcome language barriers that impede equal participation by students in its instructional programs.
>
> (cited in Garcia, 2002, p. 34)

With the backing of Congress, over one billion federal dollars have been used to develop and implement a variety of bilingual education programs in the United States.

However, increasingly the continued availability of such programs for many learners of English is diminishing. Between 1992 and 2002, when the number of ELs in grades K-12 increased by 72 percent nationwide, their enrollment in bilingual programs declined from 37 percent to 17 percent (reported in Crawford, 2006, p. 1). One reason for this trend has to do with issues of limited resources, and a national shortage of bilingual teachers. Another is the anti-bilingual backlash, and the English-only school (and out of school) initiatives in key states such as California, Arizona, and Massachusetts. California's Proposition 227 and the national No Child Left Behind (NCLB) Act have had particularly negative effects on bilingual education.

Proposition 227 was passed on June 2, 1998; it states that "All children in California public schools shall be taught English by being taught in English" (cited in Crawford, 2006). This means that the 1.4 million or more ELs in California who are not fluent in English are given no more than a year of intensive immersion in English, in a sheltered English immersion program, before they are moved to regular classes. Even within this program, instruction is to be primarily in English, with only limited support in the home language. Upon completion of the sheltered immersion program, students are to be placed in mainstream English-only classrooms. The net effect of Proposition 227 is the near elimination of bilingual education, reducing the number of bilingual programs from 29 percent of programs implemented in California to 12 percent (Cerda & Hernandez, 2006). And the percentage of ELs in bilingual classrooms immediately declined from 29.1 percent to 11.7 percent in the first year, and stayed at this level until 2002. Then, there was a further steady decline as most California schools shifted to all-English programs. For example, while a number of substantial efforts had been made to improve bilingual education for Cambodian–American students in the California school district in Wright's (2004) study, these were all eliminated after the passage of Proposition 227, and have been replaced once again by English-only instruction. The latest figures show only 6.1 percent of ELs are in California's bilingual programs (Crawford, 2006). Not surprisingly, the high school drop-out rate for ELs is substantially higher than the national average. While the national high school drop-out rate in 2005–2006 was 9.8 percent, the rate in California by ethnic group was 17 percent for Pacific Islander students, 19.7 percent for Hispanic, 25.2 percent for African–American, and 8.9 percent for white students (California Department of Education, 2007). Even more pointedly, these rates reveal an *increase* in the drop-out rates across all the ethnic groups since Proposition 227: in the 1998–1999 school year, drop-out rates were 14.0 percent for Pacific Islander, 15.2 percent for Hispanic, 18.0 percent for African–American, and 7.1 percent for white students. While we are not suggesting a causal relationship between Proposition 227 and the increase in school drop-out rates, it is significant that Proposition 227 was not able to curtail this trend.

Crawford (2006) talks about a "new and more formidable threat" to bilingual education and mother tongue maintenance that has emerged in recent years through the passing of the No Child Left Behind Act in 2001. NCLB holds schools accountable through high-stakes English-medium testing to meet targets of "adequate yearly progress" (AYP). While the policy does not explicitly mandate English-only instruction, the pressure on schools to meet their AYP targets most often results in diminished support for bilingual education. For example, (from Crawford, 2004) Highland Elementary School in Montgomery County, Maryland, offered a popular and successful two-way bilingual program, designed to cultivate bilingualism in both native English and native Spanish speakers. However, with the implementation of NCLB, the school district was concerned about EL reading scores and their "adequate yearly progress" (AYP). They mandated a 2½-hour block of English phonics every day, which had a disruptive and detrimental effect on the bilingual program. Similar decisions are being made in districts across the country as a direct result of NCLB. While NCLB could have been a platform to provide ways to improve the academic progress of ELs, it has done the opposite. As put by Crawford (2004):

> [NCLB] does little to address the most formidable obstacles to their achievement: resource inequities, critical shortages of teachers trained to serve ELLs, inadequate instructional materials, substandard school facilities, and poorly designed instructional programs.
>
> (p. 2)

He goes on to argue that the strong emphasis on test results has in effect narrowed the curriculum, and has put pressure on schools to abandon best practices and programs that have proven successful for ELs. In effect, the implementation of NCLB has moved bilingual education from being seen as a *deficit* to being a *liability* for educators, with a resulting increased tendency toward monolingualism.

In Britain, the story of mother tongue maintenance lies with the 1985 Swann Report, the government's most recent major report on linguistic and ethnic diversity in education. In chapter 2, we noted that the educational strategy proposed in the Swann Report consisted of three main strategies. First, in strong deficit-model overtones, linguistic and cultural differences were seen as disadvantages to be overcome, particularly through the teaching of English as a second language. Second, the richness of minority cultures was to be respected by all students. And third, there was to be no ethnic segregation within the public schooling system. It therefore endorsed the mainstreaming of ELs, and concurrently did not support bilingual education on the grounds that such would require the segregation of minority children. The maintenance and development of ELs' native language(s) was viewed as a responsibility of the community rather than the school. The Swann committee dismissed a European Directive on the teaching of minority languages on the grounds that these groups were British and "here to stay," and therefore it was irrelevant. The role of the schools was thus to nationalize ethnic minorities, rather than cultivate any specialized cultural or linguistic resources they might have.

Three years after the publication of the Swann Report, the government introduced the 1988 Education Reform Act and a policy of LMS—the Local Management of Schools (rather than by Local Education Authorities). By the year 2000, 82 percent of monies spent on school were controlled by headteachers and school governors. This also meant that the responsibility for allocating funds for ESL shifted to local schools, and so schools had to plan for ESL support within their own budgets. Because ESL is not mandatory, and because of competing financial priorities, there was increasing pressure on schools to reduce ESL expenditure. At the same time, and similar to pressures in the United States with Proposition 227, curriculum design and specification was centralized with the national government and with the introduction of national assessments. Also new under this policy was the freedom for parents to choose (rather than be assigned) the schools their children attended, thus increasing school accountability. The emphasis on standards fueled by national exams and market competition created a view of ELs as a liability—as a threat to a school's performance profile, lowering its published test scores, and ultimately lowering its appeal to parents and thus limiting its funding possibilities. In such a context, schools are increasingly reluctant to allocate funds and other resources to English language education, and even less to mother tongue maintenance. Most students seeking to learn their mother tongue have to look for support in community classes outside the school sector. Harris et al. (2002) observe that, "It has been suggested in some sectors of Government that in the global village, Britain's linguistic diversity provides important commercial opportunities, but so far anyway, there is little evidence of any coordinated thinking on this" (p. 45). Instead, "the emphasis has been on standard English as a common currency" (p. 45).

Summary

In this chapter we examined multilingual countries characterized by diglossia and those without diglossia, with a focus on the common themes of: incentives and support for learning English; the type of English input; the status of the mother tongue; and support for mother tongue maintenance.

In multilingual societies characterized by diglossia, it is the H-status of English that propels English language learning. Its position as an H language makes it the perceived primary means towards upward social mobility through education and language, giving the speaker of English access to the domains (and the benefits) within which English is dominant. Support for the learning of English is provided through official language-in-education policies, and through its status as an official language. Furthermore, providing English education, alongside the mother tongue languages, is seen as an important feature of nationalist policy. Within the non-diglossic multilingual societies examined, the dominant status of English is assumed, and the presence of languages other than English seen as an irritant to the goals of national identity and unity. In fact, there are strong tendencies towards monolingualism, in spite of the ethnic, cultural and linguistic diversity within their borders. The major incentive to learn English is for the purposes of citizenship and social and economic integration. Support for the learning of English comes through constitutional support and through the rhetoric of human rights.

Fishman's (1967) argument is that diglossia *maintains* languages: "Without separate though complementary norms and values to establish and maintain functional separation of the speech varieties, that language or variety which is fortunate enough to be associated with the predominant drift of social forces tends to displace the other(s)" (p. 37). On the one hand, we do see evidence of this in our contrasting accounts of diglossic versus non-diglossic multilingual societies, particularly in the increasing tendencies of English monolingualism in non-diglossic societies. Without the societal support of domain specificity, monolingualism is even a goal, as evident in the decreasing support for bilingual programs and the prevalence of transition bilingual programs where bilingualism did exist.

However, even in diglossic multilingual societies, we find a strong tendency towards a pedagogy, curriculum, and policy of English monolingualism, and often little support for mother tongue maintenance or the development of the mother tongue—even though parents strongly resist such norms. The high status accorded English, and the concurrent continued low status of mother tongue languages constantly challenge the very nature of diglossia itself.

Yet, the benefits of designing English learning environments that support the development of bilingualism, rather than monolingualism, are clear. Studies reviewed by Krashen and McField (2005) consistently show that children in bilingual programs outperform their counterparts in all-English programs on tests of academic achievement in English. We concur with their conclusion: "There is no doubt that, when it comes to English acquisition, native-language instruction is part of the solution, not part of the problem" (p. 10).

References

Annamalai, E. (2001). *Managing multilingualism in India: Political and linguistic manifestations.* New Delhi: Sage Publications.

Annamalai, E. (2004). English education in India. In J. W. Tollefson & A. B. M. Tsui (Eds.), *Medium of instruction policies: Which agenda? Whose agenda?* (pp. 177–194). Mahwah, NJ: Lawrence Erlbaum Associates, Publishers.

Bhatt, R. M. (2005). Expert discourses, local practices, and hybridity: The case of Indian Englishes. In A. S. Canagarajah (Ed.), *Reclaiming the local in language policy and practice* (pp. 25–54). Mahwah, NJ: Lawrence Erlbaum Associates, Publishers.

Bleakley, H., & Chin, A. (2004). Language skills and earnings: Evidence from childhood immigrants. *Review of Economics and Statistics, 86*(2), 481–496.

California Department of Education (2007). *Data Quest.* Retrieved on July 11, 2007, from http://data1.cde.ca.gov/dataquest/.

Cardinal, L. (2005). The ideological limits of linguistic diversity in Canada. *Journal of Multilingual and Multicultural Development, 26*(6), 481–495.

CensusScope (n.d.) Statistics on language spoken at home and English language ability. Retrieved on December 22, 2006, from www.CensusScope.org, Social Science Data Analysis Network, University of Michigan. www.ssdan.net.

Cerda, N. and Hernandez, C. M. (2006) Bilingual education. Retrieved on December 27, 2006, from http://www.freewebs.com/cerdahdz/mission statement.htm.

Chick, J. K. (2002). Constructing a multicultural national identity: South African classrooms as sites of struggle between competing discourses. *Journal of Multilingual and Multicultural Development, 23*(6), 462–478.

Cox, B. (1989). English for ages 5–16 (The Cox Report). London: DES.

Crawford, J. (September 14, 2004). No child left behind: Misguided approach to school accountability for English language learners. Retrieved on December 22, 2006, from http://ourworld.compuserve.com/homepages/JWCRAWFORD/.

Crawford, J. (2006). The decline of bilingual education: How to reverse a troubling trend. Retrieved on December 22, 2006, from http://ourworld. compuserve.com/homepages/JWCRAWFORD/. Also published in *International Multilingual Research Journal* (2007), *1*(1), 33–37.

de Kadt, E. (2002). Gender and usage patterns of English in South African urban and rural contexts. *World Englishes*, *21*(1), 83–97.

Department of Education and Science (1985). *Education for all: Report of the Committee of Inquiry into the Education of Children from Ethnic Minority Groups (The Swann Report)*. London: Her Majesty's Stationery Office.

European Commission (February, 2006). Europeans and their Languages. Special. Eurobarometer 243 / Wave 64.3—TNS Opinion & Social.

Ferguson, C. A. (1959). Diglossia. *Word*, *15*, 325–340.

Fishman, J. (1967). Bilingualism with and without diglossia; diglossia with and without bilingualism. *Journal of Social Issues*, *23*, 29–38.

Fishman, J. (1972). Domains and the relationship between micro- and macro-sociolinguistics. In J. J. Gumperz & D. Hymes (Eds.), *Directions in Sociolinguistics* (pp. 435–453). Oxford: Basil Blackwell.

Garcia, E. (2002). Bilingualism and schooling in the United States. *International Journal of the Sociology of Language*, *155/156*, 1–92.

Graddol, D. (2006). *English Next: Why global English may mean the end of "English as a Foreign Language."* London: British Council.

Gupta, A. (1992). Contact features of Singapore Colloquial English. In K. Bolton & H. Kwok (Eds.), *Sociolinguistics Today: International Perspectives* (pp. 323–345). London and New York: Routledge.

Gupta, R. (1995). English in a postcolonial situation: The example of India. *Profession*, 73–78.

Harklau, L. (1994). ESL versus mainstream classes: Contrasting L2 learning environments. *TESOL Quarterly*, *28*(2), 241–272.

Harris, R., Leung, C., & Rampton, B. (2002). Globalization, diaspora and language education in England. In D. Block & D. Cameron (Eds.), *Globalization and Language Teaching* (pp. 29–46). London and New York: Routledge.

Heugh, K. (2002). The case against bilingual and multilingual education in South Africa. *Perspectives in Education*, *20*(1), 171–196.

Hornberger, N. (1989). Continua of biliteracy. *Review of Educational Research*, *59*(3), 271–296.

Kamwangamalu, N. M. (2002). The social history of English in South Africa. *World Englishes*, *21*(1), 1–8.

Krashen, S. and McField, G. (2005). What works? Reviewing the latest evidence on bilingual education. *Language Learner*, *1*(2), 7–10, 34.

Martin-Jones, M. (1989). Language, power and linguistic minorities: The need for an alternative approach to bilingualism, language maintenance and shift. In R. Grillo (Ed.), *Social Anthropology and the Politics of Language* (106–126). London: Routledge.

McKay, S. L., & Chick, K. (2001). Positioning learners in post-apartheid South African schools: A case study of selected multicultural Durban Schools. *Linguistics and Education*, *12*(4), 393–408.

McLean, D. & McCormick, K. (1996). English in South Africa: 1940–1996. In J. A. Fishman, A. D. Conrad, & A. Rubal-Lopez, *Post-imperial English: Status change in former British and American colonies, 1940–1990* (pp. 307–337). Berlin: Mouton de Gruyter.

Myers-Scotton, C. (2006). *Multiple voices: An introduction to bilingualism.* Oxford: Blackwell Publishing.

Nieto, S. (2000). *Affirming diversity: The sociopolitical context of multicultural education. Third edition.* New York: Longman.

Ovando, C. J. & Wiley, T. G. (2003). Language education in the conflicted United States. In J. Bourne & E. Reid (Eds.), *Language Education* (pp. 141–155). London: Kogan Page.

Probyn, M. (2006). Language and learning science in South Africa. *Language and education, 20*(5), 391–414.

Ramanathan, V. (1999). "English is here to stay:" A critical look at institutional and educational practices in India. *TESOL Quarterly, 33,* 211–231.

Ramanathan, V. (2005). *The English–Vernacular divide: Postcolonial language politics and practice.* Clevedon: Multilingual Matters.

Schiffman, H. (1996). *Linguistic Culture and Language Policy.* New York and London: Routledge.

Schiffman, H. (1997). Diglossia as a Sociolinguistic Situation. In F. Coulmas (Ed.), *The Handbook of Sociolinguistics* (pp. 205–216). Malden, MA: Blackwell Publishers Ltd.

Sheorey, R. & Nayar, P. B. (2002). Learning and teaching English in India: Looking in from outside. *Indian Journal of Applied Linguistics, 28*(2), 13–24.

Statistics South Africa (2001). *Report-03-02-01—Census 2001: Key results, 2001.* Retrieved January 8, 2007, from http://www.statssa.gov.za/.

Sutton, C. (January, 2006). A case study of two teachers' understanding of and attitudes towards bilingualism and multiculturalism in a South African primary school. Master's thesis, Rhodes University, South Africa.

Thompson, L. (2004). Policy for language education in England: Does less mean more? *RELC, 35*(1), 83–103.

U.S. Bureau of the Census (2005). *2005 American Community Survey.* Retrieved December 23, 2006, from http://www.census.gov/acs/www.index.html.

University of California, Linguistic Minority Research Institute (UC–LMRI) (December 2006). The growth of the linguistic minority population in the U.S. and California, 1980–2005. *EL Facts, 8.* Retrieved on December 26, 2006, from http://lmri.ucsb.edu/publications/elfacts-8.pdf.

Webb, V. (2004). Language policy in post-apartheid South Africa. In J. W. Tollefson & A. B. M. Tsui (Eds.), *Medium of instruction policies: Which agenda? Whose agenda?* (pp. 217–239). Mahwah, NJ: Lawrence Erlbaum Associates, Publishers.

Wright, W. (2004). What English-only really means: A study of the implementation of California language policy with Cambodian–American students. *Bilingual Education and Bilingualism, 7*(1), 1–23.

Chapter 4

Language planning and policy

One of the primary issues addressed in language planning decisions is which language or languages should be designated as an official language. Three ways in which the designation of an official language has consequences for language learning and teaching are (a) the insight the designation provides into prevalent social attitudes toward particular languages; (b) the effect of approved language policies on the stated language-in-education policy; and (c) the setting of linguistic standards, particularly in relation to nativized varieties of English. Through the use of case studies, each of these consequences will be examined in depth. The case studies will also be used to show how the sometimes conflicting agendas of government officials and educators position teachers when they attempt to introduce pedagogy and curriculum that do not conform to the government-led agenda.

Language planning and politicking

Language planning versus language policy

In order to give some context to our discussion of language policy and its relationship to international English, we begin with an introduction to some of the key terms used in the field of language planning and policy. While the two terms often appear together, there are some important differences between language *planning* and language *policy*. We find the discussion by Deumert (2000) useful to make clear this distinction. Language policy, she argues (p. 384), "refers to the more general linguistic, political, and social goals underlying the actual language planning process." Language planning, a term first introduced by American linguist Haugen in the late 1950s, "refers to all conscious efforts that aim at changing the linguistic behavior of a speech community" (Haugen, 1987, p. 627 in Deumert, 2000, p. 384) in accordance with those goals and ideologies. Language planning involves things like making decisions about the status of a language, determining a new language-in-education policy, and coining a new word. Distinctions in language planning are often made between language *status* planning (the position and functions that a particular language or languages have in a country) and language *corpus* planning (the script, grammar, spelling, and so forth, of a language). For example, if several languages are spoken in a country, it is often seen necessary to select a language for official, educational and other purposes. In addition, it may be necessary to make decisions about which variety of a language will be adopted for such purposes. Governments also have to make decisions about a *national* language and about an *official* language. A national language generally is seen to represent the national identity of a country. Usually it is an indigenous language spoken as the mother tongue by at least some of the population. An official language is a language that is given unique legal status in the country. It is the language generally used for government administration and law, in the media, and as one of the languages of education. There may well be more than one official language in a country, as in India and Singapore. Through its bilingual policy, Canada has two official languages, English and French, both of which are also national languages in that they are together rooted in Canadian identity.

Once a language is chosen, particularly if it is an indigenous language, it is also often necessary to develop that language through corpus planning to meet the demands of official use. That is, it will need to be *codified*, meaning a set of rules about spelling and punctuation, alphabets and grammar will have to be chosen. When thinking of international English, governments and others involved in language planning need to make decisions about which form of English to adopt (British English? American English? The country's own form of English, such as Jamaican English?).

No matter what the language planning and policy activity, it always has direct implication for education. Which languages and language varieties will be taught in schools? From what age will these languages be taught, and for how long? Should they be taught through submersion or mainstreaming in an L2 (see chapter 2), or through the indigenous language? Bilingual education programs have proliferated around the world as a way to introduce English into the education system. However, as we discussed in previous chapters, the reasons for introducing such programs vary considerably.

As this short introduction already suggests, language planning cannot be seen (as it often is by those involved and those who study it) as if it were an autonomous entity, divorced from the circumstances of its use. To do so would limit any understanding of the particular policies put in place, as very often decisions about language in fact have very little to do with language per se. Consider, for example, Malaysia's decision to wean schools off English medium instruction immediately after independence—only to now reintroduce it into the schools. Or consider France's insistence on language purity in the face of increasing language contact with global English. Thus, in this chapter, we introduce the notion of *language politicking* to focus on the position of language in real historical and social circumstances. Particularly in discussions of international English, what becomes important is the global–local—or *glocal*—location of international English; how decisions and policies pertaining to English often become politicized in the often-conflicting demands of global (international) and local (national) concerns.

Language politicking

The underlying premise of this discussion is taken from Pennycook's (1994) notion of the "worldliness" of language. The worldliness of language suggests a view of language as located in the world: "It is impossible to deal usefully with language outside its social, cultural, historical, economic or political contexts." At the same time, he notes, this worldliness also suggests that the world is in language: "In the same way that we talk about someone being 'worldly,' language is affected by its material presence" (p. 24). Language thus has both a "constituted and constitutive role in the world: it is not merely a passive presence, nor just a language acted upon by its material circumstances, but also an active agent" (p. 24) in its material circumstances. Such a view of language has profound significance when we consider language planning and policy—activities that have particularly preoccupied actors in the nation-building agenda. This means language planning goes far beyond mere status, corpus, and acquisition concerns, but also has a direct bearing on matters of identity, economic opportunity and social status, power, human rights, and so forth. To capture this worldliness of language in the context of language planning and policy activity, we suggest the notion of *language politicking*. Indeed, very often decisions made around language have very little to do with language per se, but more to do with these larger worldly issues. Language politicking also suggests the deeply ideological nature of language policy and planning—the careful unpacking of such ideological constructs often reveals the intricate interplay of language and power. The intensification of globalization as an organizing force in human interaction has added a new layer to the previously largely nationalist-driven agenda in language planning, and has magnified the importance of understanding language as worldly—placing governments and individuals, and "language planning and policy" activities at the *glocal* nexus. And finally, the significance of the worldliness of language for language planning and the concept of language politicking is that the outcomes of such planning are not always as intended in the discourse of politicking, with often even conflicting results.

This worldly view of language planning has direct bearing on the English language classroom. Auerbach (1995) notes that the political imperatives of the language classroom are rarely acknowledged by educators:

> classrooms themselves may be seen as self-contained, autonomous systems, isolated from external political concerns. The actual teaching that goes on behind closed doors is often conceived of as a neutral transfer of skills, knowledge, or competencies, to be left in the hands of trained professionals whose job it is to implement the latest methods and techniques.
>
> (p. 9)

Yet, she continues, the "dynamics of power and domination . . . permeate the fabric of classroom life" (p. 9). Tollefson puts it this way in the Preface to his edited volume *Power and inequality in language education* (1995): "What happens in the language classroom is intimately linked to social and political forces, and practitioners must understand those links if they are to be fully effective in their work" (p. ix). These "dynamics of power and domination" are evident, for example, in the pedagogical decisions that educators make regarding curriculum development, content, materials, classroom processes, and language use.

To further explore the consequences and meanings of language politicking around English and English language classrooms, we turn to two very different countries, but with some interesting parallels: Singapore and the United States. Singapore has a national language (Malay). However, outside of the Malay community, the national language is understood and spoken by very few Singaporeans, and is active at a national level only when singing the National Anthem, giving military commands, and training and communicating with animals at the national zoo. The four official languages parallel its multi-ethnic population: English, Malay, Mandarin, and Tamil. English is the dominant official language: it is the language of government, law, and business; and through a policy of bilingual education, since the 1980s, it is the medium of instruction in all schools with the students' "mother tongue" taught as a second language. A caveat needs to be made here: ironically, the mother tongue is the language *ascribed* to one based on the ethnicity of one's father. Thus, Chinese students must learn Mandarin as their mother tongue requirement; students of mixed parentage with, for example, a Chinese father and an Indian mother must learn Mandarin. This aligning of language and race has been a central feature of Singapore's language planning. Language planning, particularly language-in-education planning, is centrally controlled by the higher echelons of government, by technocrats rather than educators. The United States, in contrast, has no national language, and there are no centrally controlled language policies. However, at the state level, language politicking is active both by government and lobbyists, and there are policies specific to language status and language-in-education particularly around making English the official language of the United States. The debates around bilingual education center on two understandings of the purposes of bilingual education: language maintenance or transitional to English only.

Singapore

Language politicking

Singapore offers an interesting analysis of language politicking. In the first place, as one observer has put it, Singapore is "small in size, big on language" (Beardsmore, 1991). In part, this is because of its densely multilingual population. Around the time of independence through merger with Malaysia (1963), the 1957 Census (Chua, 1962) reported 33 mother tongue languages in Singapore, 20 of which were spoken by more than 1,000 people. As described by the then Senior Minister (and founding Prime Minister) Lee Kuan Yew, "We were a tower of Babel, trying to find a common tongue" ("Its great contribution," 1997). Today, the Singaporean resident (citizens and permanent residents) population of about 3.6 million still comprises three major ethnic groups: about 76 percent Chinese, 14 percent Malays, and 9 percent Indians (and about 2 percent "others"; Singapore Department of Statistics, June 2005).

Furthermore, Singapore is of interest to discussions of language politicking because bilingualism is the mainstay of education policy. In fact, over 50 percent of curriculum time in primary school is spent on language learning. The result is multilingualism at the national level and, at the individual level, English-knowing bilingualism.

Another reason why Singapore contributes to our understanding of language politicking is because it has overtly and aggressively attempted to change the everyday speaking patterns of the majority (Chinese) population through an annual (begun in 1979) Speak Mandarin Campaign, and, since 2000, of the population in general through an annual Speak Good English Movement (SGEM). On the eve of independence, only 0.1 percent of the population spoke Mandarin as their mother tongue as recorded in the 1957 census (of course, more could speak Mandarin, but it was not identified as a mother tongue). Rather Hokkien and Cantonese clearly had larger representation in the population as a mother tongue (30 percent and 15.1 percent respectively) and as lingua franca within the Chinese community (Chua, 1962). Clearly, statistics alone cannot explain the decision to appoint these languages as the official languages in the nation. Notably, the language politicking has been quite successful—

today, Mandarin (and English) is continuing to replace Chinese dialects as a dominant household language, with 47 percent of the population using Mandarin at home, compared to 24 percent who continue to use mostly dialects (see table 4.1). More recent attempts at direct language intervention has come through the SGEM, targeting all Singaporeans to make Standard English, rather than Singapore's colloquial form of English (Singlish), as their habitual form of English usage. More will be said about this later.

Linguistic ecology

The linguistic ecology of this densely populated island state means that none of the languages, including English, exist in isolation. This has a number of implications. In the first place, the majority of Singaporeans use multiple language varieties in their everyday lives, depending on the particular age and educational qualifications of the persons involved, the situation, and the topic (Vaish et al., 2005).

Second, and very much related to the above discussion, even when a particular language has been identified as the dominant home language, this does not mean there is no code-switching. In fact, code-switching is so much the norm that it is often difficult to actually tease apart the different linguistic forms or to think about diglossia. Thus, the compartmentalized quadratic bilingual policy with four discrete languages (Chinese–Malay–Tamil–English) in no way reflects the complex linguistic ecology of Singapore, how these languages are used and the roles they play, nor the language repertoire of individual Singaporeans.

A third implication of Singapore's linguistic ecology has been the particular development of Singapore English. As argued by Goh and Silver (2004), this daily interaction between languages is one of the reasons for the development of a Singapore variety of English, especially Singlish. According to Gupta (1994), it is this colloquial form of Singapore English that is most likely the dominant home language, rather than Standard Singapore English. She argues that even parents who do speak Standard English tend to use the colloquial form with their children. Thus Singapore colloquial English is the first language of these Singaporean children. Standard Singapore English is generally not the language of the home, in her view, but of the school. However the reverse is also true, as anecdotally, parents have lamented that their children first learned the colloquial form upon entering school.

Before we go further in our discussion, let's look briefly at the picture of language use given by the Singapore national Census. The Census reports its data on language as it pertains to the four official languages. Table 4.1 tells us what languages respondents say they are predominantly using at home, by race. Important here for our purposes is to note

Table 4.1 Language by race, 1980–2005

Chinese	1980	2005	Malay	1980	2005	Indian	1980	2005
English	10%	29%	English	2%	13%	English	24%	39%
Mandarin	13%	47%	Malay	97%	87%	Malay	9%	11%
Chinese dialect	77%	24%				Tamil	53%	39%
						Other	14%	11%

Source: Singapore Department of Statistics, 1980; 2005.

how the use of English is increasing across all racial groups, although at different rates.

We also know from the census data that the patterns of language use are closely related to levels of educational attainment and social class. The use of English is linked to higher levels of educational attainment, while those with less than secondary education tend to use their mother tongue or a Chinese dialect as their dominant household language. As we discussed in chapter 2, a common feature in the story of international English is the lack of equal access to English, and the consequent relationship between language and social class. More will be said about this link between social class and language later.

The above discussion thus sets the stage for examining the consequences that language planning and policy have had on the learning and teaching of English in Singapore.

English in a multilingual context

There have been a series of language-in-education policies since before Singapore's independence from British colonial rule. Without going into all the details of this history (see Kaplan & Baldauf, 2003 for an overview), it is worth noting that bilingual education has been in place in Singapore since 1956, and has been the mainstay of government policy ever since. However, the policy has undergone a number of adjustments, in response to the changing linguistic ecology of the people and in response to various educational outcomes. The most notable change came in 1979/1980 after bilingual education received its first formal and thorough assessment by what is known as the Goh Committee, led by Deputy Prime Minister Goh Keng Swee. In the Goh Report the committee documented that bilingual education was essentially failing, particularly for the Chinese students who were failing miserably at both English and

Mandarin. The home environment was seen to be an impediment to the success of bilingualism:

> The majority of the pupils are taught in two languages, English and Mandarin. About 85 percent of these pupils do not speak these languages at home. When they are home, they speak dialects. As a result, most of what they have learned in school is not reinforced.
>
> (Goh, 1979, 4.4)

In 1980, a New Education System was put in place, which linked language learning to streaming—meaning that those in the bottom streams would be given a more oral-based second language curriculum, and that only the very top 10 percent of students would receive the highest level of bilingual education with both English and their mother tongue taught at the highest level. The goals of the revamped bilingual education policy were to produce graduates who are at least literate in one language if they cannot cope with two; to produce a majority of average and above average graduates who have mastered English as a first language and mother tongue as a second language; and for provisions to be made in the school system for the ablest to study two languages at the highest level and possibly a third (foreign) language such as German, Spanish, or Japanese. To support this new education policy, the annual Speak Mandarin Campaign was launched to persuade Chinese Singaporeans to replace their use of dialects with Mandarin. Finally, in 1987, English was made the medium of instruction in all schools, with the mother tongue languages taught as a second language. Thus, the goal of bilingual education in Singapore is language maintenance, to produce as far as possible an English-knowing bilingual population.

We have already noted how English does not operate in isolation in the Singapore linguistic ecology. In home, school and in society at large, multiple languages interact in complex ways. However, language politicking has made a neat binary divide of this complexity. Through a functional polarizing of language, English has been deemed the language of commerce, of international communication, of inter-racial communication, and of personal and national economic success; the mother tongue languages are the languages of ethnic and personal identity, of rootedness, of moral grounding, and of intra-ethnic communication. In addition to being ethnically neutral, English was also presented as equitable: English "is our common working language ... it provides a neutral medium, giving no one any advantage to the competition for knowledge and jobs" (Lee Kuan Yew, 1972). Of course, the claims in this statement are somewhat eroded in light of census data mentioned earlier—that English (and language-based streaming) has become a principal player in social stratification.

This then is the ideology underpinning the bilingual policy—a policy that has been tweaked slightly over the years, and an ideology that is beginning to show strains with the rising economic and global (i.e., not just mother tongue) status of Mandarin globally and in Singapore, yet continues to dominate Singapore language politicking. There are of course many nuances and paradoxes that go well beyond the discussion here. What is important here is (a) the apparent pragmatism of language politicking that gives the aura of fairness and neutrality with respect to the different languages, yet, language policy that has allowed English to gain dominance over the other languages; (b) the compartmentalization of language into discrete linguistic codes and domains, and what that means for education. Both of these pose challenges in the classroom for pedagogy and practice.

Language politicking, bilingualism and the English classroom

Under the bilingual policy, language education is definitively compart-mentalized. English is the only official medium of instruction, apart from the mother tongue classrooms. This is particularly true of English language classes, where the use of any other language is actively discouraged, as is the use of English in the mother tongue classrooms. As we have already established in our earlier discussion, this compartmentalization follows the patterns of language politicking; however, it does not follow the patterns of language use of most Singapore students. Edwin, a student quoted in Stroud and Wee (2007), is like many Chinese Singaporean youths who find it natural to use Mandarin when speaking with their Chinese friends: "It's very natural. You talk to your . . . yeah . . . Mandarin Chinese friends, ver auto one, lah. Automatically you switch to Mandarin" (p. 39). However, this happens "unless the teacher is staring at you. Then no chance, lah. Converse in English." Preliminary data from a large-scale sociolinguistic survey of 10-year-old Singaporeans (Vaish, Aman, & Bokhorst-Heng, 2005) shows that 43.98 percent of students speak with their friends of the same race at school in either just their mother tongue, or code-switch between English and their mother tongue.[1]

Apart from during group work, teachers themselves tend not to switch between languages in English nor mother tongue classes. All three reports written by the mother tongue classroom research teams at Singapore's Centre for Research in Pedagogy and Practice (CRPP)[2] report minimal

---

1 When speaking with friends of a different race, about 98 percent say they use English.
2 A description of the research being done at the Centre for Research in Pedagogy and Practice can be found at the center's website: http://www.crpp.nie.edu.sg.

code-switching by teachers (Vaish & Sam, 2006). One student in Stroud and Wee's (2007) discussion noted that her use of Mandarin may impede her learning of English: "Then at the end, the English also not very good, lah" (p. 41). One teacher would agree (Stroud & Wee, 2007): "A lot of broken English here and there. At the same time, once in a while, if you think in Chinese, you can almost hear him speaking in Chinese in the English format. So the translation wise, we can see for ourselves" (p. 43). This reductive logic is also one that dominates much debate in English language classrooms—the view that English is the only acceptable language in the classroom. For example, Stroud and Wee (2007) present data that shows "When reference to Chinese is made and when Chinese/ Mandarin fragments are actually used in the English lesson, it is in a context of derision that underscores the marginal role accorded the Chinese language and its associated identifications" (p. 43). This is a very clear example then, of how language politicking outside the classroom has direct bearing on the pedagogical practices inside the classroom, and how such practices thus reinforce the broader language politicking.

The United States

While the United States has no national language policy, there has been no shortage of language issues and debates. There are two related policy debates that dominate public discourse on language: English as an (only) official language and bilingual education.

The English-only movement

The official status of English in the United States has been a topic of debate since the founding of the nation (Collins, 1999; Shannon, 1999). Yet, throughout, there was a general reluctance to have an official language policy. However, from the early 1980s, a movement to establish English as the official language of the United States began to gain momentum, particularly at the state and local levels. This movement has largely been linked to the influence of Samuel I. Hayakawa, a Republican senator during the time of the Reagan administration.

On April 27, 1981, Senator Hayakawa proposed a constitutional amendment known as Senate Joint Resolution 72. His intent in this resolution was that English would be declared the official language of the United States. And at the same time, it would be unlawful for federal or state governments to make or implement "any law which requires the use of any language other than English" (Donahue, 1995, p. 112, citing Judd, 1987, p. 116). The amendment would have allowed languages other than English to be used in "educational instruction" and as a "transitional method of making students who use a language other than

English proficient in English" (Donahue, 1995, p. 113, citing Judd, 1987, p. 116). In practical terms, this meant that bilingual ballots would not be allowed. Neither would bilingual education for the purposes of maintaining one's L1. While this bill died in its first version before it reached any congressional committees, it is nonetheless important in how it formed the basis of the subsequent thought and influence of U.S. English—an organization that has had strong influence on federal and state language policy. Between 1984 and 1990, U.S. English launched a powerful campaign to mobilize opinion on two political fronts. First, they convinced the American public that English should be the official language of the United States. At the state level, they have been extremely successful. Since 1984, more than one third of all states have some constitutional ruling concerning "official" English. Second, without making any distinction between transitional and maintenance forms, they strongly attacked bilingual education.

The success of these campaigns has largely been through language politicking that reaches far beyond (and is even external to) language concerns per se. Donahue (1995) quotes from materials mailed by U.S. English in 1991. In a 1990 flyer entitled "A Common Language Benefits Our Nation and Its People," the group argues that:

> A common language benefits a country and its people. In our country this common bond is more important than in most because Americans continue to be diverse in origin, ethnicity, religion and native culture.
> (in Donahue, 1995, p. 114)

Hayakawa is quoted as saying, "a common language unifies, multiple languages divide," and that the English Language Amendment is "a measure to strengthen the ties that bind together all of us, of whatever national origin or race, through the magical bond of a common language." English is seen as a neutral language, devoid of ethnic identity, much as it is in India and in Singapore. A U.S. English newsletter makes the claim that "The USSR, currently torn by linguistic separatism, consists of 15 republics, 114 languages, and 300 dialects" (cited in Donahue, 1995, p. 115). Further on it charges that current legislation on bilingual education should be called "The Bilingual Dropout Law" (cited in Donahue, 1995, p. 115), arguing bilingual education is to blame for the high rates of school failure of minority students.

Because of his particular interest in language politicking around English and Spanish in the United States, Donahue (1995, pp. 118–132) provides an excellent account of language politicking in Arizona, Florida, and Colorado—all states with a large Hispanic population. What we will discuss briefly here, largely because of the long enduring debate it has had, is language politicking in California. California has a large Mexican

and Asian immigrant population. It also has a very large school population. MacKaye's (1987) analysis of the debate on Proposition 63, the
proposal to make English the official language in California, provides an
overview of the arguments presented. As summarized by Shannon (1999,
p. 177), MacKaye identified four key principles underlying the debates as
found in letters to the editor of various major newspapers in California:
(a) language was seen as a common bond unifying the nation; (b) language
was seen as a key to personal and economic success; (c) language was
viewed as a symbol of one's ethnic identity; and (d) language was viewed
as a symbol of nationhood and good citizenship. It is worth noting that
these themes were seen in Singapore's language politicking, and indeed
are echoed around the world where English is taught. These principles
materialized in a number of ways throughout the state (see Donahue,
1995, p. 132). For example, supervisors in hospitals have been reported
to spy on, and to reprimand, nurses speaking Tagalog in the Pomona Valley
Hospital Medical Center near Los Angeles. The mayor of Monterey Park
opposed a gift of Chinese books to the city library because "if people
want foreign-language [books], they can go [buy them] on their own."
Some activists in the same city pushed for a resolution targeting Korean
and Chinese grocers, demanding that all market signs be in English. As
Shannon (1999) concludes, "In the absence of an official language policy
and in the debate for such a policy, U.S. society has shifted to an ideology
of English monolingualism . . . English as a symbol of national identity,
pride, unity, support, and devotion became an important feature" (p. 179)
of the kind of nationalistic ideology that had become widespread during
the Reagan administration.

What does this all mean for education and for the language learning
classroom? The literature shows a very strong link between the debates
around official English and the various positions people take on bilingual
education policy. Donahue (1995) and Edwards (1984) are just some of
the sources documenting the extensive literature on these debates. Proponents of bilingual education argue that L1 literacy is indispensable for
forming the early emotional and intellectual health of children, and that
bicultural individuals are emotionally stable and productive in society.
Opponents of bilingual education, as reported by Edwards, argue that
bilingual education fosters an elite, and that the costs of bilingual education for the public are too high. Furthermore, they argue that bilingual
education is divisive.

Bilingual education

The Bilingual Education Act of 1968 began as a legislative movement to
address the education needs of children who spoke languages other than
English as their L1. The legislation is essentially about educational equity,

about the persistent failure in school of students whose mother tongue is not English, and about children's educational rights (as, for example, in the Lau v. Nichols case[3]). Under this act, children are educated through two languages: English and their L1. An important amendment to that legislation in 1974 narrowed this definition, stating that children would be taught in their L1 "to the extent necessary to allow a child to progress effectively through the education system" (Schneider, 1976, cited in Shannon, 1999, p. 171). Since this time, educators, scholars, politicians and the general public have debated what form bilingual education should take, and the role languages other than English should have in education and in society. That all minority language speakers should benefit from equal education and the learning of English is not the issue; rather, what is at the center of the controversy is the role of the minority language in "bilingual" education.

Central of course to this debate is the status of English in the United States. As argued by Shannon (1999): "A policy making the status of English official would make the use of other languages problematic. Thus, the debate on bilingual education with its focus on the institutionalization of the use of other languages in the schools draws much of its rhetoric from the official English debate" (pp. 171–172). Opponents of bilingual education generally take what they see as ethnic pride and ethnic consciousness as being an impediment to proficiency in English. And they generally target the use of any language other than English in educational programs as problematic. As we discussed in chapter 2, their approach is thus one of submersion, whereby "the goal of bilingual education must be English oral language proficiency and instruction through English only. To that end, time spent in a language other than English is wasted" (Shannon, 1999, p. 182). At best, supporters of the English-only movement see the goal of bilingualism to be monolingualism. Those who support bilingual education support the sustained use of and instruction in the mother tongue language for the purposes of bilingualism.

Language politicking and the bilingual classroom

As exemplified by research conducted by Shannon (1995), Wong-Fillmore (1991) and others, the practices of bilingual education are very much

---

3 Lau v. Nichols (1974) was a civil rights case brought by Chinese American students living in San Francisco, California, who had limited English proficiency. Appealing to the Civil Rights Act (1964), they claimed they were being discriminated against by not receiving the additional help they needed in school due to their inability to speak English. In a landmark decision, the U.S. Supreme Court ruled in their favor. See Wong (1988) for an excellent summary of this case and the implications it has had for language and ethnic rights in the U.S.

shaped by prevailing language ideologies. Particularly in the "absence of language policy at the federal level and its absence in bilingual education, bilingual teachers rely on language ideology to make sense of their practice" (Shannon, 1999, p. 172). In many cases, these teachers are also informed by local language-in-education policies that have in place a transitional, rather than a maintenance, bilingual education program.

In her discussion of adult ESL/literacy instruction in the United States, Auerbach (1995) examines the ways in which the ESL classroom functions as a kind of microcosm of the broader social order, looking at issues of power in pedagogical choices concerning curriculum development, instructional context, and materials. She also discusses the issue of language choice in the ESL classroom. This is a clear example of the ways in which the language politicking outside the classroom operates within the classroom. The prevailing view is that English is the only acceptable medium of communication in the ESL classroom. As soon as students enter the door, it is English only. She describes the so-called pedagogical rationale behind such a view (1995):

> Adult ESL students need to learn English as quickly as possible for survival reasons; the more they are exposed to English, the more quickly they will learn; as they hear and use English, they will internalize it and begin to think in English; the only way they will learn it is if they are forced to use it.
>
> (p. 25)

Teachers develop a variety of devices to enforce this principle, from games, to signals, to penalty systems. Auerbach (1995) cites from the *TESOL Newsletter* which supported the practice of fining students: the teacher told students, "This is an English-only classroom. If you speak Spanish or Cantonese or Mandarin or Vietnamese or Thai or Russian or Farsi, you pay me 25 cents. I can be rich" (p. 25). While this submersion approach to language education is uncritically and almost universally applied, Auerbach raises important questions about its underlying assumptions. For example, particularly for adult learners, research suggests that strong L1 literacy and schooling are key factors in successful L2 acquisition. Auerbach cites Klassen's (1987) research, which found that, without first language literacy, ESL classes were essentially inaccessible to the low-literate Latinos in Toronto. Silenced from a lack of self-confidence in such learning environments, these learners frequently drop out. And thus, she argues, a bilingual model that uses L1 as a bridge to L2 is a more effective approach, with teachers reporting quite different results. Being allowed to use L1 contributes to a safe setting, and allows for a broadened curriculum and pedagogical approach that considers critical thinking—one that queries the processes of constructing meaning in and through language. L1 becomes a resource, rather than an impediment, to the objectives of language learning.

While the logic of submersion and the prohibition of the use of L1 in the English classroom is usually framed in pedagogical terms, Auerbach (1995) points to the ideological meanings behind such framing. The English-only movement and the insistence of the exclusive use of English in the classroom are, she says, "two sides of the same coin":

> My point here is that they are two sides of the same coin: Insistence on English in the classroom may result in lower acquisition of English, a focus on childlike and disempowering approaches to language instruction, and ultimately a replication of relations of inequality outside the classroom, reproducing a stratum of people who can do only the least skilled and the least language/literacy-dependent jobs.
>
> (p. 27)

In contrast, Auerbach suggests a classroom in which students and teachers together reflect and dialogue classroom guidelines on language-use.

Shannon's (1995; 1999) case study of bilingual education in one school district provides an example of the impact of language politicking on the pedagogical practices in the classroom. Hers was an eight-year ethnographic study of bilingualism and bilingual education in a large urban school district in the southwestern part of the United States. There were 66,000 children in the schools, with over 80 home languages other than English. Forty per cent of those were from Spanish-speaking homes, with families of Mexican origin. The school district has had some form of bilingual education since the early 1970s. There are 350 bilingual teachers in the school district. Twenty-five have state endorsement, meaning they have passed a Spanish proficiency test; the rest are in the in-service program. Shannon (1999) recounts the experiences of one parent—who spoke Spanish and no English and was actively involved in the classrooms and worked closely with teachers. This parent's observations were that "Many times teachers say they are bilingual and they are not. They are not." Furthermore, in the classroom, from "the work that they do in the classroom in English and in Spanish and with this teacher one could see that it was all in English, all in English. I couldn't have a conversation with him because he didn't understand me. And then I say it's because of this that my son was more focused on English because the boy was the whole year in English only" (pp. 186–187). As Shannon comments (1999), this parent "believed that the goal of bilingual education is bilingualism. She saw this as a societal goal and not something that would benefit just her children or Mexican children" (p. 187). In another classroom, Shannon observed an in-service teacher's lesson on the topic of pre-Columbian civilization in Mexico. The richly illustrated book she read to the class was in English. Periodically she would ask a student to translate what she had read into Spanish, in summary form. After reading the books, students were asked to recall what they remembered about the Maya before they proceeded to the Aztecs. She wrote down their responses on a piece of chart paper. While students were invited to respond in English or in Spanish, she consistently wrote the response in English. Shannon sees this classroom experience, and the fact that effective Spanish bilingualism is marginalized in practice in the hiring and training of bilingual teachers, as an example of how the school district, and the teachers, are guided by the ideology of English monolingualism.

This desire for English monolingualism, and the concurrent lack of interest in maintaining the linguistic diversity of the country, is only bolstered by the rise of English dominance around the world. There is arrogance among some English speakers who question the need to learn foreign languages or to maintain the language resources that exist. Smolicz and Secombe (2003) make this point in reference to programs in Australia to promote the learning of other languages. The programs have largely been unsuccessful. And, they point out, this is "particularly striking for students from the majority English-speaking background, many of whom see no obvious benefits from investing the effort required to learn a new language, in view of the availability of what they perceive as 'easier options,' as well as the global dominance of English" (p. 16). In the United States, this same arrogance is evident in the lack of interest in maintaining the linguistic diversity of the country, and through the English-only movement.

Thus far, we have discussed language politicking within Singapore and the United States with respect to the designation of an official language and the effects that such language policy and politicking has had on language attitudes and language diversity. As we think of the impact of language politicking on classroom pedagogy, notions of language standards becomes one other area of significance. As we will discuss in the next chapter, English in different socio-linguistic and socio-political contexts typically goes through processes of nativization. This raises concerns of what *kind* of English should be promoted by governments, allowed in the media, and taught in schools. In the next section, we will discuss the effects of language politicking on attitudes toward nativized varieties of English and the effects of these attitudes on pedagogical practice. We once again turn to Singapore and the United States: Singlish as a nativized variety in Singapore, placed in opposition to Standard Received Pronunciation (RP) English; and Ebonics as a localized (and historical) variety in the United States. In addition, we will discuss the localization of English in the Expanding Circle contexts of China and Korea.

Language politicking and the nativization of English

Singapore

Singlish

In the Singapore context, there has been a hotly debated distinction between Singapore *Standard* (RP) English and Singapore *Colloquial* English/Singlish.[4] Much of the more recent debate stemmed from a controversial sitcom in which one of the lead characters, Phua Chu Kang, speaks Singlish. While there have been no specific policy statements emerging from this controversy, there has been the creation in 2000 of a Speak Good English Movement (SGEM), as well as a formal request from the Prime Minister to the producers of the sitcom to have this character go to English school (Goh Chok Tong, 1999). With the launch of SGEM, the Ministry of Education also began to conduct a 60-hour course for English language teachers for an initial group of 8,000 teachers—who were to "lead the way to better English standards in the country" (Nirmala, 1999, p. 1).

Linked to this distinction between Singapore Standard English and Singlish are very specific ideologies about the purposes of English. Like the Ebonics debate, the politicking around English and Singlish in Singapore, and the policies that emerge from it, is intimately tied to particular views of language and of what the ideal nation should be. In the United States, the debate is more internal and linked to issues of pluralism, multiculturalism, and student equity. The Singapore story shares some of these concerns, but in broad strokes, it is more about tensions emerging from Singapore's glocal position (Bokhorst-Heng, 2005) and the role English plays in that. Crystal (1995, p. 110) refers to two competing perspectives: national identity and internationalism. In the former, the nation looks within itself at its societal structure and composition, defining its needs in relation to national identity. In the latter, the nation looks outside from itself at the world and global economy, and defines itself and its needs in relation to its position within that world.

Very loosely, we can position the advocates of Standard English only on

---

4 Examples of Singlish would include, "my one, not your one" (mine, not yours); "wear your shoes" (put on your shoes); "bang! You die already" (bang! You're dead); "on the light" (turn on the light); "my one got pink also" (mine also has pink). It must be noted, however, that the distinction between these two is not always clear, leading some to describe Singapore English as a continuum between high and low, or formal and colloquial, forms of the language (e.g., Pakir, 1991).

the international perspective. English was adopted in Singapore for the purposes of accessing the international global economy. The slogan for the 2006 Speak Good English Movement reads: "Speak good English . . . not only in Singapore, Malaysia and Batam." As articulated by Rear Admiral (National Service) Lui Tuck Yew, Minister of State for Education, at the launch of the 2006 SGEM, the objective of the Ministry of Education and the SGEM is to "enable every Singaporean to speak Standard English that is intelligible to English speakers all over the world." He goes on to define Standard English as "English that is grammatical, using standard sentence structure and is commonly understood around the world. And I would like to emphasize that speaking good English is not about accent."

Parents and teachers are exhorted to be positive role models by speaking good (Standard) English. In her speech at the launch of the 2005 SGEM, the chairman of the SGEM committee, Professor Koh Tai Ann said: "Parents and teachers should immerse children in an environment where adult role models speak Standard English." In this way, she said, both home and school will play their part in "providing a supportive environment for acquiring good English." The Prime Minister noted in his SGEM inauguration speech that "sixty per cent of our children start school with little exposure to English at home. This suggests that if Singlish becomes more widely used, it could hinder our children's competence in English" (Goh, 2000). Similar to the arguments against Ebonics, saying it would "ghettoize" its speakers, Lee Kuan Yew argued in his 1999 National Day speech that "popularizing" Singlish would disadvantage "the less-educated half of the population." If they learn to speak only Singlish, "they will suffer economically and socially . . . The people who will benefit most [from eliminating Singlish] are those who can only master one kind of English. Singlish is a handicap we must not wish on Singaporeans." Those on this side of the debate consider Singlish as a form of broken English—indicated in the Sunday edition of *The Straits Times* weekly column entitled "English as it is Broken"—and as a bastardized form of English.

Those on the other side of the debate argue that Singlish needs to be recognized as a legitimate linguistic code. Rather than eliminating and devaluing Singlish, they advocate a view that positions Singlish as one code within one's linguistic repertoire. To them, Singlish is perhaps the *real* language of national identity, the language of familiarity and bonding. For example, one reader contributing to *The Straits Times* "Forum page" argued, "Speaking standard English in this era of globalisation is absolutely essential, but Singlish identifies and bonds us as Singaporeans" (Chia, 1999). Advocates of Singlish are focused on Crystal's notion of *national identity*, looking at what language means for their identity as Singaporeans. Advocates generally are those who have also mastered the standard form of English, and can code switch appropriately—which is indeed what they advocate. What they argue is not to have Singlish used at all times in all places, but rather, that Singlish be given a legitimate place in the national linguistic repertoire.

Language politicking, Singlish and the English classroom

The earlier mention of Phua Chu Kang, the Singlish-speaking sitcom character sent to grammar classes by Singapore's prime minister, has relevance as we consider what the Singlish debate has meant in the English classroom. Very quickly, the focus of the debate turned from the media to the scene of teaching—even though there had been no substantiated evidence that teachers were indeed using Singlish in their classroom teaching (Kramer-Dahl, 2003). Parents expressed concern in *The Straits Times* Forum page that teachers were failing in being "standard bearers" for the students (Lee, B.T., 1999), and called for higher standards in the classroom. And in response, the Ministry of Education announced that they would be sending 8,000 teachers for remedial English lessons.

As Kramer-Dahl (2003) notes, a parallel was established between Phua Chu Kang and the 8,000 negligent English teachers when both had to be sent to attend grammar classes: for both, the grammar classes "are as much projects of moral regulation as linguistic regulation" (p. 173). She continues, "Like Phua Chu Kang, through grammar lessons teachers were to become fine exemplars, disciplined to accept the negative value placed on the local vernacular and to 'lead the way to better English standards in the country' " (p. 173), citing a front page article in *The Straits Times* (Nirmala, 1999, p. 1). And then, after attending these classes, they would be fully trained to not only teach students "the rules how English ought to be used," again citing the newspaper article, but also "encourage them to continue to be complicit in recognizing the standard as the only legitimate language, the arbiter of the worth of any alternative ones, and the element on which the economic well-being of the nation is most vitally dependent" (Kramer-Dahl, 2003, p. 186). Furthermore, she continues, "teachers would be led to perceive those students who only know Singlish as having a lack, a deficit, which they as teachers were morally obligated to compensate for" (p. 186).

However, research emerging from Singapore schools (Gupta, 1994) is showing that, beyond the use of familiar particles such as "lah," teachers generally do not use Singlish in the English classroom.[5] When it is used, it

---

5 While English language teachers are not using Singlish in their classroom talk, teachers in content subject classrooms do, especially in mathematics and science. In such instances, Singlish is used to give emphasis, scaffolding knowledge construction, reiteration, clarification of lesson content, checking of student understanding, giving directions, focusing students' attention, inviting

is most often in situations of classroom management and discipline (Gupta, 1994). And thus, it is the language politicking by the government around the English/Singlish debate that guides their classroom practices. Echoing the language politicking discussed earlier, the English Language Syllabus 2001 (still current in 2006) is unequivocal about the position of English in Singapore and the purposes of English language proficiency:

> English is one of four official languages in Singapore. As the language of public administration, education, commerce, science and technology, and global communication, it has become the medium by which most Singaporeans gain access to information and knowledge from around the world. The ability to speak and write English effectively, therefore, has become an essential skill in the workplace, and a mastery of English is vital to Singapore's pupils.
>
> (Ministry of Education, 2001, p. 2)

It states one of the aims of the syllabus as to "speak, write and make presentations in *internationally acceptable English* ..." (2001, p. 3), which is defined as, "the formal register of English used in different parts of the world, that is, standard English." Schools themselves organize programs, activities, and in-house campaigns to encourage the use of Standard English.

The United States

Ebonics

The Ebonics debate arose when the Oakland, California School Board proposed in December 1996, that the variety of English spoken by a majority of African–Americans should be recognized and supported in the schools. The resolution stated that Ebonics was a language distinct from English, and it should be recognized, tolerated, and otherwise accounted for in the instruction of the district's predominantly African–American student body (Oakland School Board, 1997).[6] It called for resources to be allocated to preparing teachers and materials to that end. As described by Collins (1999), the school board proposed this policy as part of a strategy to improve the poor educational performance of its

---

student participation, encouraging students, disciplining students, checking of student engagement and building rapport (Gwee, 2006).

6 The Oakland School Board's attempts to legitimate Ebonics vis-à-vis Standard English were forcefully opposed, and the Resolution went through a series of amendments (Collins, 1999; Perry and Delpit, 1998).

urban (and mostly African–American) students.[7] A number of issues were raised and argued (Collins, 1999, pp. 203–204): Was Ebonics a separate language from English as stated in the proposal, or was it merely slang? Would recognizing and allowing for Ebonics in the classroom improve students' performance, or would it "ghettoize" the schools? Was the problem of minority educational performance a question of language, or was language a mere distraction from more important issues such as funding for schools, student motivation, and the quality of teaching? The Oakland School Board clearly saw a strong link between language and school performance, that "taking account of minority children's home language will help their educational performance" (Collins, 1999, p. 205). As described by Collins (1999):

> In their resolution, the Oakland School Board argued that differences between the home language of the students of the African–American majority school district and the English expected in the school played a key role in the poor school performance of the district's African–American students . . . and that better awareness of Ebonics by teaching staff, along with modifications of curriculum to build bridges between Ebonics and standard English, would enhance overall school performance.
>
> (p. 205)

During the debate what emerged was that, while Ebonics may give voice to identity and intimacy with friends and family, its status as a legitimate language was not so clear. And even less clear was its place in educational settings. As one high school teacher put it (cited in Collins, 1999), "[I accept Ebonics] but *I don't want to hear it in my classroom!*" (p. 209). As we heard in Singapore, the prevalent assumption is that "only standard English is appropriate for instruction in schools or for literate expression" (Collins, 1999, pp. 209–210). This reflects a view around the world where English is being taught—that those in power view Standard English as the only variety with any global (and national) currency.

It is important to position this debate in our earlier discussions on the English-only movement and bilingual education. The original Oakland School Board proposition argued that Ebonics was a language distinct from Standard American English, and that Bilingual Education subsidies

---

7 The average grade point average for all students in the district was 2.4. By race, it was 2.7 for white students, 2.4 for Asian–American students, and 1.8 for African–American students. African–American students made up 53 percent of the student population—yet represented 80 percent of suspensions and 71 percent of students with "special needs" (Perry and Delpit, 1998, p. xi).

could therefore be accessed to help provide special language services and curricular development for Ebonics-speaking students. Some saw this as an attempt to teach Ebonics, as language maintenance similar to that discussed under bilingualism. The argument again was for monolingualism—for English to be the only legitimate language of the nation, and for the form of that English to be Standard American English.

Throughout the debate, Ebonics was frequently defined and evaluated in terms of what it was not: Standard English. Collins traces the development of the ideologies around "Standard [American] English" in the United States. Much of the discourse smacks of what we have already seen concerning English only—notions of nationalism, of monolingualism, and of social mobility through English. Only this time, with the qualifier of *Standard* English. As with Spanish and English discussed by Shannon (1999), in discussions of Standard English and Ebonics, some languages are "empowering" while others are "ghettoizing."

Language politicking, Ebonics, and the English classroom

Once again, we think about the classroom. "What must teachers do? Should they spend their time relentlessly 'correcting' their Ebonics-speaking children's language so that it might conform to what we have learned to refer to as Standard English?" asks Delpit (1998, p. 17). She provides examples of how such attempts fail to produce the desired effect (1998, pp. 23–24) and ultimately impede language and literacy learning:

Text: Yesterday I washed my brother's clothes.
Student: Yesterday I wash my bruvver close.
Teacher: Wait, let's go back. What's that word again? [Points at *washed*]
S: Wash.
T: No. Look at it again. What letters do you see at the end? You see "e-d." Do you remember what we say when we see those letters on the end of the word?
S: "ed."
T: OK, but in this case we say washed. Can you say that?
S: Wash*ed.*
T: Good. Now read it again.
S: Yesterday I wash*ed* my bruvver . . .
T: Wait a minute, what's that word again? [Points to *brother*.]
S: Bruvver.
T: No. Look at these letters in the middle. [Points to brother]. Remember to read what you see. Do you remember how we say that sound? Put your tongue between your teeth and say /th/ . . .

Is it possible, Delpit further queries, to embrace both realities in class-room instruction—the reality that Ebonics, the linguistic form a student brings to school, is intimately connected with their loved ones, community and personal identity, and the reality that students who do not have access to the politically and socially popular linguistic form of Standard English are less likely to succeed economically than those who do? We will return to her question in a moment. But first we turn to a discussion of the localization of English in two Expanding Circle countries, China and Korea, where similar issues and questions are emerging.

Localization of English in the Expanding Circle: China and Korea

China

According to Hu (2005, p. 6), "Policies on basic English language education in China have been inextricably linked to political, economic, and social development in the country," and reflect the change in attitudes toward the outside world in general. Particularly since 1980, language politicking in China largely revolves around some of the themes we have mentioned earlier—the view that English is an important resource for modernization, for accessing global markets, for gaining scientific knowledge and technological expertise, fostering economic progress, and gaining competitive advantage. With the nation's accession to the World Trade Organization (WTO) and the Beijing Olympic Games in 2008, the popularity of English has reached new heights with government policy makers, educationalists, and the Chinese public. Because of such importance accorded to English in the nation's development agenda, very large national resources have been invested in English language education. In chapter 1, we outlined some of the major developments in English language education in China, and talked about the influence of government policies in regard to the provision and even pedagogy of English language learning. Hu (2005) provides estimates of about 80 million students studying English in general secondary schools, and an estimated 40 million learners of English in primary schools and specialized/vocational secondary schools. Language learning is happening at an increasingly younger age. A growing number of parents are enrolling their preschoolers in local English courses, and some expectant mothers are even speaking English to their unborn babies (Power, 2007).

Much of this English language education occurs through materials and pedagogy imported from outside the county. Government-led reforms of English language teaching in the late 1980s and 1990s involved revamping English language curricula and syllabi to include principles and practice advocated by Communicative Language Teaching (CLT), producing communication-oriented English textbooks and skill-oriented examinations. Hu (2002a) argues that such enbloc imports are doomed to fail. For example, his research found that CLT did not receive widespread support and for many teachers support merely stopped at lip-service. Instead, the traditional grammar-based and teacher-centered approaches dominated most classrooms. He pointedly argues that CLT has failed to make inroads in English language teaching in China because most of its key tenets and practices clash with deeply held expectations of teaching and learning in the Chinese culture of learning. For example, CLT advocates an interactive model while the Chinese is an epistemic model; CLT is premised on learner-centeredness while the Chinese culture of learning stresses teacher dominance and control; CLT values verbal activeness in contrast to the mental activeness valued in traditional Chinese learning. The incongruity between the two models has resulted in the general failure to develop an adequate level of communicative competence for a large majority of students in China's schools. Hu (2002b) predicts similar limitations in the more recent embrace of Content Based English Instruction (CBEI) in key primary and secondary schools, and argues for the need for pedagogical choices that are "grounded in an understanding of sociocultural influences" (Hu, 2002b, p. 103).

One of the results of adopted foreign teaching materials is the implicit lack of recognition of China English in English language teaching. As will be discussed in the next chapter, China English is like other forms of International English in that it comprises its own unique lexis, phonology, sentence structure, and discourse style, largely through the influence of the Chinese language (Kirkpatrick & Xu, 2002). For example, Chinese phrases such as "pay New Year calls" (a spring festival tradition) and "no face" (to be ashamed) are seen as Standard China English. Many linguists and teachers see the ascendancy of China English as unstoppable. However, through the teaching materials they endorse, both national governments and the regions implicitly endorse the British or American model as the ideal for Chinese learners (Hu, 2004, 2005). Their adherence to an exonormative model comes through even more clearly in their uncritical sourcing of native speakers of English to act as teachers, even if they have no training. According to Adamson (2002), the government's failure to support China English is because of the particular ideological politicking around English. As in Singapore, English has been selectively adopted for its pragmatic and utilitarian value, with concurrent efforts to minimize its cultural impact. In Adamson's (2002, p. 231) words, "China has had a strategy to mitigate undesirable cultural transfer in place since the mid-nineteenth century: a policy of controlled and selective appropriation, to use English for the purposes of state building, while maintaining cultural integrity." To officially accept China English, he argues, would be an acknowledgement that English has expanded into non-pragmatic and socio-cultural spheres.

South Korea

As in China, English in South Korea is consciously associated with globalization and international competitiveness—so much so that there have been repeated calls for English to be made an official language. As discussed in chapter 1, English is a mandatory subject at school (all children receive a minimum of six years of English instruction), and a major goal of the Ministry of Education is the attainment of native-speaker proficiency. In addition to its pragmatic value, English is also associated with middle class and cosmopolitan values, and progressive ideas. J. Lee (2004, 2006) documents the popular hybrid use of English and Korean in pop-culture formats, such as television commercials and popular music. There is widespread use of Korean English (also known as Konglish) throughout the media, government, and wider society and, unlike China English, Korean English has been codified in dictionaries. Thus many Koreans regard Korean English as a legitimate variety of English, and see a central role for English in the nationalist agenda. However, at the same time, there is resistance to the spread of English in South Korea and to calls for its official status, with concerns that the Korean language and national identity are at risk (Collins, 2005). Thus, as in China and in Singapore, while English is accepted and valued as a means of establishing South Korea in a global market, there is resistance to giving it any role in national and cultural identity.

Following a 1992 Ministry of Education directive, the primary method of instruction used to teach English in most schools is based on CLT models. However, numerous studies reveal the general ineffectiveness of such pedagogical imports in the South Korean classroom (e.g. Kim, 2002) for reasons similar to China. There is a gap between the principles of CLT and the Korean culture of learning, with resistance to learner-centered pedagogy and oral participation. While these issues are shared in the China context, where Korea and China differ is in the teaching materials used. Shim (1999) has found that forms of Korean English exist in some textbooks, and that the educational codification of Korean English has occurred. This is contrary to what many outsiders expect: "people all over the world believe that American English is being taught in [Korean] schools" (Shim, 1999, p. 250). Among the examples she provides is the use of non-count nouns as count nouns as in the following: "Although it is *a hard work*, I enjoy it" (Shim, 1999, p. 252) and the mixing of different tenses in one sentence, exemplified in the following excerpt: "He *seems to be* pleased when he *saw* me" (Shim, 1999, p. 253). This is not to say that the use of Konglish in the schools is uncontested. Similar to the attitudes of some towards Singlish in Singapore, there are some who argue Konglish is bad English and undermines the learning of good English. A commentary printed in the *Korean Herald* (cited by Cohen, 2001) argued, "Bad English in textbooks is particularly troubling because it helps reproduce the passivity towards good English that has permitted bad English to prosper in Korea for so long. If students are exposed to mistakes that many teachers will teach as good English, then how can English education in Korea improve?" Hagens' (2005) dissertation research shows that some teachers hold similar attitudes—that while they may accept Korean English as a legitimate form of English, they still hesitate to use it extensively in the classroom, preferring instead to defer to Inner Circle exonormative standards.

Thus, in both Outer and Expanding contexts, we see similar issues regarding the status of nativized varieties, particular in regard to their role in schools. We also see how the tensions between the concerns of globalization and nationalism shape language-in-education politicking and pedagogy. Earlier, we raised Delpit's (1998) questions about the possibility of embracing both realities surrounding Ebonics and Standard English, or more broadly, the nativized variety and Standard English, in the classroom. To answer Delpit's question (which she herself answers, of course, and which will be incorporated below), consider for a moment the points made at the beginning of the chapter. We noted that there are three main ways in which the designation of an official language has consequences for language learning and teaching: (a) the insight the designation provides into prevalent social attitudes toward particular languages; (b) the effect of approved language policies on the stated language-in-education policy; and (c) the setting of linguistic standards. Our discussion that follows will be organized around these three areas of consequence, with reference to Singlish and Ebonics.

Language politicking and EIL pedagogy

We first consider the insight the designation of an official language provides into prevalent social attitudes toward particular languages. In Singapore, English-knowing bilingualism and language-based streaming has given ascendancy to English vis-à-vis the mother tongue languages, and has linked English to higher levels of socio-economic status. Ironically, given the dominant and prestigious presence of English in Singapore, it is not a mother tongue. English is for international communication, not identity; English is for economic pragmatism, not a matter of the soul. In his 1984 Speak Mandarin Campaign Speech, then Prime Minister Lee Kuan Yew unequivocally stated: "One abiding reason why we have to persist in bilingualism is that English will not be emotionally acceptable as our mother tongue." The international position of English also is the basis by which Singlish is kept at bay—it is not internationally intelligible, and therefore has no position in the linguistic ideological landscape.

In the United States, efforts to position English and Standard English as the only official language of the nation and of the individual states is based on particular views of language. As noted earlier, in such efforts (a) language is seen as a common bond unifying the nation; (b) language is seen as a key to personal and economic success; (c) language is viewed as a symbol of one's ethnic identity; and (d) language is viewed as a symbol of nationhood and good citizenship. And thus, the presence of more than one language (especially Spanish) would be a symbol of disunity, disloyalty, and divisiveness. Where the Singaporean and U.S. stories converge is in the attempt of those in positions of power to follow a policy of homogenization through language politicking—neat linguistic quadrants in Singapore, and monolingualism with regard to English in the United States and efforts of monolingualism with respect to bilingualism and Ebonics.

Singapore and the United States also demonstrate the effect of approved language policies on the stated language-in-education policy. Singapore's English-knowing bilingual education policy means four languages are represented in the education system. All Singaporeans are somewhat bilingual, in English and their "mother tongue". However, certain characteristics of the policy and politicking have very particular realization in the classroom. Language politicking concerning bilingualism treats English and the mother tongue languages as discrete units and binary opposites. It also inextricably links language and race. What this means in the classroom is that, first of all, it is not possible to learn an official language that is not your ascribed mother tongue at school (exception is given to Indians whose mother tongue is not Tamil, and through a case-by-case appeal process). This has resulted in a form of bilingualism that in fact tends to reinforce ethnic boundaries, with students going to segregated mother tongue classes (each with their own curriculum, developed in isolation of each other), rather than unify the different ethnic communities. These aspects of language politicking have also led to a curriculum and pedagogy that teaches the languages in bilingualism in isolation of each other, in total contrast to the interwoven practices of language use within each person's repertoire. In the United States, politicking for English only at the state level translates into policies of transitional bilingualism at best, where English monolingualism is the goal. In both countries then, there is an erasure of the everyday linguistic realities of the students through classroom pedagogy. This is equally potent with regard to the non-standard form of English (Singlish and Ebonics), where the politicking pursues an aggressive agenda of "elimination" (Trudgill, 1995, pp. 185–188). As noted by Trudgill, elimination of non-standard speech is the most common approach in English language classrooms around the world, where teachers attempt as much as possible to prevent students from using their non-standard varieties and correct all instances of non-standard features. This often involves the criminalization of use of the non-standard variety, whereby the student "caught" using the non-standard variety is punished or fined. This is seen in Singapore, for example, where Bokhorst-Heng observed one teacher fining students in her English class each time they used their mother tongue.

A contrasting approach to elimination would be bidialectism (Trudgill, 1995). In this approach, teachers accept that the non-standard variety might be used in informal situations, but as much as possible encourage the use of the standard variety in the classroom and in other school situations, especially in written work. The effectiveness of such pedagogical approaches has been documented by Lin (1996) and Delpit (1995, 1998). An example would be the Standard English Proficiency program in California, which is a statewide initiative that acknowledges Ebonics as a linguistic code while helping children to learn Standard English. This view suggests building students' linguistic repertoire, whereby Ebonics is recognized as one linguistic code in this repertoire. Rather than a "fix-something-that-was-wrong" approach, it seeks to add to the funds of knowledge that students come with to the classroom (for other examples, see teacher interviews and related articles in Perry & Delpit, 1998). Delpit (1998) provides the example of Mrs. Pat, a teacher chronicled by Stanford University researcher Shirley Brice Heath, who had her students become language "detectives," interviewing a variety of individuals and listening to the radio and television to document the differences and similarities in the ways people talked. Through this process, "children can learn that there are many ways of saying the same thing, and that certain contexts suggest particular kinds of linguistic performances" (Delpit, 1998, p. 18). Other examples include teachers who have their students create bilingual dictionaries, role-play, and the use of self-critique of recorded forms.

Such a bidialectal approach has also been advocated by Singapore scholars (e.g., Kramer-Dahl, 2003; Stroud & Wee, 2007) particularly in encouraging the use of code-switching for pedagogical practices. As argued by Stroud and Wee (2007):

> A conventional pedagogical emphasis that requires the students to pay attention to correctness and standard English while simultaneously downplaying the social meaning of language(s) for them, only serves to ignore the complexity of the interactional and social structures found in the classroom. Concomitantly, such an emphasis gives rise to the marginalization of multilingualism and the stereotyping of non-standard varieties of English as well as other languages in the Singapore classroom, creating a situation where the students negoti-

ate resistant and alternative (multilingual and multicultural) personae in relation to off-site peer interaction.

(p. 50)

Ironically, even Minister Mentor Lee Kuan Yew now acknowledges the value of this approach—however, he only discusses it in the context of learning Mandarin, which is increasingly challenged by the growing dominance of English in Chinese Singaporean homes. In an interview by Ho Sheo Be (March 19 and 26, 2005 in Chua, 2005, n.p.), Lee Kuan Yew argues:

> Teachers should understand that English will be the master language of most students. If they don't relate Chinese to English and teach Chinese as a standalone, the students will lose out ... Learning two languages, with English as the master language, you need to relate Chinese to your English. It is wrong to believe that if you teach Chinese using English, you will weaken the learning of Chinese.

Lee Kuan Yew had at one time similarly held the view that knowledge of Chinese dialects, which were the "real" mother tongue of many Chinese Singaporeans, could be harnessed in the learning of Mandarin. However he subsequently took the very hardline view that the use of dialects was a "handicap" in the learning of Mandarin, and thus should be eliminated from Singaporeans' linguistic repertoire—which has indeed occurred for most young Singaporeans today, who have very little proficiency in any Chinese dialects other than Mandarin (Bokhorst-Heng, 1999). Thus, it is not clear what real support would be given to such a bidialectical pedagogical approach in policy or practice. It has never been mooted in conversations about pedagogy in the English classroom.

Kramer-Dahl (2003) goes even further to suggest a pedagogy that is anchored on an *appreciation of dialect difference* (Trudgill, 1995). The emphasis of this approach is on a recognition of the worldliness of language and a pedagogy of critical language awareness. It involves a pedagogy that teaches students how "notions of facts" about language are actually "elements of a larger narrative, an elaborate construction deployed for larger social needs and political ends, and that as such they should be questioned, and if necessary, made differently" (Kramer-Dahl, 2003, p. 186).

Going back to Delpit's (1998) question raised earlier—whether or not it is possible to embrace the worldliness of language in the classroom— the answer is, through bidialectism and through critical language awareness, yes. It is possible, and it has been proven to be an effective and empowering form of language learning.

Finally, we discuss what official language policy does for the setting of linguistic standards in the classroom. In Singapore, the only legitimate standard of English is Standard English. It is measured by international intelligibility, which in the classroom is measured and controlled by high-stakes exams and multiple layers of accountability through ranking and streaming. And it is controlled by the omnipresence of the moral obligation of teachers to be bearers of the standard. In the United States, Standard American English is the only accepted variety of English in the classroom. The setting of standards comes through the harsh realities of funding (or the lack thereof) and with no platform by which to defend any other standard. As noted by Collins (1999), "Standard English is the public, official language; speakers of other languages have individual rights to special educational provision [under 'equal opportunity' provisions], but speakers of nonstandard varieties of English have no special standing" (p. 211).

We close with a quote from Green and Hodgens (1996, p. 225), which was brought to our attention in Kramer-Dahl (2003):

> The grammar lesson needs to be understood as a form of moral training above all, linked to the disciplined and practiced formation of embodied subjects. It is never a question of grammar per se, or even of the best "method" ("tried or true") that is at the heart of the debate; rather, as is so often the case in education, it is more particularly a matter of power and ideology as realized in and through English teaching, as a distinctive form of social practice and cultural politics.
> (p. 159)

What is said of grammar can also be said of mother tongue languages in the English language classroom. It is about the worldliness of language and what that means for English classroom pedagogy and learning.

Summary

Through our discussion of the worldliness of language and language politicking, we see a number of themes emerge that are becoming familiar in our narrative of international English. One is the relationship between language and social class. Around the world where English is used and taught, unequal access to English relates to unequal access to the so-called benefits that come with speaking English. This was very clearly evident in the statistics provided by the Singapore Census, and is evident in the concurrent legislation in California of English only and the elimination of funding for English language learning. Yet, at the same time, the spread of international English is thus promoted as being a means by which to increase economic opportunity. However, and another theme we see emerging, the view that this international English can only be so-called

Standard English continues to erect barriers to the very access it supposedly provides.

Furthermore, English is presented as being neutral, devoid of any ethnic identity. Hence it can be the language of inter-ethnic communication in Singapore. And hence it can be the unifying language for the ethnically-diverse immigrant population in the United States. Once again, however, it must be the so-called Standard form of English, stripped of any ethnic (in contrast to Ebonics in the United States) and national (in contrast to Singlish in Singapore) identifier. With such a view comes the *othering* (Palfreyman, 2005) and marginalization of those who speak only linguistic forms other than the Standard—those who speak only Singlish in Singapore, particularly in the global/local nexus of language politicking; and those who speak only languages other than English in the United States, and speakers of Ebonics who are depicted as being somewhat deficient in comparison to those who speak the Standard. As an aside, it is worth mentioning that discussions of *international* English and the need to access the international community and global economy are not mentioned in U.S. language politicking—a reflection of the dominant status of the United States and American English globally.

As we continue in our next chapter, we will see these themes continue to operate in the narrative of teaching and learning international English.

References

Adamson, B. (2002). Barbarian as a foreign language: English in China's schools. *World Englishes*, 21(2), 231–243.

Auerbach, E. R. (1995). The politics of the ESL classroom: Issues of power in pedagogical choices. In J.W. Tollefson (Ed.), *Power and inequality in language education* (pp. 9–33). Cambridge: Cambridge University Press.

Beardsmore, H. B. (1991). *Business Times*, November 15, 1991.

Bokhorst-Heng, W. D. (1999). Singapore's Speak Mandarin campaign: Language ideological debates in the "imagining of the nation". In J. Blommaert (Ed.), *Language ideological debates* (pp. 235–265). Berlin and New York: Mouton de Gruyter.

Bokhorst-Heng, W. D. (2005). Debating Singlish. *Multilingua*, 24(3), 185–209.

Chia, H. K. S. (1999). Don't break the Singlish bond. *The Straits Times*, September 8, p. 45.

Chua, C. L. (Ed.) (2005). *Keeping my Mandarin alive: Lee Kuan Yew's language learning experience*. Singapore: World Scientific and Global Publishing.

Chua, S. C. (1962). *State of Singapore: Report on the Census of Population, 1957*. Singapore, Department of Statistics: Government Printing Office.

Cohen, D. (2001). "Konglish" replaces good English. *Guardian Unlimited*, April 27. Retrieved September 13, 2007 from http://education.guardian.co.uk/news/story/0,,479566,00.html.

Collins, J. (1999). The Ebonics controversy in context: Literacies, subjectivities, and language ideologies in the United States. In J. Blommaert (Ed.), *Language ideological debates* (pp. 201–234). Berlin and New York: Mouton De Gruyter.

Collins, S. (2005). "Who's this *Tong-il?*:" English, culture, and ambivalence in South Korea. *Changing English, 12,* 417–429.

Crystal, D. (1995). *The Cambridge encyclopedia of the English language.* Cambridge: Cambridge University Press.

Delpit, L. (1995). *Other people's children: Cultural conflicts in the classroom.* New York: Free Press.

Delpit, L. (1998). What should teachers do? Ebonics and culturally responsive instruction. In T. Perry and L. Delpit (Eds.), *The real Ebonics debate: Power, language, and the education of African–American children* (pp. 17–26). Boston: Beacon Press, in collaboration with *Rethinking Schools.*

Deumert, A. (2000). Language planning and policy. In R. Mesthrie, J. Swann, A. Deumert, and W. Leap, *Introducing sociolinguistics* (pp. 384–418). Edinburgh: Edinburgh University Press.

Donahue, T. S. (1995). American language policy and compensatory opinion. In J. W. Tollefson (Ed.), *Power and inequality in language education* (pp. 112–141). Cambridge: Cambridge University Press.

Edwards, J. R. (1984). Language, diversity and identity. In J. R. Edwards (Ed.), *Linguistic minorities, policies, and pluralism* (pp. 277–320). New York: Mouton.

Goh, C. C. M. & Silver, R. (2004). *Language acquisition and development: A teacher's guide.* Singapore: Pearson Education.

Goh, C. T. (1999). Prime Minister's National Day rally speech, 1999 First-World Economy, World-class home—Extract E. Education. Retrieved November 18, 2006, from http://www.moe.gov.sg/speeches/1999/sp270899.htm.

Goh, C. T. (2000). Speech by Prime Minister Goh Chok Tong at the launch of the Speak Good English Movement on Saturday, 29 April 2000, at the Institute of Technical Education (ITE) Headquarters Auditorium, Dover Drive, at 10:30 am. Document number gct20000429j. Singapore: Ministry of Communication, Information and the Arts. Retrieved October 27, 2006, from http://stars.nhb.gov.sg/stars/public/.

Goh, K. W. (1979). *Report on the Ministry of Education 1978. (The "Goh Report").* Singapore: Ministry of Education.

Green, B. & Hodgens, J. (1996). Manners, morals, meanings: English teaching, language education and the subject of "grammar." In B. Green and C. Beavis (Eds.), *Teaching the English subjects: Essays on English curriculum history and Australian schooling* (pp. 204–225). Geelong, Australia: Deakin University Press.

Gupta, A. F. (1994). *The step-tongue: Children's English in Singapore.* Clevedon: Multilingual Matters.

Gwee, S. B. Y. (2006). Teacher code-switching in a multilingual classroom. Paper presented at the American Educational Research Association Annual Meeting, San Francisco, 2006.

Hagens, S. (2005). *Attitudes toward Konglish of South Korean teachers of English in the Province of Jeollanamdo.* Dissertation Brock University, Canada.

Hu, G. (2002a). Potential cultural resistance to pedagogical imports: The case of communicative language teaching in China. *Language, Culture and Curriculum*, 15(2), 93–105.

Hu, G. (2002b). Recent important developments in secondary English-language teaching in the People's Republic of China. *Language, Culture and Curriculum*, 15(1), 30–49.

Hu, G. (2005). English language education in China: Policies, progress, and problems. *Language Policy*, 4, 5–24.

Hu, X. (2004). Why China English should stand alongside British, American and other "World Englishes." *English Today*, 20(2), 26–33.

Hu, X. (2005). China English, at home and in the world. *English Today*, 21(3), 27–38.

Its great contribution was in teaching of English language. (1997). *The Straits Times*, April 18, p. H55.

Judd, E. L. (1987). The English language amendment: A case study on language and politics. *TESOL Quarterly*, 21(1), 113–135.

Kaplan, R. B. & Baldauf, R. B. (2003). *Language and language-in-education planning in the Pacific Basin*. Dordrecht, Boston and London: Kluwer Academic Publishers.

Kim, J. (2002). Teaching culture in the English as foreign language classroom. *Korea TESOL Journal*, 5(1), 28–40.

Kirkpatrick, A. & Xu, Z. (2002). Chinese pragmatic norms and "China English." *World Englishes*, 21(2), 269–279.

Koh, T. A. (2006). Speech by Professor Koh Tai Ann, Chairman, Speak Good English Movement Committee at the launch of the Speak Good English Movement on Tuesday, 25 July 2006, 11:00am, The Plaza, National Library Building. Retrieved November 17, 2006 from http://www.goodenglish.org.sg/SGEM/archive/speech/chairman2.htm.

Kramer-Dahl, A. (2003). Reading the "Singlish debate:" Construction of a crisis of language standards and language teaching in Singapore. *Journal of Language, Identity, and Education*, 2(3), 159–190.

Lee, B. T. (1999). Teachers give up speaking good English. *The Straits Times*, July 28, p. 46.

Lee, J. (2004). Linguistic hybridizations in K-pop: Discourse of self-assertion and resistance. *World Englishes*, 23, 429–450.

Lee, J. (2006). Linguistic constructions of modernity: English mixing in Korean television commercials. *Language in Society*, 35(1), 59–91.

Lee, K. Y. (1972). Summary of Speech by the Prime Minister at the Singapore Teachers Union's 26th Anniversary Dinner held at Shangri-la Hotel on 5th November, 1972. Document number: lky19721105. Retrieved November 17, 2006, from http://stars.nhb.gov.sg/stars/public/.

Lee, K. Y. (1984). Speech by Prime Minister Lee Kuan Yew at the opening of the Speak Mandarin Campaign on Friday, 21 September 1984, at the Singapore Conference Hall. Document number lky19840921a. Retrieved November 17, 2006, from http://stars.nhb.gov.sg/stars/public/.

Lee, K. Y. (1999). Speech by Senior Minister Lee Kuan Yew at the Tanjong Pagar 34th Naitonal Day Celebration on Saturday, 14 August 1999, at the Tanjong Pagar Community Club. Document number lky19990814m. Retrieved November 17, 2006, from http://stars.nhb.gov.sg/stars/public/.

Lin, A. M. Y. (1996). Bilingualism or linguistic segregation? Symbolic domination, resistance and code-switching in Hong Kong schools. *Linguistics and Education*, 8(1), 49–84.

Lui, T. Y. (2006). Speech by RADM (NS) Lui Tuck Yew, Minister of State for Education at the launch of the Speak Good English Movement on Tuesday, 25 July 2006, 11:00am, The Plaza, National Library Building. Retrieved November 17, 2006 from http://www.goodenglish.org.sg/SGEM/archive/speech/radm.htm.

MacKaye, S. (1987). California Proposition 63 and public perceptions of language. MA dissertation, Stanford University.

Ministry of Education. (2001). *English Language Syllabus 2001 for primary and secondary schools. Curriculum Planning and Development Division, Ministry of Education.* Retrieved October 10, 2006 from http://www.moe.gov.sg/cpdd/doc/English.pdf.

Nirmala, M. (1999). Teachers to go for English upgrading. *The Straits Times*, July 25, p.1.

Oakland School Board. (1997). *Resolution of the Board of Education adopting the report of the African–American Task Force.* Board of Education, Oakland Unified School District, Document No. 597-0063.

Pakir, A. (1991). The range and depth of English-knowing bilinguals in Singapore. *World Englishes*, 10(2), 167–179.

Palfreyman, D. (2005). Othering in an English language program. *TESOL Quarterly*, 39(2), 21–233.

Pennycook, A. (1994). *The cultural politics of English as an international language.* London: Longman.

Perry, T. & Delpit, L. (Eds.) (1998). *The Real Ebonics Debate: Power, language, and the education of African–American children.* Boston: Beacon Press, in collaboration with *Rethinking Schools*.

Power, C. (2007). Not the Queen's English. *Newsweek International.* Retrieved September 12, 2007, from http://www.msnbc.msn.com/id/7038031/site/newsweek/.

Shannon, S. M. (1995). The hegemony of English: A case study of one bilingual classroom as a site of resistance. *Linguistics and Education*, 7(3), 177–202.

Shannon, S. M. (1999). The debate on bilingual education in the U.S.: Language ideology as reflected in the practice of bilingual teachers. In J. Blommaert (Ed.), *Language ideological debates* (pp. 171–199). Berlin and New York: Mouton de Gruyter.

Shim, R. J. (1999). Codified Korean English: Process, characteristics, and consequence. *World Englishes*, 23, 429–450.

Singapore Department of Statistics. (1980). *Census of Population, 1980. Resident Households by Ethnic Group of Head and Predominant Household Language, 1980.* Singapore: Department of Statistics.

Singapore Department of Statistics. (2005). Singapore Residents by Age Group, Ethnic Group, and Sex. *Monthly Digest of Stats Singapore.* June. Retrieved September 26, 2006, from www.singstat.gov.sg/keystats/mqstats/mqstats.html.

Smolicz, J. J. & Secombe, M. J. (2003). Assimilation or pluralism? Changing policies for minority languages education in Australia. *Language Policy*, 2, 3–25.

Stroud, C. & Wee, L. (2007). A pedagogical application of liminalities in social positioning: Identity and literacy in Singapore. *TESOL Quarterly, 41*(1), 33–54.

Tollefson, J. (1995). Preface. In J.W. Tollefson (Ed.). *Power and inequality in language education* (p. ix). Cambridge: Cambridge University Press.

Trudgill, P. (1995). *Sociolinguistics: An introduction to language and society. (Revised Edition).* London: Penguin.

Vaish, V., Aman, N., & Bokhorst-Heng, W. D. (2005). An introduction to the sociolinguistic survey of Singapore. *SingTeach, 2.* Available at http://singteach.nie.edu.sg/content/view/16/143/.

Vaish, V. & Sam, C. (2006). *Mother tongue languages: Specific focus projects in CRPP. A report.* September. Singapore: Centre for Research in Pedagogy and Practice, National Institute of Education, Nanyang Technological University.

Wong, S. (1988). Educational rights of language minorities. In S. McKay & S. Wong (Eds.), *Language diversity: Problem or resource?* (pp. 367–386). New York: Newbury House.

Wong-Fillmore, L. (1991). When learning a second language means losing the first. *Early Childhood Research Quarterly, 6*(3), 323–346.

Chapter 5

Linguistic variation and standards

Thus far, our discussion has focused on the social factors involved in the teaching and learning of EIL. This chapter takes a much more micro-level approach, focusing on the linguistic diversity of present-day English use. Special attention will be given here to the development of World Englishes, their features and relationship to identity issues, particularly focusing on the plurality of World Englishes in their contexts of socio-cultural diversity. We will argue that language contact necessarily leads to linguistic variation and that such variation is clearly related to issues of power.

This discussion of linguistic variation will be followed by a thorough analysis of the question of standards in EIL pedagogy. Various meanings of intelligibility will be discussed, as well as criteria for determining when a linguistic innovation should be considered as a norm. We will argue that EIL pedagogy should encourage awareness of the variation that exists in English today and recognize the validity of different varieties of English.

Interpreting language variation

As was noted earlier, the current growth of English is due largely to the increasing number of second language speakers of English who are learning English within their own country. Brutt-Griffler (2002) terms this process of second language acquisition by speech communities in their own local context *macroacquisition*. The large-scale macroacquisition that is occurring today has resulted in many speakers of English using English in contact with their other languages, sometimes on a regular basis. One result of such contact is a type of linguistic hybridization that we referred to earlier in advertising, music, movies and electronic communication. In addition, in contexts where English is used on a daily basis among bilinguals, the changes in English that are developing are being codified and accepted as standard. The result is a growing number of standardized varieties of English—not just in Kachru's Outer Circle countries but also, as Lowenberg (2002) documents, in many Expanding Circle nations as well. According to Lowenberg (2002, p. 431), in certain intranational and regional domains of language use in some Expanding Circle countries (for example, across Europe), English actually functions as a second language, and often develops nativized norms.

Finally, these processes of hybridization have resulted in not just the development of different varieties of Standard English between countries, but also varieties of English within countries. For example, Banjo (discussed by Bamgbose, 1992) distinguishes the varieties of English used in Nigeria based on the specific linguistic characteristics of the variety, its international intelligibility, and its social acceptability, resulting in the following description of Nigerian English:

> Variety 1: Marked by wholesale transfer of phonological, syntactic, and lexical features of Kwa or Niger-Congo to English. Spoken by those whose knowledge of English is very imperfect. Neither socially acceptable in Nigeria nor internationally intelligible.

> Variety 2: Syntax close to that of Standard British English, but with strongly marked phonological and lexical peculiarities. Spoken by up to 75 percent of those who speak English in the country. Socially acceptable, but with rather low international intelligibility.

> Variety 3: Close to Standard British English both in syntax and in semantics; similar in phonology, but different in phonetic features as well as with regard to certain lexical peculiarities. Socially acceptable and internationally intelligible. Spoken by less than 10 percent of the population.

> Variety 4: Identical with Standard British English in syntax and semantics, having identical phonological and phonetic features of a British regional dialect of English. Maximally internationally intelligible, but socially unacceptable. Spoken by only a handful of Nigerians born or brought up in England.
> (Banjo as cited in Bamgbose, 1992, pp. 149–150)

Bickerton's (1975) work on creolization, originally developed in relation to Caribbean and Guyanese English, has been used by a number of scholars to explain these various forms of language variation. In broad strokes, creolization occurs when a pidgin language—a language developed as a means of communication between different groups of people who do not share a common language (and hence is nobody's native language)—is passed on to the next generation and used as a native language. Because a creole is generally spoken in a country where other people speak the creole's lexical source-language, like English, the creole generally has less prestige. This situation gives rise to a *post-creole continuum.* In such situations, creole speakers will tend to shift towards the source language, with the result that there is a range of intermediate varieties. Bickerton places this whole range of varieties on a *lectal continuum.* In reference to Guyanese English, Bickerton (1975, p. 24) used the term *acrolect* to refer to educated Guyanese English, a (prestige) variety similar to other varieties of Standard English. At the other extreme of the continuum is the *basilect,* the creole. The intermediate varieties he called *mesolects.*

Bickerton's model has been applied to a number of English language contexts, and has been further modified in an attempt to capture the nuances of language variation. For example, using Bickerton's post-creole continuum, Platt and Weber (1980) described variation within Singapore English in terms of its correlation with proficiency, education, and socio-economic status. The *basilect* represents the variety of Singapore English spoken by those with low levels of education and low socio-economic status, which they describe as Singlish. The *acrolect* represents the Standard variety of Singapore English, spoken by those with higher levels of education and higher socio-economic status. In this model, the acrolect variety (which shows little difference from British Standard English) is held as desirable, and the basilect as undesirable. One of the main criticisms against this model is that it is too static, obscuring how especially the more educated speakers of Singapore English regularly switch between the basilect and acrolect forms. It therefore cannot account for this educated father's use of Singlish in the following situation. A father (tertiary educated) is telling his daughter about the "good old days" when educational experiences were pleasurable ("pleasure" and "pressure" sound similar in Singapore English) (from Pakir, 1991):

Father: You know why, in our days, ah, in our days different lah. Studying is different lah. Studying is mixed with a bit of pleasure. Pleasure. Not nowadays.
Daughter: Now no pressure? Are you telling me now no pressure?
Father: No, "pleasure", "pleasure". Not "pressure" . . . Because that time that time nobody talked about this kind of thing. Competition or what. Yah. My colleague, myself, we never compare marks . . . Ya we heard people talk about wah this fella got 8 A's. So what? Everybody still get a C. Go to Polytechnic or University or whatever.

(p. 173)

The limitations of the lectal continuum model led other Singapore scholars to see variation within Singapore English more in terms of diglossia. First introduced by Gupta (1994), the diglossic model identifies Singlish as the L-variety, and Standard Singapore English as the H-variety.

Each of these varieties, she argues, has a specific set of functions in line with the traditional diglossic framework (see chapter 3). The strength of this model is that it addresses the major flaw of the lectal model in that it accounts for the code-switching between varieties. In so doing, it "re-casts Singlish as a colloquial form of Singapore English used by educated English speakers to indicate informality or solidarity. Singlish thus becomes a variety of English with a sociolinguistic purpose and design, rather than one borne out of a lack of competence to command the standard variety" (Alsagoff, 2007, p. 41). The use of Singlish by this educated father when speaking with his daughter in the informal domain of the home is thus not unusual or unexpected. A diglossic assumption would be that, outside the home and in more formal domains, he would speak the Standard form.

A third model used to explain variation within Singapore English is the expanding triangles model developed by Pakir (1991), which draws on both the polylectal continuum and the diglossic model (see figure 5.1). It places variation in Singapore English along two clines (influenced by Kachru's (1983) "cline of English bilingualism"): the *proficiency* cline and the *formality* cline, reflecting the *users* and *uses* of English. Pakir's model is represented through a series of expanding triangles, which represent the differing ranges of styles of English-speaking Singaporeans, with education and English proficiency offering an increasing range of choice. Those users of English with higher education are located at the top ends of both the formality and proficiency clines. They often are capable of the whole range of English expression, and able to move along the whole length of the formality cline. Those at the base of the triangle have lower levels of proficiency, typically have lower levels of education, and tend to come

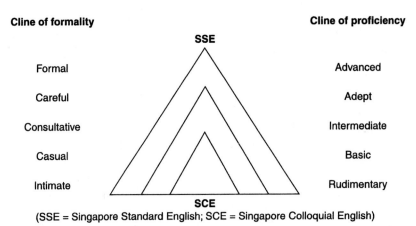

(SSE = Singapore Standard English; SCE = Singapore Colloquial English)

Figure 5.1 Pakir's expanding triangles of Singapore English.

(Source: Pakir, 1991, p. 174)

from a lower socio-economic background. They are more restricted in their movement along the formality cline, and can usually speak only the colloquial forms of Singapore English.

Applying this model to our example of the father and daughter's exchange, their conversation can be characterized as intimate or casual. However, because of the father's level of education, his proficiency can be expected to be high on the cline of proficiency, either adept or advanced. Hence, he is able to make use of the full range of language variation in accordance to the formality of the situation.

What all of these interpretations attempt to do is to develop a model that describes and legitimizes a pluricentric view of English, and one that moves away from any view of there being just one standard form against which all others are measured. As argued by Kachru (1983, 1992), English has "blended itself with the cultural and social complex" (1983, p. 139) of the country and has thereby become "culture-bound" (1983, p. 140) in it. Therefore, he argues, new Englishes cannot be characterized in terms of acquisitional inadequacy, or be judged by the norms of English in Inner Circle countries. Rather, the form and function of new Englishes must be considered according to "the context of situation which is appropriate to the variety, its uses and users" (1983, p. 215). It is because of this latter point that we prefer the term *World Englishes* over *New Englishes*. The notion of "New Englishes" continues to privilege a distinction between "new" and "old/established" varieties and thus may unintentionally perpetuate their associated power differentials. "World Englishes" attempts to place all varieties of English on par with each other without any one being a reference point.

The World Englishes paradigm thus stresses the pluricentric nature of English: as a result of its spread and contact with indigenous languages, English has acquired many centers from which norms and innovations are created. There is an emphasis in discussions of World Englishes on the cultural embeddedness of language—or, a term that Bhatt (2005) adopts, the "grammar of culture" (p. 534). D'souza's (1988) definition is helpful: "Grammar of culture is used . . . to mean the acceptable possibilities of behavior within a particular culture" (p. 160), including what is appropriate or expected in a given context. Thus, language and culture are intimately related: "The grammar of culture affects and influences the use of language in very striking ways and is in turn affected by language" (D'souza, 1988, p. 160). In his application of D'souza's definition, Bhatt (2005) describes it this way: "Nonnative English speakers . . . created new, cultural-sensitive and socially appropriate meanings—expressions of the bilingual's [and multingual's] creativity—by altering and manipulating the structure and functions of English in its new ecology" (p. 534). As a result, he continues, "English underwent a process of acculturation" (p. 534).

All of these discussions of language variation operate as a response to the Standard language ideology, and implicit in them is a debate about issues of intelligibility. We will discuss these debates more closely later in this chapter. But first, it is useful to look at some of the features of variation we are talking about, illustrated with examples taken from varieties of English in various Outer and Expanding Circle countries. The main features of variation that will be considered are: pronunciation, grammar, vocabulary/idiom, and discourse style. Our discussion will do two things: it will provide a glimpse of the scope of variation within World Englishes, and demonstrate the pluralistic nature of World Englishes; it will also provide examples of how such variation needs to be understood as emerging from its interaction with particular cultural grammars.

Features of variation

Pronunciation

Platt, et al. (1984) summarize some of the common variations that can be heard in World Englishes regarding *consonant* and *vowel* sounds (see also Jenkins, 2003, pp. 23–25). They include:

CONSONANTS (pp. 30–45)

1   Replacement of the fricatives [θ] and [ð] by other sounds, usually [d] and [t] on their own or followed by slight friction.

   The sounds [θ] and [ð] as in words such as <u>th</u>in and <u>th</u>is are pronounced in a variety of ways by speakers of New Englishes (Jenkins, 2003, p. 23).

   > Speakers of Indian and West Indian Englishes will use the sounds [t] and [d], so that the words are pronounced "tin" and "dis".
   > Speakers of Lankan (Sri Lankan), Malaysian, Singaporean, and many African Englishes will use the sounds [tθ] and [dð], so that the same words sound similar to "t-thin" and "d-this".

2   A tendency to reduce the aspiration of consonants at the beginning of words.

   The voiceless sounds [p], [t] and [k] are pronounced at the beginning of words without aspiration (a small puff of air) by speakers of Indian, Filipino, and Malaysian Englishes, such that they sound more like the voiced [b], [d] and [g]. Words such as "pin", "tin", and "cap" thus sound more like "bin", "din", and "gap" (Jenkins, 2003, p. 24).

3   A tendency not to release consonants at the end of words.

   Consonants at the end of words tend to be unreleased or replaced with glottal stops in Englishes such as Ghanaian, West Indian, and

Singaporean. A word such as "cat" may be pronounced either ca(t) with an unreleased final consonant, or ca' with a final glottal stop (Jenkins, 2003, p. 24); or "world" pronounced as worl(d).

4 The sound [w] is pronounced as [v] in Lankan and some Indian languages so that "wet" sounds like "vet".

VOWELS (pp. 31–37)

1 A tendency to shorten vowel sounds.

Shorter vowel sounds: Singaporean, Indian and African Englishes are among the World Englishes that minimally distinguish (if at all) between the short and long vowels [I] and [i:] as in the words "sit" and "seat", which both are pronounced as [I]. An example from Ghana is given by Platt et al. (1984): "People will not seat (sit) down" (p. 33).

2 A lack of distinction between long and short vowels.

Many World Englishes, including Indian, Filipino, Lankan, and Singaporean pronounce [a:] without its length. The word "staff" is thus pronounced as "stuff" (Jenkins, 2003, p. 24).

3 A tendency to replace central vowels by either front or back vowels.

In African Englishes, one hears the *schwa* sound [ə] as the full vowel [a] at the end of words. For example, matter is pronounced as [mata], and butter as [bata] (Platt et al., 1984, p. 35).

Grammar

Platt et al. (1984) also summarize the main grammatical features found in World Englishes regarding nouns and verbs. The following are some of these features, along with several of their examples:

NOUNS (p. 65)

1 A tendency not to mark nouns for plural.
   Up to twelve year of schooling. (India)
   A province will be divided into district. (Philippines)

2 A tendency to use a specific/non-specific system for nouns rather than a definite/indefinite system, or to use the two systems side by side.

   • Non-specific:
     I really want to spend some time in village, definitely if I get chance. (India)

- Specific:
  Got <u>*one*</u> *boy, morning also eat instant noodles, afternoon also eat instant noodles, night also eat instant noodles. Suddenly he died. The doctor found a lot of wax in his stomach.* (Malaysia)

3 A tendency to change the form of quantifiers.
  Don't eat so <u>*much sweets.*</u> (Singapore)
  You are expected to say <u>*some few words.*</u> (Sri Lanka)

4 A tendency to convert certain uncountable nouns to countable (examples cited by Shim, 1999, p. 252, taken from a high school English textbook).
  Although it is <u>*a hard work,*</u> *I enjoy it.* (Korea)
  An old man showed <u>*a great patience.*</u> (Korea)

5 A tendency not to make a distinction between the third person pronouns "he" and "she."
  My mother, <u>*he*</u> *live in kampong.* (Malaysia; a "kampong" is a small village)
  My husband who was in England, <u>*she*</u> *was then my fiancé.* (East Africa)

6 A tendency to change the word order within the noun phrase.
  <u>*Ninety over*</u> *cheques.* (Singapore/Malaysia)
  <u>*That your brother*</u> *will he come?* (Nigeria)

VERBS (pp. 85–86)

1 A tendency not to mark the verb for third person singular in its present-tense form. Instead of "She drinks milk," a speaker of Philippine English might say, "She <u>drink</u> milk."

2 A limited marking of verbs for the past tense.
  I <u>*move*</u> *to hostel.* (India)
  Last year I <u>*stay*</u> *three months in Germany.* (Singapore)
  Some of them are crying because teacher <u>*ask*</u> *them to read stories in Filipino.* (Philippines)

3 A tendency to use an *aspect* system (completed or ongoing action) rather than a *tense* system (past or future) or to use both systems side by side.
  It was during that time these people <u>*make*</u> *some arrangement with law enforcement agencies . . .* (West Africa)
  I <u>*still eat.*</u> (I am/was eating; Malaysia)

4 A tendency to extend the use of *be + verb + ing* constructions to stative verbs.

She _is knowing_ her science very well. (East Africa)
The squad _we are having_ here is good enough to beat Namibia.
(South Africa, from Kamwangamalu 2001, p. 58)

5 The formation of different phrasal and prepositional verb constructions.

Her name _cropped_ in the conversation. (East Africa)
You can _voice out_ what you are not satisfied with at the meeting.
(Singapore)
Each and every day one was well informed to _cope up_ with any
eventuality. (written English, West Africa)
The older generation finds it difficult _to do with_ young people.
(Korea, from Shim, 1999, p. 251)
Gardens _come on_ life again. (Korea, from Shim, 1999, p. 251)

In addition to these nativized norms in the usage of nouns and verbs,
a number of researchers have documented the nativization of norms
having to do with prepositions. For example, Lowenberg (2002, p. 432)
cites examples of English usage in China having to do with collocations
involving prepositions. The following is taken from an exercise in a textbook used by the Ministry of Education in the People's Republic of China:

Karaoke is very popular _____ (with, among) young people.
(_among_ is listed as the only correct answer)

Jung and Min (1999) document the tendency in Korean English to use
_at_ regardless of dimensional location, as in the following example taken
from an English Korean newspaper:

An earlier meeting _at_ Cheju set the stage for a renewed peace effort.
(Jung & Min, 1999, p. 34)

Vocabulary/idiom

As Platt et al. (1984) argue, "When a new variety of a language develops, it
does not develop in isolation but it depends on the communicative needs
of those who speak it and write it" (p. 87). Speakers of World Englishes
often need to develop a range of expressions to fulfill their communicative
needs in the particular cultural context within which they interact. There
are many expressions of "new" vocabulary in World Englishes (particularly in the area of food, garments, cultural ceremonies, and kinship
terms), including locally coined words/expressions; borrowings from
indigenous languages; and the creation of idioms.

Our following discussion is taken from Kamwangamalu (2001), where
he provides rich analysis of the dialectic relationship between the socio-

cultural context and language in the development of South African English vocabulary.

LOCALLY COINED WORDS/EXPRESSIONS

Kamwangamalu (2001) talks about kinship terms as being particularly prone to "nativization" in South African English due specific local meanings of family and relationship lexical expressions. For many South African communities, the word *sister* is used for any female, regardless of her relationship to the speaker. Speakers therefore will qualify the term *sister* with the expression "*same father same mother*", or "*womb sister*" (or "*sister of the womb*"). He provides the following examples:

> I went to see my sister, *same father same mother*.
>
> (from Chisanga, 1987, p. 53)

> My aunt Gladys, the one who is my *father's womb-sister*, older than him but younger than *Babamukuru* (old father), came first . . . The next minute he was drowned in a sea of bodies belonging to uncles, aunts and nephews; grandmothers, grandfathers and nieces; brothers and *sisters of the womb and not of the womb*. The clan had gathered to welcome its returning hero.
>
> (from Dangaremgba, 1988, p. 53)

The use of *Babamukuru* in the second excerpt, which also appears in its translated form "old father" in reference to uncle, is seen to be more affectionate than simply uncle. Another example of coined terms in reference to kinship involves those used to accommodate polygamy, including: *right-hand wife* (an intimate wife, one in whom the husband has more faith and confidence); *principal wife* (the first married wife); *candle wife* ("the one chosen to bear the heirs of the king").

The new socio-political circumstances of post-Apartheid South Africa have also given rise to new lexical innovations—for example, in the creation of the *rainbow-X* compound (Kamwangamalu, 2001). It refers either to "the coming together of people from previously racially segregated groups," or to "something that affects or benefits these people." Kamwangamalu (2001) provides the following example from the *Sunday Times*:

> Mrs van Reenen has taken her two older children . . . to the *rainbow-nation school* across the road, where she teaches Standard 2.
>
> (*Sunday Times*, July 1996, p. 54)

Other examples of compounding include *rainbow blanket*, *rainbow gathering*, *rainbow swimming pool*, and so forth.

BORROWINGS FROM INDIGENOUS LANGUAGES

The following text taken from a South African English newspaper article about adultery illustrates the use and purposes/effects of borrowings from indigenous languages (taken from Kamwangamalu, 2001):

> Away with this *lobola*. Why do they have to be so demanding for their daughters?
>
> (*The Times of Swaziland*, November 6, 1992, p. 49)

As Kamwangamalu (2001) explains, the word *lobola* loosely translates as "dowry" or "brideprice" in English. However, such translations do not capture the socio-cultural nuances of the word in the South African context:

- like in a brideprice arrangement, the groom must bring money and other property to the bride's parents;
- the payment of *lobola* officializes and legitimizes the marriage;
- if the marriage fails, the bridegroom can claim the *lobola* back; and the bride cannot remarry while the groom is alive;
- if the bridegroom dies, the bride will be inherited by a brother or other appointed relative;
- if the bride is infertile, the groom can claim one of her sisters to become his wife and bear him children.

(p. 50)

He argues that the need to maintain such socio-cultural nuances in reference to local marriage practices has thus resulted in the adoption of *lobola* into South African English.

IDIOMS

An example of the ways in which particular idioms bear the socio-cultural meanings of its local context is seen in the reference to various parts of the body to convey personal feelings in some South African idioms. This practice of "body symbolism," Kamwangamalu (2001, p. 56) argues, has its roots in the indigenous languages:

> *I wrote it down in my head.* (I made a mental note of it)
>
> (Dangarembga, 1988, p. 56)

> *Snakes started playing mini soccer in my spine.* (I became very excited)
>
> (p. 56)

Idioms in World Englishes also develop as translations from indigenous idioms (Platt, et al., 1984, p. 108; p. 110):

Shake legs (Singapore, Malaysia; from Malay "goyang kaki", meaning "to be idle")

To eat snake (Singapore; from Hokkien "chiáh chôa," meaning "to shirk duty")

And finally, idioms develop through combining elements from different languages:

Put sand in someone's gari (Nigeria; meaning "to threaten one's livelihood"—"gari" is a type of flour) (Platt et al., 1984, p. 109)

Discourse style

Several World Englishes have a more formal character than the Inner Circle Englishes: their vocabulary and grammatical structure are more complex. An example from Platt et al. (1984) is Indian English, which favors "lengthy constructions, bookish vocabulary and exaggerated forms which make even a formal style appear 'more formal' to a speaker of another variety of English" (p. 149). The following is an excerpt of a letter written to the editor of *The Telegraph*:

> Whatever manner the issues involved are analysed, one particular conclusion is inescapable. It was bhoomi puja [*worship of the earth*] performed on what is claimed to be still government property; it was organized by government officials qua government officials. And this is precisely where anguish begins to seize the mind. The multitude of its supporters and admirers look up to the Left Front government in West Bengal as the repository of secular ideals; they pin their faith on it to act as vanguard in the relentless fight against the fundamentalists and religious obscurantists.
>
> (*The Telegraph*, Calcutta, India, January 25, 2007)

Another example is that of different reactions to events (Platt et al., 1984, pp. 159–160). In West African English, the expression "*wonderful*" simply expresses the speaker's amazement, whether the event is good or bad:

A: *He died yesterday morning.*
B: *Wonderful!*

Another common discourse feature of many varieties of World Englishes is the use of undifferentiated question tags. In British English, for example, the use of question tags is formed by the use of a pronoun version of the subject after an appropriate modal auxiliary. A typical example would be, "*Mary is coming over for tea today, isn't she?*" The meaning is probably, or presumably. In contrast, undifferentiated question tags do not distinguish between different kinds of pronouns and auxiliaries, and are limited to one or two question tags only. The most common ones are *no?* and *is/isn't it?* An example from Singapore English is: "*You don't feel well, is it?*"

While some analysts like Kachru (1983) and Trudgill and Hannah (2002) merely identify this use of tags as one of the linguistic components of Indian English, perhaps a feature of grammatical simplification, Bhatt (2001) argues they have an important pragmatic role to play in the Indian English speech community. In particular, he argues that the use of undifferentiated question tags demonstrates how linguistic form (of the tag) interacts with the particular cultural ecology (the grammar of culture), in this case, the cultural constraints of politeness in India. He provides the following contrast to demonstrate:

Indian English	Standard British English
You said you'll do the job, isn't it?	*You said you'll do the job, didn't you?*
They said they will be here, isn't it?	*They said they will be here, didn't they?*

(p. 535)

By contrasting the use of question tags in Indian English with British English, he shows how the Indian form serves to "signal deference and acquiescence" (p. 535) with its tone of non-imposition and mitigation. Rather than an incorrect version of a so-called standard form, the use of undifferentiated question tags is thus an important component of particular socio-cultural relationships, expressed through language.

A final example of variation in discourse style comes from Kachru's (1986) analysis of matrimonial columns (see discussion in Bhatt, 2001). Kachru argues that the matrimonial columns reflect Asian and African sensitivity to color, caste hierarchy, regional attitudes, and family structure, resulting in the use of highly contextualized English lexical items with semantic nativization. The following is a Hindi example:

Non-Koundanya well qualified prospective bridegroom below 20 for graduate Iyengar girl, daughter for engineer. Mirugaserusham. No dosham. Average complexion. Reply with horoscope.

(p. 44)

[*Koundanya and Mirugaserusham are sub-caste names; Iyengar is a fairly high-caste surname; dosham means "flaw"—thus the girl has no flaw*]

Bhatt sees this as an example of how the "rhetorical-communicative styles of South Asian English . . . show that both the text and the context must be nativized in order to derive an interpretation that is faithful to the new situations in which World Englishes function" (p. 437)—a point we will come back to in our discussion of intelligibility.

Linguistic variation, cultural grammar and hybridization

To summarize our discussion of linguistic variation and its emphasis on cultural grammar, we bring in Bakhtin's (1981) and Bhabha's (1990) notion of "hybridization:"

> It is a mixture of two social languages within the limits of a single utterance, an encounter, within the arena of an utterance, between two different linguistic consciousnesses, separated from one another by an epoch, by social differentiation or by some other factor. Such mixing of two languages within the boundaries of a single utterance is, in the novel, an artistic device (or more accurately, a system of devices) that is deliberate. But unintentional, unconscious hybridization is one of the most important modes in the historical life of all languages.
>
> (Bakhtin, 1981, p. 358)

Through hybridity, then, there is "something different, something new and unrecognisable, a new area of negotiation of meaning and representation" (Bhabha, 1990, p. 211). For example, Bhatt's analysis of question tags could be seen as an example of hybridity (see his own discussion of this in Bhatt, 2005).

An example of such hybridity is found in African writer Achebe's (1975) discussion of his use of English in his writing. He quotes from his book *Arrow of God* (1969) to make his point. The Chief Priest is telling one of his sons why it is necessary to send him to Church:

> I want one of my sons to join these people and be my eyes there. If there is nothing in it you will come back. But if there is something then you will bring back my share. The world is like a mask, dancing. If you want to see it well, you do not stand in one place. My spirit tells me that those who do not befriend the white man today will be saying, "had we known," tomorrow.

He then contrasts this version with another that he could have used, using non-African Standard English:

> I am sending you as my representative among these people—just to be on the safe side in case the new religion develops. One has to move with the times or else one is left behind. I have a hunch that those who fail to come to terms with the white man may well regret their lack of foresight.

The first excerpt Achebe describes as being "in character," as reflecting the cultural context of its use. This illustrates what he wrote elsewhere (1966): "I feel the English language will be able to carry the weight of my African experience. But it will have to be a new English, still in communion with its ancestral home but altered to suit its new African surroundings" (p. 22)—a hybrid form.

Standard language ideology

Implicit in discussions of variation are the notion of standards, a standard language, and issues of power and identity that are built into such concepts. *Standard language* is the term generally used to refer to that variety of a language that is considered the norm. It is the variety regarded as the ideal for educational purposes, and usually used as a yardstick by which to measure other varieties. The related notion of *language standards* has to do with the language rules that inform the standard, and that are then taught in schools.

While this simple introduction may seem straightforward, definitions that have circulated in discussions about Standard English suggest it is in fact a much more contentious issue:

- A particular dialect of English, being the only non-localized dialect, of global currency without significant variation, universally accepted as the appropriate educational target in teaching English; which may be spoken with an unrestricted choice of accent. (Strevens, 1983, p. 88)
- The variety of the English language that is normally employed in writing and normally spoken by "educated" speakers of the language. It is also, of course, the variety of the language that students of English as a Foreign or Second Language (EFL/ESL) are taught when receiving formal instruction. The term *Standard English* refers to grammar and vocabulary (dialect) but not to pronunciation (accent). (Trudgill & Hannah, 2002, p. 1)
- We may define the Standard English of an English-speaking country as a minority variety (identified chiefly by its vocabulary, grammar

and orthography) which carries most prestige and is most widely understood. (Crystal, 1995, p. 110)

For Strevens (1983), there is no standardized accent associated with Standard English. Others, such as Trudgill and Hannah (2002) and Crystal (1995) associate Standard English more directly with the written form of the language, and by extension, with the language used by "educated" speakers of English. The "educated" speakers of the language are defined by McArthur (1998) as the "more or less middle-class range throughout the English-speaking world . . . essentially those who have completed their secondary-school education [and] may have gone on to college-university" (p. 117).

Guiding each of these views of what is "standard" are particular ideological assumptions. As Bhatt's (2001, 2005) work reveals, the Standard language ideology is embedded in the "sociolinguistic struggle between the center and the peripheries over practices, meanings, and identities of English"—and how particular discourses attempt to "suppress variation in their attempts to impose control (hegemony) and order (homogeny) on English language acquisition and use" (2005, p. 26). Bhatt (2001) calls these ideological assumptions "sacred cows of English" (pp. 538–541). For example, the "acquisitional" sacred cow embodies dichotomies such as *native–nonnative; standard–non-standard;* and *language–interlanguage*, all of which embody deficit notions of language variation and perpetuate a kind of "linguistic imperialism" (p. 539). Bhatt (2001) contends that "The teaching of English, with the entire framework and institutions that support it worldwide, is a critical site where the dominant ideology, Standard English, is constantly evolving and constantly bargaining with regional ideologies for power" (p. 541). Bhatt (2005) talks about an "ideology of standardization" within the "expert discourse," described as: "an ideology of standardization is recruited to delimit language by imposing ordered and reasoned patterns of correct usage through codification of form and function, and by minimizing variation in the grammatical structure while maximizing the allocation of social and linguistic roles" (p. 30). Schools, lexicographers, and grammarians, he argues, are among those who participate in the reproduction of such ideological constructs (see Trudgill & Hannah's (2002) definition of Standard English given earlier).

The challenge that World Englishes present to the Standard English ideology is thus one of plurality—that there should be different standards for different contexts of use; that the definition of each Standard English should be endonormative (determined locally) rather than exonormative (determined by outside its context of use). However, if there are different forms of Standard English, the concern of mutual intelligibility emerges. We will explore these issues in our following discussion.

Intelligibility

The fact that some speakers of English use a variety of English that is quite different from a standard variety of English has led some to argue that the use of these varieties of English will lead to a lack of intelligibility among speakers of English. It is this fear that has led to a widespread debate over standards in the use of English.

One of the early debates over standards occurred at a 1984 conference to celebrate the 50th anniversary of the British Council. At this conference, Randolph Quirk and Braj Kachru, two key figures in the growing debate over standards in international English, expressed conflicting views on the issue of standards in relation to international English. Quirk argued for the need to uphold standards in the use of English in both countries where English is spoken as a native language and in countries where English is used as a second or foreign language. He maintained that tolerance for variation in language use was educationally damaging in Anglophone countries and that "the relatively narrow range of purposes for which the non-native needs to use English . . . is arguably well catered for by a single monochrome standard form that looks as good on paper as it sounds in speech" (Quirk, 1985, p. 6). For Quirk, a common standard of use was warranted in all contexts of English language use.

Kachru (1985), on the other hand, argued that the spread of English had brought with it a need to re-examine traditional notions of codification and standardization. As he put it,

> In my view, the global diffusion of English has taken an interesting turn: the native speakers of this language seem to have lost the exclusive prerogative to control its standardization; in fact, if current statistics are any indication, they have become a minority. This socio-linguistic fact must be accepted and its implication recognized. What we need now are new paradigms and perspective for linguistic and pedagogical research and for understanding the linguistic creativity in multilingual situations across cultures.
>
> (p. 30)

Kachru maintained that allowing for a variety of linguistic norms would not lead to a lack of intelligibility among varieties of English; rather what would emerge from this situation would be an educated variety of English that would be intelligible across the many varieties of English.

The debate regarding the teaching of standards continues today with some arguing for the promotion of a monolithic model of English while others support a pluricentric model. Those like Quirk who argue for a monolithic model contend that native-speaker models should be promoted because they have been codified and have a degree of historical authority. The monolithic model is in keeping with one of the central tenets that Phillipson (1992) argues has traditionally informed English language teaching, namely, that the ideal teacher of English is a native-speaker. This perspective also lends support to the notion of the insider and outsider, the Self and the Other, since it is native-speakers who are seen as the guardians of Standard English. On the other hand, those like Kachru who support a pluricentric model of English contend that language contact necessarily leads to language change. They argue that the development of new varieties of English is a natural result of the spread of English. In many ways the debate reflects the tension between the global and the local brought about by the new social space of globalization. Whereas global space has brought exposure to English, local space has taken the language and modified it for the local context.

At the core of the debate is the question of intelligibility. Those who support a monolithic model argue that if localized standards are allowed to develop, English speakers will no longer be able to understand one another. In examining this concern, it is important to recognize that the question of intelligibility involves the extent to which two speakers understand one another rather than involving abstract features of the language. Bamgbose (1998) emphasizes this fact when he notes, "Preoccupation with intelligibility has often taken an abstract form characterized by decontextualized comparison of varieties. The point is often missed that it is people, not language codes, that understand one another, and people use the varieties they speak for specific functions" (p. 11). These considerations appear in Kachru's (1992) key questions concerning linguistic intelligibility:

- What is meant by intelligibility with reference to each linguistic level? Who is the judge for determining intelligibility in various varieties of English—the users of the varieties themselves, or the idealized native speaker?
- What parameters should be used to distinguish intelligibility between those varieties of English which are essentially regional or national (e.g., Indian English), and those varieties within a variety which have exclusively *international* functions?
- What role does a native speaker of English (and what type of native speaker) play concerning the judgment about the nonnative varieties?
- What is the relationship between intelligibility of formal (linguistic) exponents and the contextual exponents?

(pp. 64–65)

Given our focus on the cultural grammar of World Englishes, Smith's (1992) view of intelligibility as a continuum suggests a useful and nuanced approach. The underlying premise of his view is that "the greater the familiarity a speaker (native or non-native) has with a variety of English, the more likely it is that s/he will understand, and be understood by, members of that speech community" (p. 76). The significant point in this argument is that the focus of intelligibility is on the *interaction* between speaker and listener, rather than on a particular speaker or listener. That is to say, so-called native speakers are not necessarily the sole judges of what is intelligible, nor are they themselves always more intelligible than nonnative speakers. He suggests three categories of interaction in his continuum:

- *Intelligibility*: recognizing words and other sentence-level components of utterances.
- *Comprehensibility*: understanding meaning.
- *Interpretability*: understanding the intent, purpose, or "meaning behind" an utterance.

(p. 76)

Elsewhere (Smith & Christopher, 2001) he provides the example of "turn off the light"—a request made by an Australian woman to a taxi driver in Istanbul. The driver refused. At the word/sentence level, there was intelligibility. There was recognition by the driver of the elements "turn off" and "light." There was also evidence of comprehensibility: the driver and the woman both understood the sentence structure to be a speech act of request or command for a particular activity. However, the problem occurred with the level of interpretability: he did not interpret her request accurately—presumably seen as an invitation to flirt; and she did not interpret his refusal correctly—that by Turkish law, a male taxi driver must leave the car's light switched on. Smith thus regards the last level of intelligibility, interpretability, as being the most important component of communication. McKay (2002) similarly observes that in contexts of cross-cultural communication, "it is very possible that the speakers will work together to achieve interpretability" (p. 53).

The fact that many bilingual users of English acquire English in an educational context in which particular standards of use are emphasized will likely insure some unifying standards. Furthermore, unifying norms are needed if English is to serve purposes of wider communication. As Widdowson (1994) notes,

> As soon as you accept that English serves the communicative and communal needs of different communities, it follows logically that it must be diverse. An international language has to be an independent language. It does not follow logically, however, that the language will disperse into mutually unintelligible varieties. For it will naturally stabilize into standard form to the extent required to meet the needs

of the communities concerned. Thus it is clearly vital to the interests of the international community . . . that they should preserve a common standard of English in order to keep up standards of communicative effectiveness.

(p. 385)

Finally, it is worth noting with McKay (2002) that the global spread of English only naturally gives rise to many varieties, each with its own norms. However, as "many bilingual users of English acquire the language in an educational context in which particular standards of use are emphasized" (p. 53), there will likely always be some unifying norms. Thus, it is highly unlikely that Quirk's prediction of English dispersing into mutually unintelligible varieties would ever come true.

Innovations versus norms

Related to the question of Standard English and questions of intelligibility is the issue of determining when exactly an innovation can be considered a standard or norm. What Bamgbose said in 1998 remains true today: there are still questions about the status of innovations in the nativization process, about the continued use of native norms as a point of reference, and the ambivalence between recognition and acceptance of nonnative norms. There remains a constant pull between native and nonnative norms, with continued preference of native norms in determining nonnative norms. At issue is the need to determine when a particular feature of language use is indeed an innovation, and when it is simply an error. Kachru's (1992) distinction between *mistakes* and *deviations* applies to innovations as well:
  A mistake:

- may be unacceptable by a native speaker since it does not belong to the linguistic "norm" of the English language;
- it cannot be justified with reference to the socio-cultural context of a nonnative variety;
- and it is not the result of the productive processes used in an institutionalized nonnative variety of English.

A deviation:

- is different from the norm in the sense that it is the result of the new "un-English" linguistic and cultural setting in which the English is used;
- it is the result of a productive process that marks the typical variety-specific features;
- and it is systemic within a variety, and not idiosyncratic.

(p. 62)

That is to say, an innovation is an acceptable variant or deviation, whereas an error would be simply a mistake or incorrect usage. Clearly, if innovations are seen as errors, many varieties of English would never receive legitimacy, as is evident in the following statement about English in Ghana:

> English in Ghana is very ill. The cancerous tumors are countless: wrong collocation; false concord; poor spelling due to unfamiliarity with the word or to mispronunciation; inability to handle the third person singular in particular the tenses generally; wrong omission or insertion of articles; misuse of prepositions; errors arising from mother tongue interference; paucity of vocabulary, etc.
>
> (Gyasi, 1990, cited in Bamgbose, 1998, p. 2)

In chapter 4, we saw similar comments concerning Singlish in the Singapore context as well.

According to Bamgbose (1998), this tendency to see innovations as errors stems primarily from an exonormative view of language norms— that is, using the norms of so-called "native English" by which to evaluate linguistic practices. He offers an alternative form of assessment, one that takes into account also the pragmatic and communicative appropriateness of language usage. He suggests five "internal measures" of innovation that in his view determine when an innovation can be considered a norm:

> *Demographic* (How many people use the innovation?): In talking about demography, he specifies that it is the number of users of a form in the *acrolectal* variety, rather than in the mesolectal or basilectal, that is important. For example, while the vast majority of speakers of Nigerian English may use the expression, *"I cannot be able to go"*, it would likely be stigmatized as non-standard since it rarely, if at all, appears in the acrolectal variety.

> *Geographical* (How widely dispersed is it?): The greater the geographical spread of an innovation, the higher its acceptance as a standard form.

> *Authoritative* (Who uses it?): This relates to the use or approval of an innovation by writers, teachers, media practitioners, examination bodies, publishing houses, and so forth. Lowenberg (1990, in Bamgbose, 1998) notes the influence of authority on the acceptability of innovations: "norms of Standard English cannot be identified on linguistic grounds alone" since acceptance or rejection "frequently depends on attitudinal variables, particularly on the relative sociolinguistic status of the sources of an innovation" (p. 4).

Codification (Where is the usage sanctioned?): Codification refers to the innovation being put into a written form in a grammar, lexical or pronunciation dictionary, course books, or any other type of reference manual.

Acceptability (What is the attitude of users and non-users to it?): The acceptability factor, Bamgbose argues, is the ultimate test of an innovation becoming a norm. For, once accepted, an innovation is ensured a reasonable lifespan.

(pp. 3–5)

For Bamgbose (1998), codification and acceptance are the most important factors in determining if an innovation can be considered a norm—without them, he notes, innovations will continue to be labeled as errors. He also argues that the dearth of codification is the major militating factor against the emergence of endonormative standards in World Englishes. One exception is the *Macquarie Regional Asian English Dictionary*, which is the most comprehensive codification of Asian Englishes to date.

The importance of codification in legitimizing innovations can be seen in the all too frequent divergence between actual language use and the norms sanctioned by examining bodies. Bamgbose (1998, pp. 4–5) gives examples of common features of West African English that are deemed errors by West African examiners: *furnitures, equipments, defreeze* (defrost), *tight friend* (close friend), *discuss about* (discuss). Lowenberg (2002, p. 434) similarly provides rich examples of how tests such as the Test of English for International Communication (TOEIC) consider certain constructions ungrammatical when they are in fact nativized structures in some contexts. For example, "His proposal met with a lot of resistances" used by the English Testing Service is deemed ungrammatical, when they actually parallel structures seen in Korean and British English.

Finally, as further demonstration of the power of codification in the acceptance of innovations, some innovations originating in Outer/Expanding Circle contexts have become accepted in Inner Circle contexts. For example, the Singaporean word "kiasu," meaning "afraid to lose out to others or not to lose face", is now an entry in the Oxford English Dictionary. At the same time, occasionally innovations are accepted without codification, such as the use of "discuss about" mentioned earlier, which is now seen in British English; however, although it is widely used, it has not been codified (Jenkins, discussed by Bragg, 2003, pp. 309–310).

Summary

In this chapter, we explored the issues of standards in reference to World Englishes. We began with a discussion of the stratification of English to highlight the variation *within* individual World Englishes, and then moved on to examine variation *between* World Englishes. Our focus was on the socio-cultural embeddedness of language, and how language variation needs to be seen within the contexts of its use. We then moved on to a discussion of the Standard English ideology, and explored some of the discursive features of this ideology. Finally, we considered issues of intelligibility, and sought to answer the question of when an innovation is considered a norm. The implications of language variation and the plurality of norms for the teaching of international English is significant, as we have seen in Lowenberg's (2002) and Bamgbose's (1998) discussions about the divergence between actual language use and language norms expected on exams. Acknowledging language variation, understanding the processes of language variation, and accepting a pluralistic model of English language norms are thus key to effective EIL pedagogy.

In the next chapter, we will examine how interactional sociolinguistics can provide further insight into the use of English as an international language

References

Achebe, C. (1966). *Things fall apart*. London: Heinemann.

Achebe, C. (1975). *Morning yet on creation day*. New York: Anchor.

Alsagoff, L. (2007). Singlish. In V. Vaish, S. Gopinathan, & Y. Liu (Eds.), *Language, capital, culture* (pp. 37–58). Rotterdam: Sense Publishers.

Bakhtin, M. M. (1981). *The dialogic imagination: Four essays* (M. Holquist, Editor, C. Emerson & M. Holquist, Trans.). Austin and London: University of Texas Press.

Bamgbose, A. (1992). Standard Nigerian English: Issues of identification. In B. B. Kachru (Ed.), *The other tongue* (pp. 148–161). Chicago: University of Illinois Press.

Bamgbose, A. (1998). Torn between the norms: Innovations in World Englishes. *World Englishes, 17*(1), 1–14.

Bhabha, H. K. (1990). Interview with Homi Bhabha. In J. Rutherford (Ed.), *Identity: community, culture, difference* (pp. 207–221). London: Lawrence & Wishart.

Bhatt, R. M. (2001). World Englishes. *Annual Review of Anthropology, 30,* 527–550.

Bhatt, R. M. (2005). Expert discourses, local practices, and hybridity: The case of Indian Englishes. In A. S. Canagarajah (Ed.), *Reclaiming the local in language policy and practice* (pp. 25–54). Mahwah, NJ and London: Lawrence Erlbaum Associates, Publishers.

Bickerton, D. (1975). *Dynamics of a creole system*. Cambridge: Cambridge University Press.

Bragg, M. (2003). *The adventure of English: 500AD to 2000—The biography of a language*. London: Hodder & Stoughton.

Brutt-Griffler, J. (2002). *World English: A study of its development.* Clevedon: Multilingual Matters.

Crystal, D. (1995). *The Cambridge encyclopedia of the English language.* Cambridge: Cambridge University Press.

D'souza, J. (1988). Interactional strategies in South Asian languages: Their implications for teaching English internationally. *World Englishes, 7*(2), 159–171.

Gupta, A. (1994). *The step-tongue: Children's English in Singapore.* Clevedon: Multilingual Matters.

Jenkins, J. (2003). *World Englishes: A resource book for students.* London and New York: Routledge.

Jung, K. & Min, J. (1999). Some lexio-grammatical features of Korean English newspapers. *World Englishes, 18*(1), 23–37.

Kachru, B. B. (1983). *The Indianization of English: The English language in India.* New York: Oxford University Press.

Kachru, B. B. (1985). Standards, codification and sociolinguistic realism: The English language in the Outer Circle. In R. Quirk & H. Widdowson (Eds.), *English in the world: Teaching and learning the language and literatures* (pp. 11–30). Cambridge: Cambridge University Press.

Kachru, B. B. (1986). *The alchemy of English: The spread, functions and models of non-native Englishes.* London: Pergamon.

Kachru, B. B. (1992). Models for non-native Englishes. In B. B. Kachru (Ed.), *The other tongue: English across cultures. Second edition* (pp. 48–74). Urbana and Chicago: University of Illinois Press.

Kamwangamalu, N. M. (2001). Reincarnations of English: A case from South Africa. In E. Thumboo (Ed.), *The three circles of English* (pp. 45–66). Singapore: UniPress.

Lowenberg, P. (2002). Assessing English proficiency in the Expanding Circle. *World Englishes, 21*(3), 431–435.

McArthur, T. (1998). *The English languages.* Cambridge: Cambridge University Press.

McKay, S. L. (2002). *Teaching English as an international language: Rethinking goals and approaches.* Oxford: Oxford University Press.

Pakir, A. (1991). The range and depth of English-knowing bilinguals in Singapore. *World Englishes, 10*(2), 167–179.

Phillipson, R. (1992). *Linguistic imperialism.* Oxford: Oxford University Press.

Platt, J. & Weber, H. (1980). *English in Singapore and Malaysia: Status, features, functions.* Kuala Lumpur: Oxford University Press.

Platt, J., Weber, H., & Ho, M. L. (1984). *The New Englishes.* London: Routledge and Kegan Paul.

Quirk, R. (1985). The English language in a global context. In R. Quirk & H. Widdowson (Eds.), *English in the world: Teaching and learning the language and literatures* (pp. 1–6). Cambridge: Cambridge University Press.

Shim, R. (1999). Codified Korean English: Process, characteristics and consequence. *World Englishes, 18*(2), 247–258.

Smith, L. E. (1992). Spread of English and issues of intelligibility. In B. B. Kachru (Ed.), *The other tongue: English across cultures. Second edition* (pp. 75–90). Urbana and Chicago: University of Illinois Press.

Smith, L. E. & Christopher, E. M. (2001). Why can't they understand me when I speak English so clearly? In E. Thumboo (Ed.), *The three circles of English* (pp. 91–100). Singapore: UniPress.

Strevens, P. (1983). What is "standard English"? In L. Smith (Ed.), *Readings in English as an international language* (pp. 87–93). Oxford: Pergamon Press.

Trudgill, P. & Hannah, J. (2002). *International English. Fourth edition.* London: Arnold.

Widdowson, H. (1994). The ownership of English. *TESOL Quarterly, 28*, 377–388.

Chapter 6

Interactional sociolinguistics

In this chapter we examine how interactional sociolinguistics can provide insight into the use of English in an era of globalization. The chapter begins with an overview of the central figures and tenets of interactional sociolinguistics. Using this background, we examine existing research regarding EIL interactions. Specifically, we explore the ways in which interactional sociolinguistics has been beneficial in providing insight on:

- English as a lingua franca (ELF) interactions;
- the code-switching behavior of bilingual users of English; and
- bilingual users' attitudes toward code-switching.

In each section we will consider the manner in which the topic has relevancy for EIL pedagogy.

Defining interactional sociolinguistics

Historical development

Interactional sociolinguistics developed out of linguistics, sociology, and anthropology. Current interest in interactional sociolinguistics began largely as a reaction to Chomsky's (1957) view of language as a fixed universal property of the human mind that exists devoid of context. A major challenge to Chomsky's view of language was the work of Hymes (1974), a linguistic anthropologist, who argued that a description of language must take into account the social knowledge that individuals bring to linguistic interactions. Hymes argued that researchers interested in describing how language is used need to consider the context in which particular interactions take place and how this context affects the interaction. Specifically, Hymes (1972) maintained that the following four questions must be raised in analyzing language use.

1   Whether (and to what degree) something is formally *possible*.
2   Whether (and to what degree) something is *feasible* in virtue of the means of implementation available.
3   Whether (and to what degree) something is *appropriate* (adequate, happy, successful) in relation to a context in which it is used and evaluated.
4   Whether (and to what degree) something is in fact done, actually *performed*, and what its doing entails.

[emphasis in original] (p. 281)

It is item numbers three and four that are critical to the development of the field of interactional sociolinguistics. For the first time linguists were asked to consider whether or not a particular instance of language use was appropriate in relation to a specific context. In addition, linguists were asked to examine what was being accomplished by a particular use of language.

Another linguist who contributed to the development of interactional sociolinguistics is John Gumperz. In 1971 Gumperz published a collection of essays in which he reported on his work with various social and cultural groups as, for example, his work in India on regional and social language differences and on Hindi–Punjabi code-switching. His work reinforced a commonly held assumption in social and cultural anthropology, namely, that the meaning and use of language are socially and culturally relative. In emphasizing this idea, Gumperz analyzed spoken interactions in terms of *contextualization cues* or aspects of language and behavior that relate what is said to the background knowledge the speaker has or what Gumperz calls *contextual presuppositions*. These conceptual presuppositions allow the listener to make *situated inferences* about what the speaker intends to convey. Schiffrin (1996), using data from Gumperz's work with African–Americans, illustrates how these concepts operate in an instance of classroom interaction.

Teacher: James, what does this word say?
James: I don't know.
Teacher: Well, if you don't want to try, someone else will. Freddy?
Freddy: Is that a p or a b?
Teacher: (*encouragingly*) It's a p.
Freddy: Pen.

(Gumperz, 1982, p. 147, as cited in Schiffrin, 1996, p. 313)

The teacher's response ("Well if you don't want to try, someone else will") suggests that the teacher interprets James' comment ("I don't know") to mean that he does not know the answer and does not wish to try to answer. James, however, made this statement with a rising intonation, which, according to Gumperz, within the African–American community is understood to mean, "I need some encouragement." Because the teacher was not from the African–American community she did not make use of this contextualization cue (the rising intonation) to make situated inferences about what James meant by the comment, "I don't know." By analyzing the misunderstandings that occur in cross-cultural encounters such as the one shown above, Gumperz emphasized the idea that context (both linguistic and social) is critical to the interpretation of meaning.

The work of Erving Goffman also contributed to the development of interactional sociolinguistics. Goffman's major contribution to the development of pragmatics is his discussion of the relationship between the self (the sense of who we are) and the society at the microlevel of daily interactions and activities. Goffman contended that by choosing to speak in a certain way, individuals express their sense of who they are and who they believe others are. In this way, our daily interactions play a crucial role in "creating and maintaining the roles we fill, the statuses we occupy (our social identities), and the personalities we feel ourselves and others to have (our personal identities)" (Schiffrin, 1996, p. 309). Goffman (1967) argued that one way to view the self is through the concept of *face* or "the positive social value a person effectively claims for himself by the line others assume he has taken during a particular contact" (p. 5). For Goffman, social interactions are important in creating and maintaining both self (who we are) and face (who others take us to be).

Interactional sociolinguistics versus conversation analysis

The majority of L2 discourse analysis studies typically employ one of two qualitative research methodologies: *interactional sociolinguistics* (sometimes termed *the ethnography of communication*) or *conversation analysis* (CA). Conversation analysis involves an examination of naturally occurring talk in order to determine what is being accomplished for the speakers involved. For those doing CA and "trying to understand a bit of talk, the key question about any of its aspects is—*why that now?* . . . What is getting done by virtue of that bit of conduct, done that way, in just that place?" (Schegloff et al., 2002, p. 5).

In terms of methodology, conversation analysts generally adhere to the following principles:

1 using authentic, recorded data which are carefully transcribed;
2 using "unmotivated looking" rather than pre-stated research questions;
3 employing the "turn" as the unit of analysis;
4 analyzing single cases, deviant cases, and collections thereof;

5   disregarding ethnographic and demographic particulars of the context and participants;
6   eschewing the coding and quantification of data.

(Lazaraton, 2002, pp. 37–38)

Interactional sociolinguists adhere to all of these principles except item number five, that is, the disregarding of ethnographic and demographic particulars of the context and the participants. For interactional socio-linguists, it is essential that the social and cultural context of the interaction be considered in reaching an interpretation of a particular interaction. Interactional sociolinguists are also concerned with getting an *emic* or insider interpretation of an interaction. Because of this, interactional sociolinguists might interview the participants of an interaction regarding their understanding of what occurred in a particular interaction.

The most significant difference, however, between these two traditions is the target speakers that are involved. Conversation analysts generally focus on interactions between native speakers of a language. By doing so, they posit particular maxims that apply to all interactions. One of the most widely accepted set of maxims is Grice's (1975) Conversational Maxims. Grice assumed that speakers share certain rules or conventions that underlie their conversations. For Grice, four central conversational rules shared by native speakers are the following.

Quantity: Make your contribution as informative as is required (for the current purpose of the exchange).
Do not make your contribution more informative than is required.
Quality: Do not say what you believe to be false.
Do not say that for which you lack adequate evidence.
Relation: Be relevant.
Manner: Avoid obscurity of expression.
Avoid ambiguity.
Be brief (avoid unnecessary prolixity).
Be orderly.

(p. 45)

Grice contends that when native speakers blatantly fail to observe these maxims, they want the speaker to consider meanings other than what was said. For example, a speaker might choose to ignore the maxim of rela-tion if they wish to change the topic of conversation. What is important for our purposes, as we shall see in the section on English as a lingua franca interactions, is that there may be an entirely different set of maxims in operation when speakers do not share the same culture and have gaps in their proficiency in English. Because conversational analysis has typically focused on native speaker interactions, it has not looked at L2–L2 and L1–L2 interactions in any depth.

Methodology

In order to be able to evaluate and interpret the findings of conversation analysis and interactional sociolinguistics studies, we believe it is important to briefly consider the methodology of these disciplines.

Transcriptions

For both conversation analysts and interactional sociolinguists, the research process begins by selecting natural interactions and recording and transcribing these interactions. Whereas it may appear that transcribing is a very simple process of writing down what is said, ten Have (1999) argues that a transcription is best seen as a "*translation*, made for various practical purposes, of the actually produced *speech* into a version of the standardized *language* of that particular community, with some selective indication of the actual speech production" [emphasis in original] (p. 76). Because spoken language conveys a good deal of meaning through intonation, pauses, overlaps and so on, which cannot be fully captured in the written word, transcripts cannot be taken as equal to the recordings of spoken language. For this reason, transcripts are not considered as the data of the analysis; rather the recording itself is what the researcher must consider.

In an attempt to capture some of the features of spoken interaction, transcriptionists rely on coding systems that symbolize several features of spoken interaction. The following are some commonly used transcription symbols (adapted from Atkinson & Heritage, 1984; ten Have, 1999).

SEQUENCING

[A left bracket indicates the beginning of an overlap in speech.
]   A right bracket indicates the end of an overlap in speech.
=   An equal sign at the end of one line and an equal sign at the beginning of another indicates that there is no gap between the lines. This is called *latching*.

TIMED INTERVALS

(.)   A period in parenthesis indicates a micropause, that is, a pause of less than 0.2 seconds.
(0.0)   Numbers in parentheses indicate the length of a pause by tenths of a second.

CHARACTERISTICS OF SPEECH PRODUCTION

Word   Underlining indicates some form of stress from pitch or loudness.
:   A colon indicates a lengthened sound or syllable. More colons indicate a more prolonged sound.
-        A dash indicates a cutoff, usually a glottal stop.
.   A period indicates falling intonation.
,   A comma indicates continuing intonation.
?   A question mark indicates a rising intonation.
.hhh   This symbol indicates inhalation.
hhh   This symbol indicates exhalation.

TRANSCRIBER'S DOUBTS AND COMMENTS

()   Empty parentheses indicate the transcriber's inability to hear what was said.
(())   Double parentheses indicate the transcriber's description of details of the scene.

Data analysis

Once recordings are transcribed, both conversation analysts and interactional sociolinguists begin the task of analyzing the data by searching for patterns and explaining the logic of the interaction. In order to accomplish this, the researcher starts with a process of "unmotivated looking," which entails noticing what may at first seem unremarkable features of the interaction. The idea is to approach the data not with any preconceived ideas of what the data are about but rather with an open mind. Starting with an open mind, researchers typically do the following.

- First, a sequence of the interaction is selected for analysis.
- Next, the researcher characterizes the actions in the sequence on a turn-by-turn basis by considering what the participants are doing in each turn. In order to accomplish this task, the researcher considers "how the timing and taking of turns provide for certain understandings of the actions and matters being talked about" (ten Have, 1999, p. 106).
- Finally, the researcher, at least in the case of interactional sociolinguists, considers how the manner in which the actions were accomplished reflects certain identities, roles, and relationships for the participants.

In the following discussion, we examine how an analysis of interactions between L2 speakers of English has provided insight into how bilinguals use English for both international and intranational purposes.

English as a lingua franca interaction

Research findings

Recently a good deal of attention has been focused on an analysis of interactions between L2 speakers of English, termed *English as a lingua franca* (ELF) talk. Firth (1996) provided one of the earliest definitions of ELF, stating that ELF interactions are those in which English is used as "a 'contact language' between persons who share neither a common native tongue nor a common (national) culture, and for whom English is the chosen *foreign* language of communication" [emphasis in original] (p. 240). Such interactions occur frequently in Expanding Circle countries where English is used for business, political, academic and travel purposes. This type of interaction can also occur in Inner Circle countries where international students use English as their contact language.

Pragmatic features

Some of the current research on ELF has focused on identifying the pragmatic features of ELF interactions, as was done in Firth's (1996) seminal article on ELF. One of the purposes of Firth's paper was to question the application of conversational analysis (CA), originally designed to analyze monolingual talk, to ELF interactions. Firth argued that although CA does provide a basic methodology for describing "in detailed ways how lingua franca interactions are sequentially and thus socially constructed, consideration of the data type itself allows us to cast new light on CA's methods and assumptions" (p. 240). One of the outcomes of his paper was to delineate conversational principles that appear to be unique to ELF interactions.

Firth's data involved a collection of telephone calls from two Danish international trading companies involving Danish export managers and their international clients. As Firth points out, one of the major advantages of analyzing such discourse from a CA perspective rather than as "foreigner talk," "interlanguage talk," or "learner interaction" perspective is that the participant is viewed as "a *language user* whose real-world interactions are deserving of unprejudiced *description* rather . . . than as a person conceived *a priori* to be the possessor of incomplete or deficient communicative competence, putatively striving for the 'target' competence of an idealized 'native speaker' " [emphasis in original] (p. 241). Firth contends that an unprejudiced description of ELF interactions clearly demonstrates that "lingua franca talk is not only meaningful, it is also '*normal*' and, indeed, '*ordinary*' " [emphasis in original] (p. 242). The following excerpt illustrates several common features of ELF interactions.

(1)
```
 1  H  fine than(k) you (.) you know now the summer time had-
       t-come to D'nmark
 2     as well (.) hh:uh ((laugh))=
 3  G  =((laughing)) huh hh:eh heh heh heh:.hh
 4  H  so for:: the:- us here in Denmark it's hot (.) it's uh twenty five
       degree, (.) .hh
 5     but for y[ou it will be-
 6  G           [ya:h,
 7  H  it would be ↑ cold (.) I think
 8  G  no, here in this pwu:h forty- forty two
 9  H  yes?
10     (1.0)
11  H  [[well
12  G  [[yes
13     (1.0)
14  H  well I prefer twendy five. (.) it's better to me
15     (0.9)
16  G  yeah
```
(p. 242)

To begin, the interaction includes grammatical errors, unidiomatic clause constructions and pronunciation variants. But more significantly is the apparent misunderstanding that occurs in lines 4–9 when it appears that G has failed to understand that H is using *cold* in a comparative sense with the temperature in Denmark. What is remarkable is that the conversation continues in an orderly way with no recognition of the misunderstanding. Firth argues that one common phenomenon of ELF talk is the "let it pass" principle in which participants appear to determine that during a particular interaction, a misunderstanding is "non-fatal" so is allowed to pass. The problem, however, is that from the analyst's point of view, it is unclear whether or not the problem was missed by the participants or whether it was understood and allowed to pass.

Whereas the let-it-pass principle is evident in some ELF interactions, on other occasions, when mutual understanding is deemed essential, misunderstandings are not allowed to pass, as is evident in the following interaction.

(2)
1 B . . . so I told him <u>not</u> to u::h send the:: <u>cheese</u> after the- (.) the
    <u>blow</u>ing (.) in
2   the ↑ <u>cus</u>toms
3   (0.4)
4   we don't <u>want</u> the order after the cheese is u::h (.) <u>blow</u>ing.
5 H <u>I</u> see, yes.
6 B so I don't know <u>what</u> we can uh do with the order <u>now</u>. (.)
    What do <u>you</u>
7   think we should uh do with this is all ↑<u>blo:w</u>ing Mister Hansen
8   (0.5)
9 H I'm not uh (0.7) <u>blow</u>ing uh what uh, <u>what</u> is this u::h too <u>big</u>
    or what?
10 (0.2)
11 B <u>no</u> the cheese is ↑<u>bad</u> Mister Hansen
12 (0.4)
13 it is like (.) <u>fermen</u>ting in the customs' cool <u>rooms</u>
14 H ah it's gone <u>off</u>↑.
15 B yes it's <u>gone</u> off↓
16 H we::ll you know you don't have to uh do uh <u>any</u>thing because
    it's not . . .
    ((turn continues))
                                                    (p. 244)

When in lines 6–7 B asks H a direct question regarding the blowing of the
cheese, H is compelled to display his unfamiliarity with the term *blowing*.
Because of a need for mutual understanding, the let-it-pass principle is
not adequate.

Firth's data also showed that on some occasions participants formally
recognize their lack of competence in the language, sometimes as a means
of achieving comity, as is evident in the following excerpt.

(7)
1 L ((Hungarian: name of company))
2   (0.4)
3 H yes he ↑<u>llo</u>: this is <u>Hanne</u> from ↑CellPhone
4   (0.2)
5 L oh↓ ↑hello [how <u>are</u> you?]
6 H   [h e: ↓<u>ll</u> o::]
7   (0.2)
8 H ↑fine↓ thank you an <u>you</u>::↓
9 L .hh oh <u>fine</u> thank ↓you
10 H how are sales going in ↑<u>Bu</u>dapest
11 (0.3)

```
12  L  oh (.) ↑sorry↑
13     (0.2)
14  H  how are sales going in ↑Budapest=
15  L  =o:h I think now its- its a little bit ↑middle h(h)h. hh. middle
       power hu(h)
16     hu(h)h [h(h)u(h)
17  H         [(h)o:k(h)a(h)y::↓
18  L  it's not- it's not so ↑ni::ce
19     (0.2)
20  L  .hh=
21  H  =so [why's that
22  L      [but it's going hh. h(h)hu(h)
23  H  okay:
```
(p. 254)

In lines 15–16, L laughs at his own marked usage of *a little bit middle ...
power* which displays his recognition of his own marked usage. This
invites H to do the same and creates a feeling of camaraderie.

For Firth (1996), one of the most significant insights provided by his
analysis is that although lingua franca interactions are linguistically
marked, "the parties nevertheless *do interactional work* to imbue the talk
with orderly and 'normal' characteristics" [emphasis in original] (p. 256).

Subsequent research on ELF has yielded additional findings on the
pragmatic characteristics of ELF interactions. House (2003), for
example, studied the interactions of international students at the
University of Hamburg in Germany. The students were asked to interact
with one another as they expressed their opinions on a reading text
discussing the role of English as a lingua franca. House noted several
common features of these exchanges. First, there was a lack of discourse
markers like *well* or *I think* when students started or completed a new
turn or opportunity to speak. The most common feature of turn-taking
was what House terms *represents*, that is, a repetition of the previous
speaker's comments, as shown in the exchange below.

Mauri: Yes but the grammar is quite differ[ent very different]
Wei: [it is very different]
Mauri: between Chinese and Japanese.
(House, 2003, p. 145)

House points out that using these repetitions may be one strategy the
students used to make the processing of English easier. In addition, it
signals acceptance and understanding of the previous speaker's statement.

A second feature in many of these exchanges was a high use of starting
a turn with conjunctions like *and* and *but* rather than more common

items like *yes, well,* or *I see.* Also, when speakers did disagree, they tended not to use any phrases to soften the disagreement such as "I hate to disagree with you but. . . ." Rather they used raw negation, rejection and disagreement, instead of face-saving strategies. Fourth, the participants often took little account of their interlocutors' expectations, violating turn transition points. This is evident in the following interaction when Joy does not answer Mauri's question but proceeds to make her own comment on the use of English.

Mauri: But don't you agree that all people of the world that they should speak English?

Joy: I would like to know erm what is English so important for the people in the globe.

(House, 2003, p. 146)

Meierkord's (2000) work highlighted additional aspects of the pragmatic features of ELF interactions. Based on her analysis of conversations of overseas students in Great Britain, collected in a student hall of residence, Meierkord (2000) delineates the following characteristics of ELF conversations.

- Pauses often occur between conversational phrases, especially at the end of a conversation to make the transition from one phase of the conversation to the other.
- Participants prefer to discuss safe topics like talking about the meals and life in the hostel rather than more controversial and complex topics.
- Participants tend to keep the topics very short and to deal with them rather superficially.
- Participants display frequent and long pauses both within and between turns.
- The participants make considerable use of politeness phenomena such as routine formulae in openings and closings, back-channels, and other gambits. Most of their routines, however, were restricted to common phrases like "How are you?" and "Bye."

Meierkord (2000) points out two possible explanations for these characteristics. The first is that they reflect the participants' own gaps in English proficiency. For example, the choice of safe topics could be interpreted as a reduction strategy employed because of a lack of vocabulary for dealing with more complex philosophical or political themes. On the other hand, it could be explained as being due to the participants' insecurity regarding the acceptability of the topics they introduce. Clearly both interpretations are possible depending on the proficiency and intention of the participants, leading Meirkord to argue for a differentiated interpretation of interactional data "which takes into account both the intercultural situations as well as the fact that speakers need to be regarded as learners of the language they use."

Summarizing the findings of existing data on ELF interactions, Seidlhofer (2004) provides the following generalizations regarding the pragmatics of ELF.

- Misunderstandings are not frequent in ELF interactions; when they do occur, they tend to be resolved either by topic change or, less often, by overt negotiation using communication strategies such as rephrasing and repetition.
- Interference from L1 interactional norms is very rare—a kind of suspension of expectations regarding norms seems to be in operation.
- As long as a certain threshold of understanding is obtained, interlocutors seem to adopt what Firth (1996) has termed the "let-it-pass principle," which gives the impression of ELF talk being overtly consensus-oriented, cooperative and mutually supportive, and thus fairly robust.

(p. 218)

In reaching overall generalizations regarding ELF interactions, it is essential to fully define the contextual features of the exchange. This should include the demographics of the participants, including the speakers' level of English language proficiency, as well as the social context and purpose of the interaction. This information is necessary for two reasons. First, an understanding of the language proficiency of the speakers allows the researcher to determine if the features delineated are typical of proficient bilingual users of English or if they are rather a feature of learner discourse. Second, because social context is typically used by speakers in making a choice as to what to say and how to say it, it is important that such background information be provided to correctly interpret the findings, as was evident from the fact that the "let-it-pass" principle seems to be put aside when speakers believe that a clarification of terms is warranted. The advantage of approaching EFL discourse from an interactional sociolinguistics perspective is that interactional sociolinguists fully recognize the importance of context in understanding discourse.

Grammatical features

Current work is also underway to identify the grammatical and phonological features of ELF interactions. Although our discussion of these features could have been dealt with in chapter 5 in relation to standards, we decided to include them here to provide a comprehensive coverage of ELF interactions. In addition, frequently it is the grammatical and phonological features of ELF that trigger the specific pragmatic features of ELF interactions. Significant contributions to the endeavor to identify the grammatical features of ELF are under way through the compilation of the Vienna–Oxford International Corpus of English (VOICE) now in progress at the University of Vienna under the supervision of Siedlhofer. The corpus includes face-to-face interactions among fairly fluent speakers of English from a wide range of first language backgrounds in a variety of settings in which participants have various roles and relationships. At this point, an initial data analysis has highlighted particular grammatical items which, though emphasized in language classrooms, do not appear to cause problems in communicative success. These include:

- dropping the third person present tense -*s*;
- confusing the relative pronouns *who* and *which*;
- omitting the definite and indefinite articles where they are obligatory in ENL [English as a native language], and inserting them where they do not occur in ENL;
- failing to use correct tag questions (e.g., *isn't it?* or *no?* instead of *shouldn't they?*);
- inserting redundant prepositions, as in *We have to study about . . .*;
- overusing certain verbs of high semantic generality, such as *do, have, make, put, take*;
- replacing infinitive constructions with *that* clauses, as in *I want that*;
- overdoing explicitness (e.g., *black color* rather than just *black*).

(Seidlhofer, 2004, p. 220)

It is important to note that many of the terms used in this description (e.g., *confusing, omitting, failing, overusing*), whether or not intentionally used by the author, suggest that the variety is being compared to "standard" English used by "native speakers" rather than being considered as a variety in its own right.

Phonological features

Finally, research on ELF interactions has also led to the identification of the phonological features of ELF interactions. Jenkins (2000), in her work on the phonology of English as an International Language, analyzed the interactions of six learners of English—two Japanese, three Swiss–German and one Swiss–French—all at the upper-intermediate to low-advanced level who were recorded as they practiced for the Cambridge Certificate in Advanced English speaking examinations. Some learners of other L2 backgrounds who were not engaged in examination practices were also included in the data. Some of these interactions were between interlocutors with the same L1, others were between speakers of different L1s. Using this data, Jenkins identified 40 occasions where there was a breakdown in communication due to pronunciation, lexis, grammar, world knowledge or ambiguity. All of the breakdowns in the data occurred between speakers of different L1 backgrounds. In addition, the vast majority of breakdowns (27) were due to pronunciation problems, with another eight due to lexis. The data also showed that occasionally the speakers used top-down, context-based strategies to resolve difficulties.

Based on her investigation, Jenkins (2000) delineates what she terms a phonological Lingua Franca Core, that is, phonological features that appear to be most crucial for intelligibility among L2 speakers of English. Based on her data, the central features of this core appear to be the following

1   Most consonant sounds.
2   Appropriate consonant cluster simplification.
3   Vowel length distinction.
4   Nuclear stress.

(Jenkins, 2000, p. 132)

She argues that since these features have the greatest potential for causing breakdowns in communication between speakers of different L1 backgrounds, the pedagogical focus in EIL classrooms should be on the production of most consonant sounds, initial consonant clusters, vowel length and nuclear stress. Less attention needs to be given to word stress, rhythm, and features of connected speech. What then do findings on the pragmatic, grammatical and phonological features of ELF interactions suggest for EIL pedagogy?

Implications for EIL pedagogy

The delineation of key features of ELF interactions has resulted in a good deal of consensus regarding what the pragmatic goals of an EIL curriculum should entail. Among these goals are the following.

1   Explicit attention should be given to introducing and practicing repair strategies, such as asking for clarification and repetition, rephrasing, and allowing wait time.
2   A variety of conversational gambits or routines should be introduced and practiced, including such items as expressing agreement and disagreement, managing turn-taking, and taking leave.
3   The curriculum should seek to promote students' understanding of how pragmatic norms can differ cross-culturally.
4   Students should be free to express their own pragmatic norms but to

recognize that, to the extent these standards differ from the norms expected by their listener, there may be cross-cultural misunderstandings.

In her discussion on pragmatic competence in ELF, House (2003) argues that since ELF research suggests that the participants belong to a rather vague but existing community of ELF speakers, in which negotiation of meaning is paramount, it is inappropriate to teach the pragmatic norms of an Inner Circle country. Rather the curriculum should "focus on the learners' need to be flexibly competent in international communication through the medium of the English language in as broad a spectrum of topics, themes, and purposes as possible" (p. 149).

Whereas the delineation of pragmatic goals for ELF interactions has raised little controversy, this is not the case with regard to the grammatical goals of an ELF curriculum and to a lesser degree to phonological goals. Many agree that in terms of phonological emphasis, ELF classrooms should give primary attention to the Lingua Franca core delineated by Jenkins. Prodromou (2006), for example, points out the difficulty of attaining native-like pronunciation, and thus believes it is reasonable to focus primarily on those phonological features that can impede communication. In a like manner, Prodromou (2006) states that once it is clear which grammatical items do not impede comprehension, some educators may conclude these features need not be addressed in the English classroom. In terms of Seidlhofer's (2004) findings on the grammatical features of ELF interactions, this would suggest that ELF classes need not focus on items like the deletion of the third person singular -s or the distinction between *who* and *which*. It is important to note, however, that Seidlhofer (2006) herself makes no claim as to the pedagogical implications of her work. As she says,

> I should also like to emphasize that I have never made any general pronouncements as to what should be taught and what shouldn't be—this is a complex pedagogic matter which will have to be decided by teachers for their particular contexts and their particular learners ... When doing empirical research into ELF I am doing this as a descriptive linguist, and it is not my task, and indeed impossible, to pre-empt any local pedagogic decisions.

(p. 44)

Nevertheless, some have assumed that her findings should be used as a basis for deciding what should be taught in a grammar classroom, with ELF features rather than Standard English as the target. Some, however, take issue with this stance. Timmis (2002), for example, contends that many learners want to attain native-like grammatical proficiency and so it would be inappropriate not to teach the norms of a standard variety of English. He bases this conclusion on a survey he undertook of 400 students and 180 teachers on their pronunciation and grammatical goals. In terms of pronunciation, both students and teachers tended to want to attain native-like pronunciation. This tendency, however, was less prevalent among students from South Africa, Pakistan and India, suggesting that pronunciation goals may be context specific. In reference to grammatical goals, once again students and teachers preferred attaining native-speaker norms. Based on his survey results, Timmis argues that "while it is clearly inappropriate to foist native-speaker norms on students who neither want nor need them, it is scarcely more appropriate to offer students a target which does not meet their aspirations" (p. 249).

Kuo (2006) also argues against not teaching native-speaker grammatical standards, pointing out that whereas English serves an important role in functional international interactions, English also is "the language for international, and in fact intra-national competition" (p. 219). For many learners of English, English is being learned as an important school subject to attain academic and professional goals. As such, learners need access to forms that will be used to determine their proficiency in English. Kuo argues that it is "because English is now used extensively for international and intercultural purposes that in order to ease or smooth the flow of conversation, to reduce the listener's burden of processing information, and to satisfy learners' needs that stretch beyond merely international intelligibility, L2 learners should be allowed, if not encouraged, to follow a native-speaker phonological or grammatical model" (p. 220).

The debate over grammatical standards in the teaching of ELF illustrates the complexity of determining grammatical norms for an ELF curriculum. In the case of the ELF debate it is essential to distinguish several central issues in the debate. The first issue is one of learners' goals and needs. For some bilingual users of English, English will be used mainly for functional transactions such as placing an order in a restaurant or clarifying a travel arrangement. For other bilingual users of English, however, English will play an important role in their immediate and long-term academic and professional goals. A well-designed ELF curriculum must address these differences in goals. Second, it is helpful to separate phonological and grammatical goals. Although there is growing consensus that native-like pronunciation is rarely achieved by most bilingual users of English nor desired by many of them, this is not the case for grammatical norms. Many bilingual users of English wish to achieve native-like grammatical proficiency in order to attain personal goals. This fact should also inform the design of an ELF curriculum. Finally, in highlighting the features that emerge from a corpus of ELF interactions, it is critical that the participants' level of proficiency and communicative goals be clearly delineated so that the corpus in question can be taken as representative of a particular type of bilingual user of English.

Approaches to code-switching

Definition

Another prominent concern of interactional sociolinguistics that has important implications for EIL pedagogy is the investigation of code-switching. Code-switching, as we will use the term, is the alternation of linguistic codes in the same conversation undertaken by proficient bilinguals. Myers-Scotton (1993) distinguishes the codes involved in code-switching, terming one the matrix language and the other the embedded language or languages. The language which sets the grammatical frame of the conversation is the matrix language (sometimes termed the *host* language) while the embedded language (sometimes termed the *guest* language) plays a lesser role. In general the speakers perceive that the matrix language is the language they are speaking. Some sociolinguists also distinguish intrasentential code alternation, termed *code-mixing*, and intersentential code alternation, termed *code-switching*. However, for our purposes we will consider both intrasentential and intersentential code alternation as code-switching.

Code-switching differs from *borrowing* in several ways. First, borrowing is typically related to single lexical items. Second, borrowed words can be used by monolingual speakers while code-switching necessitates bilingual competence. Third, borrowed expressions typically represent semantic features outside of the borrowing language, filling a lexical gap in the language. In addition, borrowing involves a restricted set of expressions while code-switching can draw on the entire grammar and lexicon of another language. Finally, borrowing typically involves nouns and a few adjectives whereas code-switching can include all constituents of a sentence (Sridhar, 1996).

Code-switching also differs from what Rampton (1995) terms *crossing*. Rampton's work entailed an analysis of the use of Panjabi by young people of Anglo and Afro-Caribbean descent, the use of Creole by Anglos and Punjabis, and the use of stylized Indian English by all three types of speakers in the context of a British neighborhood. In this context, he defined crossing as "code alternation by people who are not accepted members of the group associated with the second language they employ. It is concerned with switching into languages that are not generally thought to belong to you" (p. 280). Crossing, then, differs from code-switching in the sense that code-switching involves speakers who are considered legitimate user of the languages involved, whereas this is not the case for crossing. Crossing, however, can occur in EIL interactions when non-proficient speakers of English make use of English as a way of signaling their affiliation with an English-speaking community and the modernity and westernization associated with it.

Code-switching research is based on quite different assumptions from second language acquisition research. With code-switching research, code alternation is typically viewed as a skillful and appropriate strategy enacted by fluent speakers of the languages involved. In second language acquisition research, on the other hand, code-switching is often viewed as an error and an indication of a lack of competence in the language (see Rampton, 1995). In our discussion we will focus on code-switching in the sense of code alternation by speakers who are legitimate and fluent speakers of the languages involved.

Historical development

An interest in code-switching is a relatively recent phenomenon. This is due perhaps to the negative social attitudes often associated with code-switching. For many, code-switching is viewed as an indication of a lack of bilingual proficiency, resulting in a random alternation of linguistic codes. One of the early challenges to this perspective was the work of Blom and Gumperz (1972) who studied the social functions of code-switching in Norway. In this seminal investigation, Blom and Gumperz examined speakers' alternation between two dialects of Norwegian: Bokmål, the variety used in formal education, and Ranamål, a more informal variety of Norwegian spoken in northern Norway. Based on their investigation, Blom and Gumperz contend that code-switching serves "to symbolize the differing social identities which members may assume" (p. 421). However, there is not a simple one-to-one relationship between a particular variety and a specific social identity since speakers often shift the identity they want to convey on different occasions. Blom and Gumperz maintain that three factors can affect the choice of the code used: the participants, the ecological context, and the topic. In accounting for code-switching behavior, Blom and Gumperz make a distinction between two types of code-switching: *situational* code-switching in which relevant social factors affect the alternation and *metaphorical* code-switching in which rhetorical reasons account for the alternation. Situational code-switching might occur when a new participant enters the scene or the topic of conversation changes. Metaphorical code-switching, on the other hand, could be used to mark a change in tone, to signal a quote, or to emphasize a particular fact.

The study by Blom and Gumperz set the stage for a growing interest in examining why individuals switch from one code to another. During the 1980s and into the 1990s many researchers studied the social function of code-switching on a micro-level, maintaining that code-switching is a strategy speakers use to influence interpersonal relationships. During the 1980s there was also interest in characterizing the morphosyntactic constraints on code-switching so that researchers focused on identifying where in a sentence it would be permissible for speakers to shift codes.

Current approaches

We begin our discussion of current approaches to code-switching with Myers-Scotton's (1993) markedness model since it is this model that many interactional sociolinguists object to because of its psychological and innatist emphasis. In the process they offer an alternative approach to code-switching.

Although Myers-Scotton (1993) fully recognizes the contribution of Blom and Gumperz to both legitimize code-switching as a research topic and provide a model for analyzing interpersonal interactions, she questions whether or not code-switching is primarily locally negotiated. If this is the case, she asks, how are speakers "able to do this unless their interactions are conducted against a common social backdrop of shared views of salient situational values" (p. 61)? The aim of her markedness model is to explain how the larger social context affects individual choices in code-switching. Specifically her markedness model proposes that "speakers have a sense of markedness regarding available linguistic codes for any interaction, but choose their codes based on the persona and/or relation with others which they wish to have in place" (p. 75). She views this sense of markedness as part of what Hymes (1972) terms communicative competence, namely the ability to judge the appropriateness of a given utterance in a particular social context.

A central argument of the markedness model is that "code choices are understood as indexing rights-and-obligations sets (RO sets) between participants in a given interaction type. The unmarked RO set is derived from whatever situational features are salient for the community for that interaction type" (Myers-Scotton, 1993, p. 84). Saliency, however, has a dynamic quality since it can be affected by the following factors:

1   It varies across communities so that age may be significant in some communities but not others.
2   It varies across interactions so that sex may have low salience in service encounters but high salience in other social encounters.
3   It has relative salience in comparison to other factors so that socio-economic status may have more salience than ethnic group in job situations.
4   The salience of any factor is open to negotiation.

Just as Grice posited a set of maxims to account for the cooperative aspect of conversations, Myers-Scotton (1993) argues that the following negotiation principle underlies all code choices,

> Choose the form of your conversation contribution such that it indexes the set of rights and obligations which you wish to be in force between speaker and addressee for the current exchange.

(p. 111)

Speakers employ this principle following one of three strategies. In the first instance, "the unmarked choice," speakers use the code that is typically expected in such encounters, reinforcing expected rights and obligations. In the second instance, "the "marked choice," speakers choose the code not typically expected in a particular encounter as a way of challenging the presumed rights and obligations. Such a choice might be made to increase the social distance between the interlocutors or to signal authority or anger. Finally, there is the "exploratory choice." This choice typically is used when there is a clash of norms such as when a brother and sister are conversing in a formal business context rather than in a home.

Various interactions taken from Myer-Scotton's (1993) African data, gathered in Kenya and Zimbabwe, illustrate how the options are enacted. First there is the case of the unmarked code choice. With family members, most Africans speak their mother tongue, making it the unmarked choice in this context. With friends of one's own ethnic group, the mother tongue is also used, although there is some code-switching to Swahili and English in Nairobi and to English in Harare depending on the speaker's age, educational level and occupation. With friends from other ethnic groups, the unmarked choice is typically Swahili and English in Nairobi and Shona and English in Harare. The same is true for most service encounters and work contexts. The unmarked code, however, could change based on who is being addressed. For example, when workers are speaking with superiors, they tend to use the language associated with education and authority, which in many cases would be English. In general, Myers-Scotton contends that urban African workers may well speak a second language like English more than their first language. This is because "the multi-ethnic nature of African cities and an accompanying sensitivity to ethnic rivalries only find resolution in neutral linguistic choices" (p. 43).

In some cases consistently alternating between two languages is the unmarked choice. Myers-Scotton (1993) provides a variety of examples in which switching between English and the local indigenous language is the unmarked choice and points out certain conditions that typically exist for code-switching to be the unmarked choice. These include the following.

1   The speakers must be bilingual peers so that typically the speakers
    are of the same socio-economic background and are not strangers.
2   The interaction has to be such that the speakers want to symbolize
    their dual membership in two communities.
3   The speakers must positively value for their own identities the sym-
    bolic values of each of the codes involved.

Nevertheless, situations do occur when speakers use the marked choice
for the context. Myers-Scotton (1993) provides several examples of when
such a choice is made. In the following passage, the passenger switches to
English, the marked code, in signaling his annoyance at not getting his
change. The conductor, by responding in English, demonstrates that he
has equal status with the passenger.

(A passenger on a bus in Nairobi and a bus conductor (a person who
collects fares, not the driver) enter into an interaction. The conductor
asks the passenger where he is going in order to determine his fare.
English is italicized; the rest of the interaction is carried out in Swahili,
the unmarked choice for such a transaction.)

Passenger: Nataka kwenda Posta. ["I want to go to the post office."]
Conductor: Kutoka hapa mpaka posta nauli ni senti hamsini.
               ["From here to the post office, the fare is 50 cents."]

(Passenger gives the conductor a shilling, from which he should get
50 cents in change.)

Conductor: Ngojea *change* yako. ["Wait for you change."]

(Passenger says nothing until some minutes have passed and the bus
is nearing the post office where the passenger plans to get off.)

Passenger: Nataka *change* yangu. ["I want my change."]
Conductor: *Change* utapata, Bwana. ["You'll get your change."]
Passenger: *I am nearing my destination.*
Conductor: *Do you think I could run away with your change?*
                                                          (p. 133)

Finally, there are some instances in which the speakers are unsure
which code to use because of a clash in norms and thus, select the
exploratory code choice. According to Myers-Scotton (1993), this is
the least common alternative since in most bilingual communities, the
speakers have a sense of what the unmarked choice of code should be for
a particular situation. Still, there are instances when the speakers are

unsure which code is most appropriate for a particular context and hence explore which code to use. The following example illustrates this. In this case a young man is asking a young woman to dance at a Nairobi hotel. He is unsure which code to select so he starts with the most neutral choice, Swahili. However, when this choice is not successful, he follows the woman's lead and switches to English, eventually getting her to dance. (English is in italics.)

> He: Nisaidie na *dance*, tafadhali ["Please give me a dance."]
> She: Nimechoka. Pengine nyimbo ifutatayo. ["I'm tired. Maybe the following song."]
> He: Hii ndio nyimbo ninayopenda. ["This is the song which I like."]
> She: Nimechoka! ["I'm tired!"]
> He: Tafadhali—["Please—"]
> She (interrupting): *Ah stop bugging me.*
> He: *I'm sorry I didn't mean to bug you, but I can't help it if I like this song.*
> She: *OK, then, in that case, we can dance.*

> (p. 146)

As mentioned earlier, Myers-Scotton's model has been criticized by interactional sociolinguists because of its failure to recognize the localized nature of code-switching. Auer (1984), for example, presents an alternative approach to code-switching, one more in line with interactional sociolinguistics. Auer contends that a bilingual interaction should not be seen as a locale for enacting a set of norms that act as a constraint on linguistic performance, which he contends is what the Myers-Scotton model advocates. Rather it should be seen as an interactive endeavor. As he puts it, in bilingual conversations, "whatever language a participant chooses for the organization of his/her turn, or for an utterance which is part of the turn, the choice exerts an influence on subsequent language choices by the same or other speakers" (p. 5). Because of this, "the meaning of code-switching must be interpreted with reference to the language choice in the preceding and following turns by the participants themselves" (p. 3). In the end, he argues for a conversation-analytic approach to code-switching that highlights the local nature of code-switching.

Based on his work with the code-switching of the Chinese Cantonese-speaking community in Newcastle, England, Wei (1998) also questions Myers-Scotton's markedness model. He states,

> The notion of "indexicality" in Myers-Scotton's "markedness" theory of code-switching may be a convenient tool for the analyst to predict code choice and assign some social value to particular

instances of code-switching. It is, however, hardly the way conversation participants themselves interpret each other's linguistic choices and negotiate meaning. In conversational interaction, either bilingual or monolingual, speakers are often faced with the fact that the situation is simply not defined unambiguously. The participants do not always have "similar precedents" with which they can compare the current interaction. Even when the situation is fairly clear to the co-participants, they simply do not have the time to inspect the current case for common features with similar precedent cases. Instead, their attention is paid first and foremost to the "new case" itself and each and every new move by their co-interactants . . . While their experiences in other situations may be useful in helping them achieve mutual understanding, speakers' on-line focus is on the local production of meaning.

(p. 159)

He concludes that "the significance of code-switching, as far as the participants themselves are concerned, is first and foremost its 'otherness.' Bilingual speakers change from one language to another in conversation not because of some external value attached to those particular languages, but because the alternation itself signals to their co-participants how they wish their utterances to be interpreted on that particular occasion" (p. 161).

In terms of how a conversational-analytic approach to code-switching can be helpful in interpreting classroom code-switching, let us consider Jorgensen's (1998) study of the code-switching behavior of Turkish children in Denmark. Jorgensen's concern was with how Turkish primary school children use Turkish and Danish as it relates to issues of power and dominance. The Turkish school children in Denmark are typical of many language minority children who speak a first language that has less power in the social context in which they live and go to school. As Jorgensen (1998) points out, "for linguistic minorities the difference in status between languages is indeed an important factor. What Gumperz (1982) labels the 'we-code' is, in the case of minorities, usually related to low prestige, its use restricted to private spheres, and at the same time a sign of belonging to the minority" (p. 239).

Jorgensen (1998) contends that Turkish children's use of code-switching is affected by both global and local factors:

On the one hand we have a kind of code-switching which is basically determined by apparently relatively long-term factors outside of the particular communication undertaken by the speakers, i.e. *globally determined* switching. On the other hand we have a kind of code-switching which is basically determined by apparently relatively short-term factors within the particular piece of communication, i.e. *locally determined* switching. This distinction is of course not a geographical one, but rather the switches are locally or globally determined with respect to a particular communication situation vis-à-vis a totality of communication situations.

(Italics in the original, p. 239)

He maintains that whereas for parents the "we-code" may be Turkish, for children, if there is a "we-code," it may be code-switching itself.

Based on his longitudinal examination of Turkish children's code-switching between the ages of 7 and 12, Jorgensen (1998) found that the children developed their linguistic skills tremendously over this time span. In terms of code-switching, they switched codes for a wide range of purposes. In some instances, Danish was used because it is the language of the school and has more power on a "global" level. However, at other times,

> code-switching in itself, in one direction or the other, is also used simply as a way of countering the claims of the opposite part of a discussion . . . It is the use of the opposite language of the interlocutor which is in itself an instrument in the power struggle, and the direction of these inter-utterance code-switches is unimportant. In this respect the code-switching does not draw on global factors, but solely on the particular constellation of points of view in the particular part of the conversation.

(p. 254)

Jorgensen ends the article by arguing that children "one way or another . . . develop a comprehension of the global factors which give power and casting rights in conversations. They also develop skills in manipulating these factors to influence events according to their own desires. This they do in a complicated interplay of global and local factors" (p. 256). This interplay between global and local factors affects the code-switching behavior of many English language learners, particularly those who recognize the global significance of English yet see the local value of their other language(s).

Implications for EIL pedagogy

Current theories on code-switching highlight its regular and productive nature. The use of two or more codes is a central aspect of bilinguals' rich linguistic repertoire, which allows them to make statements as to who they are, what they wish to accomplish, and how they view the individuals they are interacting with. The fact that most users of English today are bilinguals, many of whom code-switch on a regular basis, has several implications for the EIL classroom, among them the following:

- Educators need to work to minimize negative attitudes toward code-switching. The promotion of English-only classrooms will in many cases only increase negative views toward code-switching. Because of this, educators need to consider how students' other language(s) can productively be used within the educational context and encourage a view of bilingualism as a resource. In addition, teachers need to examine their own attitudes toward code-switching and put aside notions that such behavior is random or a sign of deficiency.
- More research is needed regarding how students make use of the languages they speak outside of the classroom. The findings of such research will be useful in designing an EIL curriculum that complements students' use of English. In many contexts, it may be that English is used more in formal rather than informal contexts.
- Classroom activities should be designed that increase students' own awareness of the linguistic choices they make and the significance of these choices. This could involve having students record instances of their own language use for discussion within the EIL classroom.

Attitudes toward code-switching

The work of interactional sociolinguistics has also proven useful in assessing bilingual speakers' attitudes toward the use of code-switching. In the following section, we discuss how hypothetical L2–L2 interactions have been used to assess young Singaporeans' attitudes toward the use of code-switching.

Language attitudes in Singapore

As we discussed in chapter 4, bilingualism in Singapore has a distinct meaning, reflecting the ethnic and linguistic diversity of the country. Bilingualism refers to English plus one's mother tongue, which is Mandarin, Malay, or Tamil. Such bilingualism is achieved through the bilingual education policy, whereby all students learn English, the medium of instruction, at "first language" level, and their mother tongue (depending on their ethnicity—Mandarin for Chinese, Malay for Malays, and Tamil for Indians) at "second language" level. The result is what is now widely referred to as "English-knowing bilingualism" in a large part of the population. The terms "first" and "second" language here do not have the same meanings they do elsewhere in linguistics. English, the "first language," is actually spoken at home by only 23 percent of the population (Singapore Department of Statistics, 2000). And the "mother tongue" has to do with one's father's ethnicity, and may not even be one's native language or the language spoken habitually at home (see table 1 in chapter 4). Code-switching is a dominant feature of speech patterns in Singapore—certainly in non-formal domains, but even in formal domains such as religion, parliament, and work (Gopinathan, 1988; Pakir, 1993; Vaish, forthcoming).

Our discussion of young Singaporeans' attitudes towards the use of code-switching is based on research underway at Singapore's Centre for Research in Pedagogy and Practice (CRPP), involving an on-going sociolinguistic survey of 10-year-old Singaporeans, grouped by ethnicity (Chinese, Malay, and Indian) and by socio-economic status (a composite measure of family income, housing type, and parents' levels of education, divided into High, Middle, and Low). The Sociolinguistic Survey of Singapore, 2006 (henceforth SSS 2006) gathers self-report data on patterns of language use ("who speaks/writes what language, to whom, and in what contexts"), proficiency and language attitudes. Thus far, 515 of the targeted 1,000 children have been surveyed; 59 percent Chinese, 25 percent Malay, and 15 percent Indian.

People's reactions to language varieties reveal much of their perception of the speakers of these varieties (Edwards, 1982). The major dimensions along which views about languages can vary are social status (the social prestige associated with a language variety and speaker of that variety) and group solidarity (loyalty to a particular language variety and sense of affinity with the speakers of that variety). The measure of language attitudes used in this study is an adaptation of the indirect matched-guise method used by Lambert and Tucker (1972): participants were asked to evaluate recorded speech samples of three different recordings involving the same 10-year-old speaker. Participants were not informed that the same speaker was used in all three recording. In each recording, the scenario and dialogue script is the same: a phone conversation in which the speaker is asking a friend to come to his/her house to do homework together. The variations in the three recordings have to do with language use:

Recording 1 (ENG): The person speaks in English/Singlish throughout the recording.

Recording 2 (MT): The person speaks in the mother tongue (Malay, Tamil, or Chinese) throughout the recording.

Recording 3 (MIX): The person begins speaking in English, but code-switches to the mother tongue (Malay, Tamil, or Chinese) at various points in the conversation.

The objective was as much as possible to capture natural speech in these recordings. Thus the script was based on recordings of actors role-playing the scenario, and subsequently translated. Six sets of recordings following the same script were prepared—a male and a female recording prepared for each of the three main language groups in Singapore: Malay, Tamil, and Chinese. The Malay participants listened to the Malay set of recordings, the Indians the Tamil set, and the Chinese the Chinese set. To control for any effect of gender, the male and female versions were administered randomly.

Participants were given the following instructions: "Imagine you are listening to someone speaking on the telephone with his or her friend. After each recording, we will ask you what you think about the speaker." After listening to each recording, participants were asked to evaluate the speaker on a four-point Likert scale (strongly disagree to strongly agree, with no "neutral" option) on a series of measures relating to status and solidarity (eight items each). Rather than merely listing speaker attributes (e.g. smart, powerful, beautiful) as is common on match-guise questionnaires, attributes were couched in situational sentences, reflecting contexts familiar to 10-year-old Singaporeans. Status items included statements such as "This student is popular at school" and "This student is studying at a top primary school;" solidarity items included questions such as "This student is helpful" and "This student is likeable." Post-survey factor analysis reduced the number of items from eight to five for both status and solidarity. Subsequent to the matched-guise test, participants were also asked a series of direct questions further measuring their language attitudes and language ideology. For example, on a four-point Likert scale (4 representing strongly agree and 1 strongly disagree), they were asked to indicated how strongly they agreed or disagreed with statements such as: "I enjoy reading in my mother tongue when I have time" and "My friends and I have more fun joking in English than in our MT."

Preliminary data analysis found that, for the 10-year-old Singaporeans in the study, there was no statistical difference in their attitude towards the use of their mother tongue only and code-switching. However, their attitude toward the use of English was significantly lower than code-switching. While the ethnicity of the respondent was significant for the solidarity factor—the Malay participant held a greater sense of solidarity towards the use of code-switching, and the Chinese the lowest—ethnicity did not have a significant effect on attitudes related to status. There were, however, significant differences in their attitudes toward code-switching concerning solidarity and status between respondents of different socio-economic groups. The data shows that the higher the socio-economic status (SES), the lower the sense of solidarity with the use of code-switching. Similarly, the higher the SES of the respondent, the lower the status they gave to the use of code-switching.

The more positive attitudes among all respondents for code-switching rather than for English were also evident in their responses to a series of direct questions regarding their language attitudes. For example, proficiency in English and mother tongue were almost equally seen to be necessary to "do well in school" (mean scores of 3.39 and 3.11 respectively, with 4 representing strongly agree and 1 strongly disagree) and students expressed almost equal enjoyment in studying English and their mother tongue (3.23 and 3.06 respectively). When asked to respond to the statements "I wish I could speak English/my mother tongue better," responses were almost equal (3.37 English, and 3.30 Chinese).

As we noted in chapter 4, the Singapore government has focused on the importance of bilingualism for national identity, for instrumental and economic utility, and for community (ethnic) and personal identity, values and cultural grounding. From this analysis, it appears that at one level the Singapore government's language politicking concerning the importance of bilingualism has worked. These 10-year-olds clearly had more positive attitudes towards the use of both their mother tongue and English than they did towards the use of English only. That is, there is a strong sense that the use of both English and their mother tongue had important value, both in terms of solidarity and status. They also appear to have accepted the general allocation of language functions and meanings that the government has assigned to English and to the mother tongue languages. The government identifies the mother tongue languages as being the languages of cultural identity and ethnic cohesion, and English the language of commerce, global connectedness, and modernization. This functional allocation of languages was evident in the students' responses to direct questions such as (means are in brackets—the highest value being 4):

> In order to learn about my own culture, it is important to know my mother tongue (3.14)
> In order to learn about my own culture, it is important to know English (2.65)

> In order to understand the world better, it is important to know my mother tongue (2.74)
> In order to understand the world better, it is important to know English (3.28)

These responses thus mirror the government's functional allocation of language meanings and use, with both English and the mother tongue languages having a valued position in society.

However, at another level, by giving higher status and having a stronger sense of solidarity with the use of *code-switching*, the participants have also complicated the government's diglossic polarization of language. While discursively and ideologically they understand the particular meanings associated with mother tongue and English, in practice their patterns of language use do not follow the clearly marked domains allocated by the government. Indeed, as we noted in chapter 5, as is often the case in Outer Circle countries, language use is much more fluid than official diglossia would suggest.

This fluidity of language use, captured by some as hybridity (see chapter 5), has important implications for language learning. If indeed language use were neatly compartmentalized, one could potentially conceive of ambilingualism as a goal of language learning. However, the interaction between English and the other languages in a society and an individual's speech repertoire instead suggests the need for a pedagogy that recognizes these complex and fluid ways in which languages are used. As we have noted throughout this book, in many Outer Circle countries the language situation suggests a need for a pedagogy that recognizes that English is acquired and used alongside the other languages in the learners' linguistic repertoires; that learners of English also desire support for their mother tongue languages; and that English is associated with particular ideologies, attitudes, and purposes. All of these factors need to be taken into account in a socially sensitive EIL pedagogy.

Summary

In this chapter we examined how the work of interactional sociolinguistics has been useful in illuminating the use of EIL. We began by describing the historical development of interactional sociolinguistics, indicating in what ways this approach differs from conversation analysis. We pointed out that although both disciplines take the examination of natural interactions as central to the field, interactional sociolinguists, unlike conversation analysts, consider the ethnographic and demographic background of an interaction as central components of their analysis.

We then examined three areas in which interactional sociolinguistics has provided valuable information on EIL interactions, namely research on ELF, code-switching, and language attitudes. In discussing ELF interactions, we summarized the existing research on the pragmatic, grammatical and phonological features of ELF interactions and explored the pedagogical implications of these findings. Our examination of code-switching research began with a definition of the term followed by an account of the historical development of code-switching research. We discussed Myers-Scotton's markedness model because it is often criticized by interactional sociolinguists for its psychological and innate emphasis and then presented a conversation-analytic approach to code-switching. We also highlighted the pedagogical implications of code-switching research. In closing we examined how the use of hypothetical EIL interactions can be beneficial in discovering more about speakers' attitudes toward code-switching. We turn now to a discussion of the overall pedagogical implications of the preceding chapters.

Acknowledgements

Thanks to Khoo Boon Suan and Tan Teck Kiang for assisting in the statistical computation and analysis of the SSS 2006 data.

References

Atkinson, J. M. & Heritage, J. (Eds.) (1984). *Structure of social action: Studies in conversation analysis*. Cambridge: Cambridge University Press.

Auer, P. (1984). *Bilingual conversation*. Amsterdam: John Benjamins.

Blom, J. & Gumperz, J. (1972). Social meaning in linguistic structures: Code-switching in Norway. In J. Gumperz & D. Hymes (Eds.), *Directions in sociolinguistics* (pp. 407–434). New York: Holt, Rinehard and Winston, Inc.

Chomsky, N. (1957). *Syntactic structure*. The Hague: Mouton.

Edwards, J. R. (1982). Language attitudes and their implications among English speakers. In E. B. Ryan and H. Giles (Eds.), *Attitudes towards language variation: Social and applied contexts* (pp. 20–33). London: Arnold.

Firth, A. (1996). The discursive accomplishment of normality. On "lingua franca" English and conversation analysis. *Journal of Pragmatics*, 26, 237–259.

Goffman, E. (1967). *On face work*. New York: Anchor Books.

Gopinathan, S. (1988). Bilingualism and bilingual education in Singapore. In C. B. Paulston (Ed.), *International handbook of bilingualism and bilingual education* (pp. 391–404). New York: Greenwood Press.

Grice, H. P. (1975). Logic and conversation. In P. Cole & J. L. Morgan (Eds.), *Syntax and Semantics 3: Speech acts* (pp. 41–58). New York: Academic Press.

Gumperz, J. (1971). *Language in social groups*. Stanford, CA: Stanford University Press.

Gumperz, J. (1982). *Discourse strategies*. Cambridge: Cambridge University Press.

House, J. (2003). Teaching and learning pragmatic fluency in a foreign language: The case of English as a lingua franca. In A. Martinez Flor, E. Usó Juan & A. Fernández Guerra (Eds.), *Pragmatic competence and foreign language teaching* (pp. 133–159). Castelláo de la Plana, Spain: Publicacions de la Universitat Jaume I.

Hymes, D. (1972). On communicative competence. In J. Pride & J. Holmes (Eds.), *Sociolinguistics* (pp. 269–293). Harmondsworth: Penguin.

Hymes, D. (1974). *Foundations of sociolinguistics*. Philadelphia, PA: University of Pennsylvania Press.

Jenkins, J. (2000). *The phonology of English as an international language*. Oxford: Oxford University Press.

Jorgensen, J. N. (1998). Children's acquisition of code-switching for power wielding. In P. Auer (Ed.), *Code-switching in conversation: Language, interaction and identity* (pp. 237–261). London: Routledge.

Kuo, I.-C. (2006). Addressing the issue of teaching as a lingua franca. *ELT Journal, 60*(3), 213–221.

Lambert, W. and Tucker, G. (1972). *Bilingual education of children: The St. Lambert experiment.* Rowley, MA: Newbury House.

Lazaraton, A. (2002). Quantitative and qualitative approaches to discourse analysis. *Annual Review of Applied Linguistics, 22*, 32–51.

Meierkord, C. (2000). Interpreting successful lingua franca interaction: An analysis of non-native/non-native small talk conversations in English. Retrieved April 21, 2005 from http://www.linguistik-online.de/1_00/MEIERKOR. HTM.

Myers-Scotton, C. (1993). *Social motivations for code switching.* Oxford: Claredon Press.

Pakir, A. (1993). Two tongue tied: Bilingualism in Singapore. In G. M. Jones & A. C. K. Ozog (Eds.), *Bilingualism and National Development* (pp. 73–90). Clevedon, UK: Multilingual Matters.

Prodromou, L. (2006). Defining the "successful bilingual speaker" of English. In R. Rubdy & M. Saraceni (Eds.), *English in the world: Global rules, global roles* (pp. 51–70). London: Continuum.

Rampton, B. (1995). *Crossing: Language and ethnicity among adolescents.* Singapore: Longman.

Schegloff, E., Koshik, I., Jacoby, S., & Olsher, D. (2002). Conversation analysis and applied linguistics. *Annual Review of Applied Linguistics, 22*, 3–31.

Schiffrin, C. (1996). Interactional sociolinguistics. In S. L. McKay & N. H. Hornberger (Eds.), *Sociolinguistics and language teaching* (pp. 307–328). Cambridge: Cambridge University Press.

Seidlhofer, B. (2004). Research perspectives on teaching English as a lingua franca. *Annual Review of Applied Linguistics, 24*, 209–239.

Seidlhofer, B. (2006). English as a lingua franca in the expanding circle: What it isn't. In R. Rubdy & M. Saraceni (Eds.), *English in the world* (pp. 40–50). London: Continuum.

Singapore Department of Statistics (2000). Singapore Census of population, 2000. Advance Data Release No. 3. Language and Literacy. Retrieved October 2, 2007, from http://www.singstate.gov.sg/pubn/papers/people/c2000adr_literacy.pdf.

Sridhar, K. (1996). Societal multilingualism. In S. L. McKay & N. H. Hornberger (Eds.), *Sociolinguistics and language teaching* (pp. 47–70). Cambridge: Cambridge University Press.

ten Have, P. (1999). *Doing conversation analysis.* London: Sage.

Timmis, I. (2002). Native-speaker norms and international English: A classroom view. *ELT Journal, 56*(3), 240–249.

Vaish, V. (forthcoming, 2007). Bilingualism without diglossia: The Indian community in Singapore. *International Journal of Bilingual Education and Bilingualism.*

Wei, L. (1998). The "why" and "how" questions in the analysis of conversational code-switching. In P. Auer (ed.), *Code-switching in conversation: Language, interaction and identity* (pp.156–179). London: Routledge.

Chapter 7

Towards a socially sensitive EIL pedagogy

Throughout the book we have argued for the need to consider the social and sociolinguistic context of L2 classrooms in making pedagogical decisions. In this chapter, we begin by summarizing the manner in which L2 classrooms are affected by:

- the extent of multilingualism in the country and the local speech community;
- the degree of official recognition afforded to English in the society and the educational structure;
- linguistic variation and local standards in the use of English; and
- typical interactional patterns of bilingual users of English within the local speech community.

We then examine how two of the themes emphasized throughout the text, the global/local tension and the discourse of Othering, have informed ELT methods and materials. We do so as a way of suggesting how these themes might be addressed in the teaching of EIL. In closing we set forth principles that we believe should inform an EIL pedagogy in an era of increasing globalization.

The sociolinguistic context

Multilingualism

Our discussion of the multilingual contexts of English language learning highlighted a contrast between the growing number of bilingual users of English and the strong emphasis and underlying assumptions of monolingualism in EIL pedagogy. In chapter 3 we examined both diglossic multilingual societies and non-diglossic multilingual societies. Diglossia most often characterizes the linguistic situation in Outer Circle countries that have adopted English in addition to their other languages. English is acquired through the formal education system, and is given high status through its allocation to formal domains. English is most often used for very specific purposes—to access and contribute to the vast amount of information available in English, and to access the economic, political, and social benefits that come with English language proficiency. Indigenous languages continue to be supported socially, politically and through the education system as a medium of instruction and/or through language learning. Yet, at the same time, we demonstrated how the pedagogy and curricula used in English language classrooms are often modeled on the monolingual and monocultural assumptions of the Inner Circle, with the result that indigenous languages are marginalized and English-language learning becomes alienating.

Non-diglossic multilingual societies, typically in the Inner Circle, tend to support English monolingualism: there is no social or institutional support for bilingualism; local and national language policies and ideologies often overtly adopt an English-only stance; support for bilingual education is often ranked last in budget priorities and thus most vulnerable to elimination; and English language pedagogy is preoccupied with rapid transition to English only. Yet most learners of English make clear that monolingualism is *not* their preferred goal, and do desire support for their other languages.

There is thus a tension between the realities of multilingualism and multiculturalism and the monolingual assumptions and goals dominating English language pedagogy. We argued in chapter 3 for the benefits of designing English learning environments that support the development of bilingualism rather than monolingualism. What is needed is a productive theory of bilingual teaching and learning that recognizes the various ways in which English is used within multilingual communities, and the specific purposes learners may have for using the language. For example, one dominant assumption in a good deal of English language pedagogy is "ambilingualism" (see chapter 5), whereby full fluency in both languages is seen as the goal of second language acquisition. With this comes another assumption, that the goal of English language learners is to develop native-speaker competence—which, as we will elaborate in our section on English standards, is often not the case. A socially sensitive EIL pedagogy would recognize the other languages used by EIL learners, as well as take into account the specific ways in which English is used in their sociolinguistic contexts.

Official recognition of English

In chapter 4 we gave attention to the degree of official recognition afforded to English in a given society and the educational structure, and the impact this recognition has on the EIL classroom. In diglossic societies, the official allocation of English in particular domains generally includes English language education in the national education system—either through English as a medium of instruction or English as a subject taught. This official recognition of English thus ensures the widespread learning of English. However, we also noted that the distinction between English-medium instruction versus learning English as a subject often resulted in different standards of pedagogy, learning and proficiency for different sectors of society. In India, for example, the stratification of Indian English mirrors the social class structures of the society. Those in English-medium schools typically learn a more standard form of English, whereas those who learn English as a subject typically acquire a more colloquial form. The official recognition of English in Inner Circle multi-lingual societies has had the opposite effect of what is seen in diglossic societies. As noted in the previous section, the official recognition of English often means the official recognition of English *only*, with the ultimate result of monolingualism. This tendency is particularly pronounced in the United States, epitomized in the English-only movement. Ironically, while there is a massive effort discursively and politically for English only, financial and institutional support to provide learners access to English is constantly under threat and is often marginalized in competing budget demands. The result is often a sink or swim pedagogical practice, or English submersion. We also noted how, in some Expanding Circle countries, the rising status of English is often tied to the particular ideological imperatives underpinning the country's development agenda. There is unease in any official status given to English, yet at the same time, it has prominent presence in educational policy in the classroom. The nativization of English in these countries brings an added dimension to the debates, the nativized variety often being marginalized in favor of exonormative standards and pedagogy.

English standards

The topic of linguistic variation and local standards in the use of English, and the impact such variation has on EIL pedagogy and learning, was the focus of chapter 5. Because English bilingual speakers use the language on a daily basis alongside one or more other languages, their use of English and their variety of English is often influenced by these other languages. We noted how new lexical items, new grammatical standards, and new pronunciation patterns emerge from the particular socio-cultural and sociolinguistic contexts within which new varieties of English are used. Thus, rather than being seen as "errors," interlanguages, or fossilized forms of incomplete acquisition of Standard English, these forms of World Englishes need to be seen as languages in their own right. We examined how English language pedagogy has typically been modeled on the native speaker, and on the myths of the Standard English discourse.

We argued that EIL pedagogy should instead encourage awareness of the variation that exists in English today and recognize the validity of different varieties of English.

Interactional patterns

In chapter 6 we discussed some of the features of ELF interactions. We emphasized that any generalizations regarding ELF interactions must take into account the purpose of the interaction and the proficiency level of the speakers since there are various reasons that may account for a particular use of English. For example, bilingual speakers may employ the "let-it-pass principle" because they do not have the language proficiency to repair a breakdown in communication or they may do so because they feel repairing the misunderstanding is not necessary in light of the overall goal of the interaction. Nonetheless, we pointed out that, in general, an EIL pedagogy would benefit from attention to repair strategies and conversational gambits.

Chapter 6 also summarized various theories that account for code-switching. Such research demonstrates that code-switching is not only a regular occurrence among bilingual speakers but that it also provides a mechanism for speakers to signal both their personal identity and their perceived relationship with their interlocutor. Given the usefulness and pervasiveness of code-switching we argued for more research on code-switching within the local community so that educators can learn how English is being used in the local speech community. We also argued that teachers need to promote students' awareness of their own use of code-switching and to consider how the local languages can be productively used in the English classroom.

Globalization and Othering in ELT materials

Throughout the text we emphasized two issues that are often evident in EIL pedagogy. The first is the tension between global and local concerns and the second is a discourse of Othering (Palfryman, 2005). The first is demonstrated in a good deal of literature that deals with the choice of EIL methodology, in which CLT is promoted as a modern method that meets global needs whereas grammar-translation and other methods are viewed as parochial and local methodologies. The theme of Othering is evident in many discussions of native and nonnative English-speaking teachers in which nonnative speakers are viewed as lacking skills in comparison with native English-speaking teachers. In the following section we carefully examine how these themes manifest themselves in ELT methods and materials. Our purpose is twofold. The first is to illustrate how these themes can affect English teaching on a day-to-day basis; and the second is to suggest ways to deal with the potentially negative effects globalization and Othering discourses can have.

One of the major ways in which global–local tensions manifest themselves in pedagogical materials is in the choice of content. In many instances, as we saw in the case of China in chapter 2, the teaching of English is promoted as a way of developing international awareness and of helping the country to become part of a global economy. With this goal in mind, many texts approved by Ministries of Education promote global themes and a discussion of other cultures, particularly those of the Inner Circle. The appropriateness of such themes for the local context is generally not examined. Local teachers, however, aware of the interests and needs of their learners, may find such materials unsuitable for their students. A second issue that is evident in a good deal of ELT materials is a discourse of Othering in which those from Western Inner Circle cultures are portrayed as having modern and desirable behavior while those from other cultures, who exhibit other ways of doing things, are seen as backward and lacking. Such polarization can inform classroom texts dealing with a variety of topics, ranging from gender issues to family relationships.

In the following section, we exemplify how global–local tensions and a discourse of Othering are evident in classroom materials. We deal specifically with how these themes are evident in the cultural content of classroom materials since it is often through the choice of cultural content that classroom materials position local teachers and learners. We also suggest possible approaches for minimizing these problems.

Stated views: rejection of Westernization

As we noted in several chapters, in many countries throughout the world today there is tremendous pressure to learn English. Along with pressures to learn English come concerns about how English should be taught and what role culture should play in the teaching of English. Many language educators support the inclusion of a cultural component in the teaching of English, arguing that having a cultural component in language teaching can promote international understanding, deepen an understanding of one's own culture, facilitate learners' visits to foreign countries, and motivate learners (Adaskou et al., 1990). For those who support explicit attention to culture in language materials, a typical question is, which cultures should be represented in textbooks and how should they be portrayed?

In some contexts, there is support for including a cultural component in language teaching materials, but only if it teaches about the local culture. For example, in reference to Morocco, Adaskou et al. (1990) argue that the inclusion of culture, specifically western culture, in teaching materials is not motivating or beneficial to students. Drawing on interviews with Moroccan teachers, Adaskou et al. maintain that, in general, Moroccan educators believe that including information about Western culture contributes to students' discontent with their own culture. Teachers also point out that some patterns of behavior that exist in English-speaking social contexts are ones that many Moroccans would prefer their young people not see. Finally, the teachers believe that students will be more motivated to learn English if the language is presented in contexts that relate to their lives as young adults rather than in the context of an English-speaking country.

Likewise in Chile, the Ministry of Education has decided that it would be more motivating for students to focus on their own culture and country. Hence, the Ministry has designed a series of textbooks for the public schools entitled *Go for Chile* (Mugglestone et al., 1999, 2000), which features a group of students from various countries on board a ship sailing along the coast of Chile. The scenario of the sea voyage enables the textbook writers to deal with Chilean places and concerns, resulting in a good deal of information about various areas of Chile and issues facing the country.

One of the strongest rejections of the inclusion of Western culture in EIL teaching materials appears in a Japanese bestseller entitled *Why the Japanese people are no good at English* by a well-known sociolinguist, Suzuki (1999). Suzuki offers several reasons why he believes the teaching of English should be separated from information about Western cultural values. First, he argues that Japan, as an international power, has no need to teach Western culture. Second, he believes that Japan must fight against the subtle form of Western imperialism that suggests the need to emulate everything Western, including the English language. For him, such emulation is a form of mental colonization. As he puts it:

> When Japanese come into contact with foreigners [Westerners, specifically, Americans], they have been historically predisposed to accepting that person's way of thinking and acting, that person's value system, and even that person's habits. And if they seem better than one's own, they don't hesitate to imitate them and take these differences in as their own, even hoping to become like them. This is the mental predisposition to what I referred to earlier as auto-colonization.
>
> (p. 145)

As illustrated by the examples above, in a variety of countries today educational leaders are expressing an explicit rejection of the promotion of Western culture and values in English teaching.

Actual policies: idealization of Westernization

While some educational leaders explicitly reject the inclusion of Western culture in English teaching, many textbooks approved by official government bodies do in fact promote Western characters and values. Japan is a case in point. In an analysis of all 7th grade ministry-approved texts, Matsuda (2002) found an Inner Circle emphasis in the textbooks' representation of users and uses of English. Of the 74 characters shown in the textbooks, Matsuda's analysis showed that most characters were from Japan (34), followed by Inner Circle country speakers (30) and the remaining from Outer and Expanding Circle countries (10). What was most telling, however, was who talked the most among these characters. Although there are more Japanese characters than Inner Circle characters, the Japanese speakers produce far fewer words than Inner Circle country speakers. In addition, those from Outer and Expanding Circle countries hardly speak at all. In a subtle way, then, these texts suggest that it is Inner Circle native speakers who have the right to use English.

The context of English uses portrayed in the textbooks is also revealing. In terms of English being used intranationally, the majority of these cases are among Inner Circle English users. There is only one example of intranational use within an Outer Circle country, even though English is often used as a lingua franca in Outer Circle countries. In terms of international uses of English, the overwhelming majority of examples are between native speakers and nonnative speakers of English with only a few examples of English being used among nonnative speakers of English, even though L2–L2 interactions represent the majority of current interactions in English. Learners of English then are provided with few models of the present-day use of English.

More telling than the nationalities of characters in textbooks is what the characters say and do in the textbooks. In many countries where Western characters are introduced in textbooks, it is often in the context of presenting differences between Western culture and local cultures, often accompanied by a subtle emulation of Western culture and traditions. The following examples from Ministry of Education texts dealing with gender issues demonstrate this tendency.

In one Moroccan textbook (*English in Life*), students are introduced to an American engineer, Steve Lynch, and his family of three children. In terms of gender roles, the family is fairly traditional since the wife, Barbara, doesn't work outside of the home. However, in one of the readings, the family's activities are described in such a way that traditional gender roles are questioned.

> *Example one:*
> After work Steve comes back home. He likes to be with his family in

the evening. Usually he or Nancy [his daughter] cooks dinner for the family. Then they wash the plates. Barbara [his wife] just likes to eat. She doesn't like to work in the kitchen. She thinks it takes a lot of time and it isn't interesting. Steve never criticizes her. Do you think he's right?

(p. 41)

In this case, although the wife plays a traditional role in that she doesn't work outside of the home, nonetheless she is unusual because she doesn't participate in the traditional female role of making meals. Steve, on the other hand, by undertaking domestic duties, illustrates a male role that is often encouraged in Western cultures. Hence, not only does the book depict gender roles advocated by many Western cultures, but it also opens a discussion of gender roles by asking whether or not Barbara should be criticized for not playing a traditional female role.

A very vivid example of the promotion of Western gender roles appears in the following dialogue from a Japanese Ministry approved textbook.

Example two:
Rye: Jim?
Jim: What?
Rye: Is your father always doing the dishes like that?
Jim: Yes. My parents take turns cooking and doing the dishes.
Rye: My father never helps with the housework. He's too tired after a long day's work.
Jim: I think the Japanese work too much and too long. What do you think?
Rye: I think so too. But people are taking more holidays than before. My father stays home longer.
Jim: What does he do on holidays?
Rye: Usually, he just relaxes. But you know what? He started to learn cooking.
Jim: Does he cook well?
Rye: Yes, he cooks very well. Everything is very very well-done.
     (Source: *Echo*. 1997. Tokyo: Sanyusya, Lesson 18, "Housework," as cited in Shimako 2000)

The dialogue is a clear example of what Suzuki (1999) refers to as auto-colonization, in which Japanese are depicted as emulating and accepting Western values. In the dialogue, Rye not only appears to apologize for aspects of his own culture, agreeing with Jim that Japanese "work too much and too long," but he quickly points out that his father is emulating Western traditions by learning to cook. As if this is not sufficient evidence of a type of auto-colonization, he goes on to say that his father, however, has not managed to undertake this Western pattern very effectively since everything he cooks is "very very well-done."

Responding to Othering

The previous discussion illustrates the ambivalent attitude that exists in some countries today in which an explicit rejection by educational leaders of globalization and Westernization is not actually manifest in classroom materials. Rather, in subtle ways, ministry-approved textbooks are promoting an idealization of Western cultures and values and a marginalization of the local culture. While textbooks may depict this marginalization, it is ultimately local classroom teachers who determine how such materials will be realized in a classroom. Teachers who decide to balance attention to global and local concerns and to reject a position of the Other can approach these materials in ways that challenge a marginalization of the local culture. What are some ways they might do this?

Let us begin with the textbook examples on gender. The Moroccan text exemplifies what Cortazzi and Jin (1999) call an *open text* in that it invites a range of possible interpretations and learner responses. In this way it encourages a discussion of cultural values. If, however, the use of the text is to proceed in a manner that achieves a balance between global and local concerns and reduces Othering, several additional features are necessary. First, the presentation needs to illustrate the diversity that exists within all cultures. Students should be encouraged to see cultural diversity as part of the cultural flow that exists today and not as a simplistic distinction depicted along the lines of Us (Center) and Them (Periphery). Second, students need to approach diversity as a means of reflecting on their own position and culture, establishing what Kramsch (1993) terms a "sphere of interculturality," in which the process of learning about another culture entails a reflection on one's own culture. In this way the global–local tension can be explicitly addressed. How might this be done with the example texts noted above?

In the case of the Moroccan example, in order to illustrate the diversity of values within Western society, there could be more than one example of a family at dinner time in which in some scenarios the wife cooks or works outside the home and in other scenarios the husband cooks or works outside the home. In other words, the texts need to illustrate that gender roles can differ within Western culture. In addition, the texts need to encourage students to make a connection between the family roles depicted in the text and their own situation, not as a way of making judgments as to the worth of a particular type of gender roles, but as a way of illustrating the diversity that exists within their own culture. In this way both the global and local are depicted as diverse and neither one is afforded more status than the other. In a similar manner, the Japanese example could include scenarios of different gender roles within a cooking context so that diversity of gender roles is illustrated in both the Inner Circle context and the Japanese context. In addition, the text needs to become an open text in which students are invited to interpret and react to the roles assigned to the characters in the dialogue.

Local teachers can also address the global–local tension and a tendency towards Othering by examining the representation of uses and users of English that exist in the materials they are using. If, like the Japanese context, their textbooks provide few examples of anything other than L1–L2 interactions and provide a dominant role for the native English-speaking characters, then local teachers can try to achieve more diversity in the uses and users of English by supplementing the textbook. This could be achieved by writing texts and dialogues that depict L2–L2 interactions among speakers from a variety of countries. These examples could be companion dialogues and readings to those that exist in the textbook, using the same topics and themes but exemplifying more diversity in the users of English.

In addition, teachers and students can undertake what Peirce (1995) terms *classroom-based social research (CBSR)*. Such research involves collaborative projects carried out by language learners in their local community under the guidance and support of the teacher. In such projects, students are asked to gather examples of when they see individuals in their local community using English with other L2 speakers. They can also gather examples of their own use of electronic written English with other L2 writers. The point of such assignments is to encourage students to become aware of how they can use English for communication across international borders, often with other L2 speakers. Teachers also can contribute to the project by gathering and audio-taping examples of L2–L2 interactions. The reason for stressing L2–L2 interactions in such projects is that in general language learners have been exposed, through classroom materials, to many examples of L1–L2 interactions. What they now need is an awareness that English is an international language that can be used not only with native speakers but also with L2 speakers in a wider variety of cultural and social contexts.

Globalization and Othering in ELT methods

As we pointed out in chapter 2, in many countries today there is tremendous pressure to implement CLT because it is considered a modern, global method. In addition, it is typically advocated by many ELT specialists from Inner Circle countries, who, because of their status as native-speakers, are looked to as models for both language standards and pedagogy. In considering the implementation of CLT, it is helpful to note the distinction made by Holliday (1994) between what he terms the *weak* and *strong* version of CLT. The weak version is often implemented in Britain, Australasia, and North American (BANA) countries while the strong version is typically implemented in state institutions in the rest of the world. In the weak version of CLT, language practice and student oral participation, particularly in groups, is highly valued and student talking time is the measure of a successful lesson. This method works in many BANA language teaching contexts where classes tend to be relatively small and classroom space can accommodate group work.

In the strong version of CLT, a premium is put on learning about how the language works in discourse. The lesson input is language data that the students use to form generalizations about the language: "the student works out how the text is constructed and how it operates—the language rules which it incorporates—making and adjusting hypotheses very much as children do when they acquire language naturally" (Holliday, 1994, p. 171). Whereas in the weak version communication typically involves students communicating with the teacher and other students, in the strong version communication involves communicating with a text. The task does not have to be undertaken in groups but can be done individually. When students do solve the language tasks in groups, the mother tongue can be used to solve the problem concerning the use of the target language. Holliday argues that the strong version does involve meaningful communication, a key component of CLT, in that students are meaningfully engaged with a text.

In many contexts in which CLT is advocated by the Ministry of Education and by Inner Circle ELT specialists, it is the weak version that is promoted. In addition it is the weak version of CLT that is associated with globalization and modernization. The problem, however, which we will consider shortly, is that the weak version of CLT in many cases is not in keeping with local pedagogical conditions. Before we consider the question of local feasibility, it is important to consider the discourse that surrounds the implementation of CLT in current language pedagogy.

The discourse of Othering

Often in discussions of the implementation of CLT in Outer and Expanding Circle countries, there is a suggestion that the culture of learning in these countries is not conducive to the weak version of CLT. Educators like Ballard and Clanchy (1991) go so far as to argue that different cultures have different attitudes regarding the nature of knowledge and its function in society. They contend that there is a continuum of attitudes toward knowledge ranging from what they term a *conserving* attitude toward knowledge to an *extending* attitude toward knowledge. In the case of the former, the learning approach is highly reproductive and learning strategies involve memorization and imitation. Activities often involve summarizing and applying formulae and information in order to achieve correctness. On the other hand, as the continuum moves to an extending attitude, the learning approach is analytic and speculative, involving critical thinking and a search for new possibilities. Activities entail questioning, judging, speculating, and hypothesizing with the aim of creativity and originality. Ballard and Clancy go on to argue that although there are individual differences within a culture, a conserving attitude toward knowledge is prevalent in many Asian societies:

> it remains true that the reproductive approach to learning, favoring strategies of memorization and rote learning and positively discouraging critical questioning of either the teacher or the text, is the dominant tendency in formal education in much of Southeast Asia and other Asian countries. And it is the case that in the Australian system, even at the primary level, the dominant tendency is to urge students toward an ultimately speculative approach to learning, to encourage them to question, to search for new ways of looking at the world around them.
>
> (p. 23)

Such Othering discourse regarding approaches to knowledge and learning styles is evident in a good deal of the discourse surrounding the implementation of CLT. Flowerdew (1998), for example, discusses the use of group work and students' oral participation, central components of the weak version of CLT, in reference to Chinese learners. She begins by asking,

> Why is it that when one poses a question to a group of Arab students the whole class is clamouring to answer, while a question addressed to a class of Chinese learners may elicit no response, followed by a stony silence or, as the Chinese say, "dead air"? Even if one nominates a particular student to reply in a class of Chinese learners, the question may still be met with a muffled reply and averted eyes. The answer lies, to some extent, in certain cultural and psychological factors deriving from Confucian philosophy.
>
> (p. 323)

Flowerdew goes on to discuss the use of group work with Chinese learners and argues that group work can be implemented with Chinese students if the group is viewed as a collective body which offers suggestions to one another not as individuals but as a group. Underlying her argument are the assumptions that group work in a classroom is admirable and conducive to language learning and that a particular group of learners, in this case Chinese students, are not open to group work and oral participation.

An Othering discourse is also evident in some discussions of critical thinking, a key component of an extending view of knowledge that appears to inform the weak version of CLT. Atkinson (1997), for example, argues that critical thinking, while extremely difficult to define, is clearly a social practice and that some cultures promote such learning while others do not. He then goes on to compare "critical thinking and nonnative thinkers" (a powerful Othering discourse), arguing that "cross-cultural research into the early socialization and educational practices of non-European peoples" suggests that there are "three areas of potential discontinuity between cultural assumptions that may underlie critical thinking and modes of thought and expression prevalent among non-Western cultural groups" (p. 79). These involve notions of relations between individuals and society, differing norms of self-expression, and different perspectives on the use of language as a means for learning. Underlying the discussion is a clear Othering between Westerners who engage in critical thinking and non-Westerners or "nonnative thinkers" whose social practice may not have encouraged critical thinking. At issue is exactly what is meant by critical thinking and if it is necessary for "nonnative thinkers" to engage in Western concepts of critical thinking in order to learn English.

Resistance to implementing the weak version of CLT

In instances where educators have tried to implement the weak version of CLT in contexts where group work is typically not used, they have often met with resistance from both students and teachers. Shamin (1996), for example, recounts her experience of trying to implement a new methodology, one involving more student participation and group work, in her class in Pakistan. She notes that the traditional style of teaching in Pakistan is largely teacher-centered, using a lecture method in which students are "passive listeners with virtually no opportunities to become active participants in the teaching/learning process" (p. 106). She contends that "this style of pedagogy, on the one hand, does not allow the learners to be creative and independent in their thinking, while, on the other hand, it encourages the rote learning of vast amounts of material which are useful only on the day of the final exams" (p. 106). Evident in such discourse is the assumption that listening to a lecture and absorbing the content is not conducive to creative and independent thinking and that not being verbally active in a classroom is rote learning.

After having a one-year training program on the theory and practice of English language teaching, Shamin (1996) felt that she should try to implement greater student participation and group work in her class. She realized that because of local conditions such as a formal system of examinations, a prescribed text and large numbers in the classes, such a methodology might not be feasible with most classes. Thus, she decided to try this approach with a small class of postgraduate students enrolled in a course in linguistics and language teaching. The innovation involved less lecture time and more time devoted to group work in which students were given specific questions to address in their group. What Shamin found over the course of the semester were various types of student resistance. For one thing, students asked for more lectures and less group work, they also frequently did not read the materials before the class, and on one occasion they stayed away from the class. In the end Shamin found that she began to assume more and more authority in the class, which seemed to make the class more relaxed. She concludes that it was ironic that the very techniques she "had been trying to use to create, supposedly, a non-threatening and relaxed atmosphere in the classroom had, in fact, become a potential source of tension and conflict" (p. 109).

In assessing her attempt at implementing innovations in her classrooms, ones largely brought on by the belief that the weak version of CLT is the most productive methodology, Shamin (1996) notes the roles of learners in implementing change. She points out that planners and outside change agents often view the teacher as the key to implementing change whereas the role of the learner is largely ignored. She argues that, from her experience,

> Learners do not always passively accept an innovation. In fact, learner resistance can be a very effective barrier to change. This resistance can be manifested explicitly in overt forms of behavior and/or by following a policy of "silent non-co-operation" in the classroom. The failure of learners to share the teacher's perception of the benefit of the innovation can lead to a situation of constant conflict between the teacher and the learners in the classroom ... and force the teacher to compromise or even totally abandon the innovation effort half-way, in the interest of harmony.
>
> (p. 111)

Teachers also can resist the implementation of new methods brought on by globalization. Canagarajah (1999), for example, describes the resistance of Sri Lankan teachers in implementing a task-based pedagogy involving more group work. In this case teachers of a first year General Purposes English course were troubled by a lack of student involvement and improvement in communicative competence. They decided to try to implement a task-based method that was being used in local secondary schools with the help of foreign experts. The tasks involved information, opinion and reasoning gap activities that demanded more student participation. The teachers recognized that this pedagogy was in conflict with the grammar-based pedagogy they were using. While some teachers tried to implement the method with great enthusiasm, they found that local conditions made this difficult.

For example, one teacher, Malathy, designed a task-based lesson in which students were given a list of 18 bibliographical entries that were organized according to a consistent bibliographical convention but were not alphabetically arranged. According to the plan, students were to put the entries in order by engaging in verbal interactions. Several practical issues, however, affected the enactment of the activity. Since it was not possible to duplicate the entries, Malathy had to write them on the board, but because the board was quite small she could only write four entries on the board at a time. This meant the students had to copy each entry down in their notebooks, a time-consuming and tedious task. While copying down the entries, students complained that some of the words in the entries were quite difficult so they asked Malathy to explain them. She did this in the form of a mini-lecture in which students wrote down the meanings and pronunciation in Tamil. She then asked students some questions to check their comprehension of the entries (e.g., On what subject did Toulmin write books?). Students replied in complete sentences and Malathy corrected their syntax, helping them to form complete sentences. At one point she took time to do a mini-lecture on the present tense.

In discussing her lesson afterwards with Canagarajah (1999), Malathy noted that it was impossible to do the activity as she had planned as a small group task due to a lack of duplicating facilities and an inability to move the chairs around. When asked why students had to answer her questions in complete sentences and why it was necessary to correct their grammar, Malathy replied that without a linguistic component, students would have considered the lesson a waste of time. Canagarajah goes on to note that

> Although the class had been organized around tasks, its format was clearly teacher-fronted, and somewhat product-oriented. Even when the teacher employed certain exercises and material suitable for a task-based approach, her values and practices showed the considerable influence of the traditional approaches (the grammar-translation method, in particular) that she had used before. Although tasks were provided, the "deep structure" of the lesson showed a form-oriented, teacher-fronted style of instruction.

(p. 114)

The actual enactment of this lesson is a clear example how global–local tensions can result in the development of what might be called a hybrid method, which arises out of global pressure to enact a CLT method matched with local practical constraints and classroom expectations. In the end the "teacher and students are negotiating an alternate pedagogy—a third approach that is neither traditional nor novel, neither grammar-translation nor task-based—that suits their learning context" (Canagarajah, 1999, p. 114). Other teachers, however, were less committed to implementing a new method and adopted subtle strategies so that the basic structure of the lesson was still a teacher-fronted grammar lesson with a short added on task or group activity. Some of the more senior teachers refused to try the new method, saying that the students were at such a low level of proficiency that they wouldn't understand the directions for the task.

While one can interpret the experiences narrated by Shamin (1996) and Canagarajah (1999) as resistance on the part of some learners and teachers to the implementation of the weak version of CLT, they can also be viewed as instances of teacher and student coping strategies in which, for example, students decide not to come to class rather than face a teaching context that is not in keeping with their expectations. In both instances, change was introduced into the language classroom by conditions of globalization in which foreign experts from Inner Circle countries promoted a particular methodology and in both instances, local conditions, including student expectations, large classes and lack of resources, made the implementation of such a methodology inappropriate. Both classrooms illustrate a global–local tension in which a global push for CLT is challenged by local conditions; they also illustrate how learners and teachers can adopt various coping strategies to deal with changes brought about by globalization.

Principles for a socially sensitive EIL pedagogy

In light of the social and sociolinguistic context of EIL pedagogy, as well as pervasive global–local tensions and the discourse of Othering, what principles should inform a socially sensitive EIL pedagogy? In the following section, we enumerate what we see as key principles.

EIL curricula should be relevant to the domains in which English is used in the particular learning contexts.

In the chapter on multilingualism we examined the manner in which English is used within particular countries. We noted that in many Outer Circle countries there is a diglossic situation with English being used in more formal domains and the local languages used in informal and intimate domains. A similar situation can occur within immigrant groups in English-speaking countries where English is used primarily in work and educational contexts and the first language is used among family and friends. If a language curriculum is to be relevant to learners' lives, local educators need to examine the manner in which English is being used in the larger social context and design curricula that are in keeping with the English demands of the students.

> *EIL professionals should strive to alter language policies that serve to promote English learning only among the elite of the country.*

In many countries we have seen how those with privilege are most likely to have access to English learning. It is often those who have both the economic resources and time for language learning who gain proficiency in English. If English is to become a truly international language, educational leaders and planners need to establish policies that afford English access to learners of all economic backgrounds. This may well mean establishing more government-funded opportunities for English learning for all citizens. In contexts in which gaining proficiency in English may threaten mother tongue use and development, English programs should be established in such a way that the local language is fully supported.

> *EIL curricula should include examples of the diversity of English varieties used today.*

In chapter 5 we documented the diversity of English use today, illustrating both the regularity of these varieties and the manner in which they are a source of personal and social identity. In light of this diversity, a socially sensitive EIL pedagogy needs to first of all afford equal status to all varieties of English and second, promote an awareness of variation in English use. Which particular varieties are dealt with should depend on the local context. It may well be that for many learners familiarity with varieties spoken in their geographical region will be the most useful. Promoting an awareness of the varieties of English in EIL classrooms will serve two purposes. First, it may enhance learners' receptive skills in processing different varieties of English. And second, it will promote an awareness that English, as an international language, no longer belongs solely to speakers of the Inner Circle. Recognition of the hybridity and fluidity of modern day English use will afford full status to second language speakers of the language.

> *EIL curricula need to exemplify L2–L2 interactions.*

Given that the majority of English interactions today are among L2 speakers, EIL curricula need to include far more examples of L2–L2 English interactions. Including examples of actual L2–L2 interactions will be beneficial in several ways. First, it will create an awareness that one important value of English is that it allows individuals to communicate across a great variety geographical and cultural boundaries and not merely with speakers from Inner Circle countries. Second, including actual examples of L2–L2 interactions can provide a context for discussing various means by which individuals can seek clarification and establish relationships when they may have gaps in their knowledge of English.

Full recognition needs to be given to the other languages spoken by English speakers.

For too long a good deal of ELT pedagogy has been informed by an English-only discourse. Yet as we have shown in several chapters, bilingual speakers of English have a rich linguistic repertoire which they often use to signal their personal identity and social relationships. Code-switching is an important means by which they do this. Encouraging code-switching in EIL classrooms is beneficial in several ways. First, it will provide equal status to all of the languages learners speak. Second, it offers a context for students to investigate the reasons for code-switching. And most importantly it allows for a well-planned use of the first language as a means of developing proficiency in English.

EIL should be taught in a way that respects the local culture of learning.

As we pointed out in this chapter, in many instances globalization has led to the introduction of materials and methods that are not in keeping with the local culture of learning. When this occurs, local teachers may be placed in a situation in which their credibility as competent teachers is challenged because they do not know about some aspect of Western culture that appears in a textbook or they are encouraged to use group work when this is not in keeping with typical student roles. Local teachers are the ones most familiar with local expectations regarding the roles of teachers and learners. They are also familiar with the manner in which English is used in the local context. Because of this, they are in a strong position to design a pedagogy that respects the local culture of learning.

In summary, we began this book by highlighting how present-day globalization, migration, and the spread of English have resulted in a great diversity of social and educational contexts in which English learning is taking place. Our basic assumption throughout the book is that, because English is an international language, effective pedagogical decisions and practices cannot be made without giving special attention to the many varied social contexts in which English is taught and learned. An appropriate EIL pedagogy is one that promotes English bilingualism for learners of all backgrounds, recognizes and validates the variety of Englishes that exists today, and teaches English in a manner that meets local language needs and respects the local culture of learning. It is our hope that by enacting such a pedagogy, EIL educators can mitigate local and global tensions and reduce the Othering that currently exists in EIL pedagogy.

Acknowledgements

Thanks to David Malinowski for his translation of Suzuki (1999).

References

Adaskou, K. & Fahsi, B. (1990). Design decisions on the cultural content of a secondary English course for Morocco. *ELT Journal, 44*(1), 3–10.

Atkinson, D. (1997). A critical approach to critical thinking in TESOL. *TESOL Quarterly, 31*(1), 71–95.

Ballard, B. & Clanchy, J. (1991). Assessment by misconception: Cultural influences and intellectual traditions. In L. Hamp-Lyons (Ed.), *Assessing second language writing in academic contexts* (pp. 19–36). Norwood, NJ: Ablex Publishing Corporation.

Canagarajah, A. S. (1999). *Resisting linguistic imperialism in English teaching.* Oxford: Oxford University Press.

Cortazzi, M. & Jin, L. (1999). Cultural mirrors: Materials and methods in the EFL classroom. In E. Hinkel (Ed.), *Culture in second language teaching* (pp. 196–219). Cambridge: Cambridge University Press.

English in Life (1990). Casablanca: Royaume du Maroc, Ministère de L'Education Nationale [Morocco's Ministry of Education].

Flowerdew, L. (1998). A cultural perspective on group work. *ELT Journal, 52*(4), 323–329.

Holliday, A. (1994). *Appropriate methodology and social context.* Cambridge: Cambridge University Press.

Kramsch, C. (1993). *Context and culture in language teaching.* Oxford: Oxford University Press.

Matsuda, A. (2002). Representation of users and uses of English in beginning Japanese EFL textbooks. *JALT Journal, 24*(2), 182–201.

Mugglestone, P., Elsworth, S., & Rose, J. (1999, 2000). *Go for Chile, Book 1 and 2.* Santiago, Chile: Addison Wesley Longman.

Palfreyman, D. (2005). Othering in an English language program. *TESOL Quarterly, 39*(2), 211–233.

Peirce, B. N. (1995). Social identity, investment and language learning. *TESOL Quarterly, 29*(1), 9–32.

Shamin, F. (1996). Learner resistance to innovation in classroom methodology. In H. Coleman (Ed.), *Society and the Language Classroom* (pp. 105–121). Cambridge: Cambridge University Press.

Shimako, I. (2000). Evaluating cultural context and content in EFL materials: A study of high school level oral communication (OCA) textbooks in Japan. Paper presented at the international convention of Teachers of English to Speakers of Other Languages, Vancouver, Canada.

Suzuki, T. (1999). *Nihonjin wa naze eigo ga dekinai ka* [Why the Japanese people are no good at English]. Tokyo: Iwananmi.

Index